New Constellations

Movie Stars of the

1960s

★★★★★★★★★★★★

EDITED BY

PAMELA ROBERTSON WOJCIK

RUTGERS UNIVERSITY PRESS

NEW BRUNSWICK, NEW JERSEY, AND LONDON

LIBRARY OF CONGRESS CATALOGING-IN-PUBLICATION DATA

New constellations : Movie stars of the 1960s / edited by Pamela Robertson Wojcik.
    p.   cm.   — (Star decades : American culture / American cinema)
    Includes bibliographical references and index.
    ISBN   978-0-8135-5171-5   (hardcover : alk. paper)
    ISBN   978-0-8135-5172-2   (pbk. : alk. paper)
    1. Motion picture actors and actresses—United States—Biography.   I. Wojcik, Pamela
Robertson, 1964–   .
    PN1998.2.N48   2011
    791.4302'80922—dc22
    [B]
                                                                        2011010857

A British Cataloging-in-Publication record for this book is available from the British
Library.

Visit our Web site: http://rutgerspress.rutgers.edu

Manufactured in the United States of America

that brought us Bob Dylan, Timothy Leary, and Robert Kennedy is also the decade in which the soundtrack for *Mary Poppins* topped the charts, *My Fair Lady* won the Academy Award for Best Picture, and figures such as Phyllis Schlafly, Barry Goldwater, Ronald Reagan, and Richard Nixon created a strong conservative opposition to the New Left. Moreover, the degree to which the counterculture can be seen as truly oppositional has come under some scrutiny. As Thomas Frank argues in *The Conquest of Cool: Business Culture, Counterculture, and the Rise of Hip Consumerism*, the counterculture not only existed alongside mainstream corporate culture, but also quickly became the cultural dominant, as the business world embraced signs of the counterculture as "hip" tools for marketing. Further, the revolution, some would argue, never came, and corporate culture and many of the conservative values that predated the sixties, like "family values" and "togetherness," as well as numerous cultural objects, like Sinatra and martinis, continue to flourish.

Introduction
Stardom in the 1960s

PAMELA ROBERTSON WOJCIK

Conventional (and often nostalgic) views of the American sixties tend to portray the decade as one of unique change, a decade in which ideologies, morality, culture, and politics were all upended and radically transformed. In line with this view, the decade is sometimes characterized through a series of displacements in which the Man in the Grey Flannel Suit is replaced by the hippie, the housewife superseded by the feminist, the martini supplanted by LSD and marijuana, Sinatra unseated by the Beatles, Dylan, and the Doors, and so on. The sense of the sixties as uniquely unsettling has a time-capsule familiarity signaled through famous events of the decade—the Bay of Pigs in 1961; the Cuban missile crisis in 1962; the March on Washington and the assassination of John F. Kennedy, both in 1963; the British Invasion beginning in 1964; passage of the Civil Rights Act of 1964 and the Voting Rights Act of 1965; 1967's Summer of Love; the litany of crisis-events in 1968, including the assassinations of Martin Luther King Jr. and Robert Kennedy, the Tet offensive, the My Lai Massacre, police attacks on the Black Panthers, the violence at the Democratic National Convention in Chicago, the Prague Spring, and the events of May 1968 in France; and the banner events of 1969: Woodstock, Stonewall, and *Apollo 11*.

Of course, the sixties did witness deep social unrest and a tumult of political and cultural activity. Sixties politics comprised anti–Vietnam War protests, the civil rights movement, Black Power and the Black Panthers, student movements, the New Left, a rising women's liberation movement, emergent gay liberation, and sprouting environmentalism. Culturally, the sixties stands out for developing a new *counter*culture represented by hippies, drugs, psychedelia, and charismatic singer-songwriters working in rock, folk, and protest genres; through painting and underground newspapers, comics, and films; in festivals, clubs, movie theaters, and more.

However, while the leftist and countercultural elements of the sixties are certainly key to the decade, they do not fully characterize it. The decade

New Constellations

ACKNOWLEDGMENTS

☆☆☆☆☆★★★★★

I wish to thank the Star Decades editors, Murray Pomerance and Adrienne L. McLean, for initiating and shaping the series, and also, along with Leslie Mitchner at Rutgers University Press, for their guidance and patience with this volume. Thanks as well are due all the contributors for sharing their insights and for their patience with the process of putting this book together. We owe a collective debt to all the scholars who have written about stars and actors before us, especially to Richard Dyer, whose influential study *Stars* still informs our work.

CONTENTS

★★★★★★★★★★★

New Constellations

STAR

 AMERICAN CULTURE / AMERICAN CINEMA

DECADES

Each volume in the series Star Decades: American Culture/American Cinema presents original essays analyzing the movie star against the background of contemporary American cultural history. As icon, as mediated personality, and as object of audience fascination and desire, the Hollywood star remains the model for celebrity in modern culture and represents a paradoxical combination of achievement, talent, ability, luck, authenticity, superficiality, and ordinariness. In all of the volumes, stardom is studied as an effect of, and influence on, the particular historical and industrial contexts that enabled a star to be "discovered," to be featured in films, to be promoted and publicized, and ultimately to become a recognizable and admired—even sometimes notorious—feature of the cultural landscape. Understanding when, how, and why a star "makes it," dazzling for a brief moment or enduring across decades, is especially relevant given the ongoing importance of mediated celebrity in an increasingly visualized world. We hope that our approach produces at least some of the surprises and delight for our readers that stars themselves do.

ADRIENNE L. McLEAN AND MURRAY POMERANCE
SERIES EDITORS

Jennifer M. Bean, ed., *Flickers of Desire: Movie Stars of the 1910s*

Patrice Petro, ed., *Idols of Modernity: Movie Stars of the 1920s*

Adrienne L. McLean, ed., *Glamour in a Golden Age: Movie Stars of the 1930s*

Sean Griffin, ed., *What Dreams Were Made Of: Movie Stars of the 1940s*

R. Barton Palmer, ed., *Larger Than Life: Movie Stars of the 1950s*

Pamela Robertson Wojcik, ed., *New Constellations: Movie Stars of the 1960s*

James Morrison, ed., *Hollywood Reborn: Movie Stars of the 1970s*

Robert Eberwein, ed., *Acting for America: Movie Stars of the 1980s*

Anna Everett, ed., *Pretty People: Movie Stars of the 1990s*

Murray Pomerance, ed., *Shining in Shadows: Movie Stars of the 2000s*

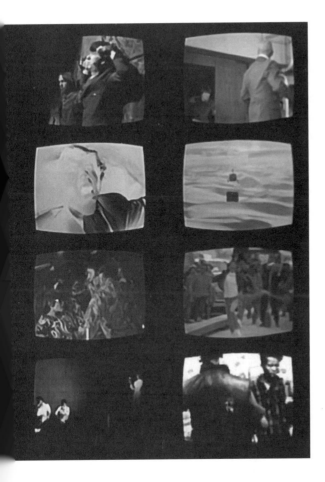

Bob Rafelson's loosely composed film *Head* (1968), starring (and effectively killing) the TV band The Monkees, captures the counterculture with psychedelic imagery, music, drug references, hippies, anticommercial and anti–Vietnam War slogans and skits, and, here, the use of multiple screens within the frame. (Digital frame enlargement)

The sixties are also a time of unprecedented economic prosperity. The Swinging Sixties, while linked to the counterculture's recreational drug use, can be seen as supremely superficial and shallow, evidence of a youthful, hip sensibility and style rather than any deep political commitment. This side of the sixties encompasses mod fashions, Mary Quant, Twiggy, Carnaby Street, James Bond films, Frankie Avalon and Annette Funicello beach movies, and so on. In this context, it is no accident that Susan Sontag's famous "Notes on 'Camp'" first appeared in 1964 and was quickly popularized and main-streamed in *Time* magazine. Camp partakes of the counterculture's challenge to dominant taste and, in its association with gay subcultures, with counter-cultural sexual freedom. But camp also underscores the superficiality of the Swinging Sixties. Camp, for Sontag, was about failed seriousness, aesthetics, exaggeration, and privileging style over content. Against the moral serious-ness of activism, camp celebrated the frivolous. Crucially, Sontag's essay on camp appears in the context of Pop Art. Standing, on the one hand, as a countercultural affront to "taste," collapsing high and low culture, Pop's espousal of Madison Avenue vernacular can also be seen as commercializing art and creating a taste for commercialism.

Thus, rather than consider the sixties as wholly revolutionary, it is perhaps more accurate to view the decade as remarkably pliant and contradictory. Without denying that the times, they were a changin', we can see that the changes, while they may have felt dramatic and all-encompassing, were, in retrospect, more gradual and uneven. Raymond Williams's understanding of residual, dominant, and emerging cultures provides a productive lens for understanding the sixties. In *Marxism and Literature*, Williams argues that at any given moment, culture consists not only of the dominant but also of residual effects of seemingly outmoded, but nonetheless active, aspects of the culture, and, at the same time, emergent elements that offer a substantial alternative to the dominant. Williams's notion provides a means to consider how residual, dominant, and emergent ideologies coexist while hegemonic discourse is challenged and eventually or potentially displaced by counter hegemonies; and also opens up a way of talking about technologies, business practices, media, and more. In the sixties, we can consider how conservative politics interact with New Deal liberalism and radical activism, and how counterculture coexists with but does not dislocate corporate culture.

The sixties film industry, like the culture as a whole, is often viewed as radically transformed. For instance, in *American Cinema of the 1960s: Themes and Variations*, Barry Keith Grant claims that "the decade was one of profound change and challenge for Hollywood, as it sought to adapt to both technological innovation and evolving cultural taste," and, he argues, "by the end of the 1960s movies were made, distributed, and exhibited differently than when the decade began" (Grant 10). Certainly, the Hollywood film industry underwent numerous changes in the sixties, and new forms of filmmaking, distribution, and audience emerged. But while some effects were drastic and lasting, many were transitional or temporary. The industry shifted in various ways: in the rise of conglomerates and package deals, in runaway, underground, avant-garde, and independent production, and in art cinema aesthetics. At the same time, it maintained a cultural dominant of large-scale studio production and distribution, television production, and continued residual practices and effects such as genre films, the screen player contract system, and the Hays Code. The relations among these dominant, emergent, and residual modes of filmmaking and distribution together shape the context for understanding stars of the 1960s and their shifting constellations.

★★★★★ Alternate Modes of Production

The sixties witnessed the emergence of a few new modes of production. Starting in the 1950s, following the historic Paramount Decision, foreign films gained increased entry to the American market and a prominent art cinema circuit developed. In the sixties, this circuit was well established, with such films as Federico Fellini's *La Dolce Vita* (1960), François Truffaut's *Jules et Jim* (1962), Michelangelo Antonioni's *Blow-Up* (1966), and Claude Lelouch's *A Man and a Woman* (1966) causing a sensation in major cities and college towns across the United States. This European art cinema created new box office competition for Hollywood and also created new standards for "sophistication and artistic achievement" that would prove to have an influence on Hollywood aesthetics (Monaco 3). Additionally, the various New Waves pointed to a new mode of production in which the director was the auteur, or author, of a film, rather than a hired hand for the studios. The aesthetics and mode of production in European art cinema created the model and conditions for the New American Cinema of the late 1960s and 1970s.

In addition, the Paramount Decision had forced the doors open for independent production. Prior to 1948, the major studios produced nearly all first-run films and about two-thirds of the total output in America. By 1958, more than half the films made were independently produced (Monaco 24). Some films were wholly independent. As studio production fell, independent American International Pictures, home to director Roger Corman, turned out twenty-five feature films a year during the decade and launched the careers of Jack Nicholson, Peter Fonda, Dennis Hopper, Ben Vereen, Talia Shire, and Bud Cort, among others (Monaco 27–29).

More commonly, "independent" production involved packages or deals. The package or deal was a new mode of film production, signaling the demise of the studio *system* but not the death of the studios. Under the classical Hollywood studio system, a studio would "own" a star, director, and technicians. Pictures would be generated through production units headed by studio production heads, like Arthur Freed, whose unit made many of the most successful musicals at MGM, working with directors such as Vincente Minnelli, Stanley Donen, and Charles Walters, writers Betty Comden and Adolph Green ,and stars such as Fred Astaire, Judy Garland, and Gene Kelly. In the 1960s, the studio system effectively expired. As Paul Monaco explains, when Rock Hudson's player contract with Universal Pictures ended in 1965, the system that had bound actors to specific studios also expired (19). In the 1960s, the film business increasingly adopted freelance business arrangements. Rather than drawing from talent within a single studio, producers would now freelance and put together deals or packages—contractual agreements among stars, director, director of photography, and others to produce a particular script (Monaco 19–25).

The package deal gave stars increased power that enabled them to become increasingly involved in production. Many stars established themselves as producers and set up production companies. Most often, star's production companies were effectively subsidiaries of the studios, reliant on them for financing and distribution, as was the case with Rock Hudson's Seven Pictures Corporation at Universal. Others, like John Wayne's Batjac Productions, were more truly independent. In some cases, a star's production company was independent but could make a deal with the studio. For example, Marlon Brando was producer, director, and star of *One Eyed Jacks* (1961), Paramount financed the film, and Brando got 100 percent of the profits while Paramount took distribution fees (Monaco 20–21).

While foreign and independent production companies were gaining ground in Hollywood, Hollywood was shifting its attention overseas. Faced with declining box office receipts at home, Hollywood was placing new emphasis on marketing films abroad. In addition, Hollywood adopted a practice, known as runaway production, of moving production to foreign countries where labor was abundant and inexpensive, and where local governments offered substantial subsidies, tax breaks, and other incentives. In some cases, a Hollywood major worked with a locally owned subsidiary and, in others, Hollywood studios could work more directly in foreign countries. Great Britain, France, and Italy were especially aggressive in offering incentives for runaway productions. As Monaco points out, of the three Great Britain was the most attractive to and welcoming of Hollywood studios, due not only to a shared language but also due to a loophole in a British subsidy scheme for moviemaking that allowed any British producer to apply for funding, regardless of whether the primary financing came from non-British sources (11–13). Among the ten Academy Award–winning films for Best Picture in the 1960s, four—*Lawrence of Arabia* (1962), *Tom Jones* (1963), *A Man for All Seasons* (1966), and *Oliver!* (1968)— were released with British producing credit, as well as British talent on and offscreen. Thus, while creating labor tension in the United States, as trade union workers found themselves under-utilized and marginalized, runaway production created new opportunities for foreign, and especially British, actors to penetrate the U.S. market in Hollywood films as well as through the art cinema circuit.

★★★★★ Changing Aesthetics and Tastes

These new modes of production led to some different aesthetics in film. Runaway productions produced an emphasis on location shooting and spectacular scenery, and competition with television led to a renewed emphasis on spectacle and theatrical experience, with widescreen, Technicolor, and long running times, often with built-in overtures and intermissions! Consider *Lawrence of Arabia*, which was shot in Super Panavision 70 widescreen and Technicolor, and in numerous locations across Spain, Morocco, the United Kingdom, the United States, and Jordan, and which clocked in at 227 minutes in its roadshow edition. Often, in this vein, Hollywood turned to lengthy, big-budget, widescreen, Technicolor musicals, like *Mary Poppins* (1964, 139 minutes), *My Fair Lady* (1964, 170 minutes), *The Sound of Music* (1965, 174 minutes), *Funny Girl* (1968, 155 minutes), and *Oliver!* (153 minutes).

Counteracting these big-budget, widescreen, Technicolor, roadshow productions, documentary, underground, and avant-garde filmmaking aesthetics went in the opposite direction, away from the glossy spectacles of Hollywood toward a rougher, edgier style of filmmaking. The development of increasingly lightweight cameras allowed the emergence of direct cinema, where the documentarian functions as an observer, shooting with a handheld camera and lightweight sound equipment. Direct cinema eschews voiceover narration and explanatory titles and does not add music or otherwise interfere in the presentation of events. Films like *Primary* (1960)

My Fair Lady, winner of the Academy Award for Best Picture in 1965, exemplifies the glossy big-budget side of 1960s filmmaking. The film has Broadway credentials, British talent, and a classical Hollywood director, and offers a Technicolor extravaganza of fantastic sets, costumes, stars, and musical numbers, clocking in at 170 roadshow minutes. (Digital frame enlargement)

allowed filmmakers to create an intimate view of public events without commenting on those events, following the candidates as they wound their way through crowds, into hotel rooms, and across public speaking engagements. Underground and avant-garde cinema figures such Stan Brakhage, Jack Smith, Andy Warhol, and Jonas Mekas also aimed for a more low-tech, low-budget mode of filmmaking, using handheld cameras and a variety of new techniques, such as painting directly on celluloid, scratching film, using recycled footage, rapid editing, editing in camera, using 8mm film, and making static one-shot films, all intended to break free from Hollywood style and create new aesthetics, whether privileging camp, kitsch, and trash, exploring boredom, or offering intensely personal and lyrical expressions. The aesthetics of direct cinema and underground cinema penetrated feature film production among independent and Hollywood filmmakers. John Cassavetes's independent *Faces* (1968), for example, adopted cinéma vérité techniques such as handheld camera and lightweight sound equipment, enabling actors the freedom to move without strict blocking and creating a feeling of spontaneous improvisation and modern realism. Sidney Lumet's studio film *The Pawnbroker* (1964) combined gritty realist black-and-white location footage with rapid editing and a jazz score by Quincy Jones to juxtapose the present-tense alienated life of a Jew in Harlem running a pawnshop with his painful, intrusive memories of the Holocaust.

Along with these different techniques for making films, the content of films changed somewhat in the 1960s. As the classical studio system broke down, and, along with it, the classical style of filmmaking (Bordwell et al.), other aspects of the studio system came under some pressure. Notably, the industry's self-censoring Production Code, commonly referred to as the Hays Code (or just the Code), was challenged, starting in the 1950s and increasingly across the 1960s. In 1953, *The Moon Is Blue* was refused a seal of approval because it used the word "virgin." Released without a seal, the film was a financial success. In 1961, Kazan's *Splendor in the Grass* was released with a seal, even though its frank depiction of youthful eroticism was explicitly forbidden by the Code, especially insofar as the lovers are not punished for their transgressions. Other films, notably *Who's Afraid of Virginia Woolf?* (1966), passed on a second review, even with its frequent use of vulgar language and mature marital situations. From 1966 forward, in his role as head of the Motion Picture Association of America, Jack Valenti lobbied to replace the Hays Code with a ratings system. Finally getting support from the National Association of Theater Owners, who would have to enforce the new system, Valenti put in place a new ratings system in Octo-

Sidney Lumet's *The Pawnbroker* (1964), shot on location and in black and white, shows the alienated life and unraveling of a Jew in Harlem, coming to terms with his memories of Nazi Germany. (Digital frame enlargement)

ber 1968 (Monaco 56–66). This created the opportunity for filmmakers to create more mature content and also officially segregated the film audience by age group, thus altering film audience demographics permanently.

★★★★★ Star, Celebrity, and Actor

Many of the changes in the industry changed the status of the actor and star in the 1960s. As part of package deals and as producers, actors gained more power over the process of production. Actors were also compensated differently, getting residuals from films broadcast on TV. Actors made fewer films than under the classical studio system, but they had more choices. Actors had increasing opportunity to work in television, even moving back and forth between media. Actors also had more opportunities to work in foreign film industries as part of runaway productions. American actors faced competition from foreign stars who appeared both in European art cinema and in U.S. runaway productions. And actors were faced with a diverse range of possible film styles to work in, often moving between Hollywood genre films and independent features.

The newfound power of stars, to make deals or function as producers, contributed to what Foster Hirsch has termed the rise of "the actor as auteur." For Hirsch, the actor is an auteur insofar as she "contributes to a film's personality," which she does through her acting style, personality, and "predilection for particular kinds of scripts" (33). While star studies would suggest that stars imprint aspects of their star text on every film, even working within the classical Hollywood studio system, Hirsch suggests that in the postclassical cinema, the actors' imprint, like the more self-consciously auteurist directors, relates more directly to the actor's choice of roles. This choice is enabled by the package deal system and advanced through the star's role as producer.

At the same time, the definition of a star underwent some modifications. First, the 1960s enabled many actors who might not have been stars in the classical Hollywood system to become stars. Among these, Barbra Streisand was the first major Jewish female star and Sidney Poitier the first major black male star to work consistently in Hollywood films with white casts. In addition, a number of quirky, not conventionally attractive actors became stars, modifying somewhat Hollywood's ideals of beauty (there had always been room for some stars, such as Humphrey Bogart, with less conventional looks)—Streisand, of course, with her prominent Jewish nose and unconventional looks, Dustin Hoffman, whose short Jewish looks were not conventionally handsome, and others like Jack Nicholson, Rod Steiger, and Sandy Dennis. Of course, Hollywood also had many more stars with typical matinee idol or glamour queen looks—Paul Newman, Jane Fonda, Steve McQueen, Faye Dunaway, Warren Beatty, Robert Redford, and others.

There were also new categories of star. Foreign stars entered the American market to a greater degree than before, via runaway productions and through the art-house circuit. Richard Burton, Sophia Loren, Albert Finney, Peter O'Toole, Julie Andrews, Julie Christie, Maggie Smith, Rex Harrison, Peter Sellers, Marcello Mastroianni, Anouk Aimee, and many others became truly global stars. While the British, French, and Italian stars who permeated American culture were still serious working actors, other kinds of celebrity emerged. Whereas stardom hinges on an interplay between an audience's sense of a star's "private" self and public roles, but always filters the image through their roles in film—reading the private person into the film roles and vice versa—celebrity plays off public fascination with people's private lives and does not depend upon there being a body of work to anchor the image. Cult stars such as Edie Sedgwick and other Superstars who were born through Andy Warhol's factory were better known for their appearances in the New York party and art scenes than for their relatively obscure film appearances. Some stars, like Brigitte Bardot and Mia Farrow, had greater celebrity than their relatively scant film work in the sixties would suggest. And TV provided some stars, such as Eva Gabor, with a profile and celebrity that extended their stardom. In line with my argument that the sixties comprised gradual and uneven change, it is important to remember that this is also a period in which there were still many prominent stars who had been groomed through the classical Hollywood system, like Rock Hudson, Elizabeth Taylor, and Doris Day (who remained one of the ten most profitable stars from 1960 to 1965).

In addition, the category of the star came into conflict with new ideas about acting and especially the Method, which changed the stakes for actors, turning them away from the desire to be stars and toward a desire to be actors, and particularly character actors. In part, this was a rebellion against the seeming conservatism and blandness of the Hollywood star—an anti-establishment posture. As Hirsch writes in *A Method to Their Madness*, "The typical Method actor, then, is the opposite of a straightforward, conventional he-man like John Wayne. . . . Method actors instinctively distrust the smooth good looks of the movie star as male model; a regulation handsomeness is read as the sign of a bland spirit" (313, 315). But it was also more deeply reflective of ideas about what acting should be. In Hollywood, there was historically an official distinction between stars and character actors in acting manuals, casting guides, contracts, and payment practices (Wojcik "Typecasting"). Generally speaking, in Hollywood, stars were white and good looking, and their characters were the active agents in a plot and the key players in romantic plots. By contrast, in Hollywood, character actors tended to be the repository for difference (ethnic difference, queerness, regional accents, physical quirkiness, etc.); they were somewhat marginal to the narrative; and they were generally left out of romantic plots, though they often served as enablers for the leads (White). Typically, stars adopted a more restrained acting style, whereas character actors could be more broadly gestural, expressive, and theatrical. And, as Hirsch points out in "The Actor as Auteur," there is traditionally a sense that "the actor accommodates his personality to the demands of the role; the star wrenches the role to the demands of his personality" (34).

In the 1960s, increasingly, Method-influenced actors who would be characterized as stars in terms of their billing, payment structure, producing power, and celebrity, speak increasingly of themselves as character actors and resist the category star. In contrast to the stereotypical star, Method actors tend to be dedicated to asserting their versatility and to resist typecasting. They flaunt rather than hide their ethnicity, regional background, and working-class identities through accent, posture, costuming, and more. They resist the star system because they want to play a variety of roles, and, in particular, characters who reflect the American vernacular, not its idealized dreams.

Many stars in the sixties, then, have a prickly relation to stardom. In the case of a star like Paul Newman, there is a tension between his stardom and his own ideal of being a versatile character actor. Other stars, like Dustin Hoffman, who in an earlier incarnation, perhaps, would have been a more marginal character actor (perhaps akin to Elisha Cook Jr.), find that changing tastes push them into stardom against their own desire to be character actors. A star like Liz Taylor will become victim to her own celebrity, her excellence as an actress often overshadowed by her personal trials writ large. For other stars, there is a perception that they are too old-fashioned, too tied to older models of Hollywood stardom. A star like Julie Andrews, for instance, while immensely popular, will quickly seem outdated, due to her attachment to old-fashioned genres, like the musical, and her British musical theater background (as opposed to the authenticity attributed to Method work in the New York theater, or Shakespearean acting on the British stage for an actor like Burton). A landmark star like Sidney Poitier will struggle with his status as role model, always feeling the pressure to be a role model but also the limitations of that position.

Thus, in the sixties, we have new constellations of stars, new kinds of stars, and new ideals of what the star ought to be. Some of these new constellations, especially the cult star and celebrity, will continue growing well past the sixties. But rather than underground cinema, the cult star will emerge through reality TV, the Internet, and other celebrity vehicles that are nonexistent in the sixties. The crossover of film stars into TV will dip, then intensify markedly again in the 2000s, especially through the rise of premium cable TV and the aura of quality attached to it. Some, such as the foreign star, will not have such prominence again after the sixties, because the foreign art house circuit will dwindle dramatically in coming decades. The dominant echelon of stars (as recognized through Academy Awards, box office, and other markers of stardom) will continue to integrate more African American, Jewish, and, ultimately, more Latino and Hispanic actors in the decades following the sixties. But the most lasting legacy of the sixties in relation to stardom may be the idea of the actor as auteur, the star with producing power, who chooses roles for versatility and moves between large-scale studio and smaller independent films.

This collection aims to provide a representative sampling of some of these new constellations. Inevitably, readers may feel that some different sixties stars ought to be here. Stars such as Audrey Hepburn and Julie Christie seem to signify sixties cool femininity. I regret their absence here. Other stars are also absent—Doris Day, Sandra Dee, Cary Grant, John Wayne, Rock Hudson, Elvis Presley, Jack Lemmon, Sean Connery, Dean Martin, Frank Sinatra, and Lee Marvin—who were each repeatedly among the top ten box office stars during the 1960s. Many of these stars seem to be definitive for a different decade and are included in earlier volumes. We did not have space for others. Some stars such as Jane Fonda, Barbra Streisand, and Warren Beatty are "in the wings," emerging in the sixties but having their peak stardom in the 1970s, and are discussed at the end of the book. The stars chosen here reflect the changing conception of stardom in the sixties. They range from old-school stars like Elizabeth Taylor and Julie Andrews to more Method-inflected actors like Paul Newman and Dustin Hoffman. Steve McQueen emerges from television stardom to become an icon of cinematic masculine cool, straddling Method-style authenticity and old school Hollywood glamour. Mia Farrow also begins in TV, and her Hollywood parentage and marriage to Frank Sinatra mark the gap between new and old styles of stardom. Peter Sellers is chosen here as representative of runaway production stardom and Brigitte Bardot for foreign art house celebrity. Sidney Poitier's relation to the civil rights movement and his status as role model is reevaluated. The Gabors speak to camp taste, new modes of celebrity, and the role of television. And Edie Sedgwick stands as representative of cult and avant-garde fame. Together they suggest some of the range and contradictions of what we call the sixties.

I ✯✯✯✯✯✯✯✯✯✯
Paul Newman
Superstardom and Anti-Stardom

CHRISTINE BECKER

In a 1970 *Los Angeles Times* article entitled "How to Be a Cool Hand Imitating Paul Newman," Joseph P. Devlin dispensed advice on "how to be: (a) cool, (b) a red-blooded-American boy, (c) win friends, and (d) influence women by imitating Paul Newman." Devlin advised that to be as admirable as Newman, one should draw from his example the following characteristics: "break away from the yoke of the Establishment . . . unshackle yourself from all contemporary banalities—and be FREE . . . buy your wardrobe at Goodwill Industries . . . Most importantly be effortless. Don't work at being cool. Wear your clothes in as unaffected a way as possible . . . In a social situation, remain totally disinterested. Always slump, always appear totally disinterested." The article closed, "If you've scrupulously followed the steps in this manual, you are now a super-cool guy. You are subtly masculine, irresistible to women, a cynical loner, and totally independent" (10 May 1970, C10). Of course, this "cynical loner" had been happily married for more than a decade, this "totally disinterested" man had devoted his time to numerous social causes, and this "totally independent" star had just appeared in one of the most popular studio films of the decade. But Paul Newman's 1960s star power resided in how he was able to reconcile these contradictions within his persona, much as the biggest stars of any era articulate the complexities and tensions of the social world and its dominant ideologies (see Dyer, *Heavenly Bodies* 7–10).

Given that the social world of the 1960s was more complex and tense than most, Newman's variety of contradictions was fitting, and how they were reconciled was also appropriate to the era. Rather than a true break from the yoke of the establishment, Paul Newman embodied a mainstream version of 1960s nonconformity, one that echoed the ways in which the counterculture itself was gradually assimilated into dominant sensibilities across the decade. Newman's vast popularity was indicative of how it was "super-cool" to seem independent, individualistic, and iconoclastic, without being subversive enough to truly represent a subcultural alternative. His most celebrated characters, typically classified as antiheroes, were transgressive rebels, but conventional film form coupled with Newman's classical star charisma made them broadly appealing. Correspondingly, Newman's off-screen life was depicted in publicity as an amalgam of the traditional and the unorthodox, from his idyllic marriage to Joanne Woodward to the couple's rejection of typical Hollywood customs. Those customs were a frequent target of Newman's tirades against the expectations placed upon him as a movie star, which reinforced both his rebel cool and a codified star image against which he chafed, even as it translated into box office success. Indeed, for as much as Paul Newman fought against the constrictions of Hollywood's star system, he was a symbol of its enduring power and efficacy.

★★★★★ Antihero Worship

Following an Actors Studio education in New York and successful stints on Broadway and in television, Newman began his film career in the mid-1950s under contract to Warner Bros. This was a contentious relationship, however, as Newman fought against Warner Bros.' desire to develop him as a traditional matinee idol. Newman's first feature, the sword-and-sandal epic *The Silver Chalice* (1954), was a classic star vehicle genre piece that required him to do little more than look gorgeous and stoic. Warner Bros. also followed previously successful publicity models by selling the young actor as a sex symbol, exemplified by a *Movie Life* profile that touted how Newman's "animal magnetism, intensity, and brooding eyes are driving all the girls crazy" ("Paul Newman: Call Him Tiger!" November 1956, 61). Newman bristled at the reduction of his performance abilities to his looks, and heopenly proclaimed his desire to be appreciated as an actor rather than a star.

This was a familiar cry among Newman's fellow Studio-trained Method actors, and Newman was initially dismissed as a pale imitation of Marlon Brando and James Dean. But what set Newman apart from those two stars, and would ultimately push him beyond their popularity, was his ability to combine the matinee idol looks that Warner Bros. so valued with expressive acting skills that conveyed considerable depth of meaning. More beautiful than Brando and more articulate than Dean, Newman was a highly attractive symbol of youthful yet intellectualized angst and rebellion that would resonate strongly with sixties audiences. Three films in particular, *The Hustler* (1961), *Hud* (1963), and *Cool Hand Luke* (1967), defined Newman's unique onscreen combination of iconoclastic sensibilities and classical star allure.

The Hustler presents Newman as "Fast Eddie" Felson, a cocksure pool shark with his mind set on taking down the legendary Minnesota Fats, played by the effectively offcast comedian Jackie Gleason. Felson fails in his first attempt at defeating Fats, subsequently drives away his manager in striving for another, and finally pushes his disillusioned girlfriend to suicide while pursuing an ultimately successful yet hollow victory. Felson shared key elements with characters Newman had played in the 1950s, primarily arrogant, ambitious menwho are at odds with those around them, but *The Hustler* surpassed Newman's previous films in fully acknowledging the human damages these selfish, antisocial tendencies could cause, while still eliciting audience sympathy for its central character. What made Felson work was Newman's ability and willingness to combine rough-edged, amoral cold-heartedness with classic star sex appeal, self-assuredness, and charm. With *The Hustler* and many of his subsequent films, a dynamic balance resulted from the tension between Newman's unblemished handsomeness and the flawed man within.

Newman's desire to play such aberrant characters was well publicized from the start of his career. He reportedly told the *World-Telegram and Sun* that "an actor has got to watch and be aware of his 'loveability' rating with the audience. When you find it you stick with it to protect yourself. This is the commercial demand of the movies. . . . When you're no longer interested in improving yourself, you become content with the status quo—then you're in trouble" (John Ferris, "Paul Newman Says He Doesn't Enjoy It Because He Lacks Intuition," 12 September 1959, 3). Newman's efforts with

Felson indicated to appreciative fans that he was not content with status quo loveability. Further, Newman acknowledged in a 1961 publicity piece that he enjoyed playing "pretty nasty" men, explaining that "although it would be disastrous to admit it, they're much more fascinating than the good guys" (Albin Krebs, "Paul Newman Enjoys Work," *Los Angeles Mirror*, 18 December 1961). His reference to potential disaster indicates a reason why so few stars were historically willing to portray "bad guys" on a regular basis: they feared alienating audiences. But the willingness of 1960s audiences to increasingly accept and even revel in antiheroic characters signaled a hallmark societal change as counterculture sensibilities grew across the country. Newman's persona was effectively poised to appeal to those sensibilities using the broad appeal of his star allure.

In fact, that very allure made possible the popular success of the most antiheroic of his antiheroes, Hud Bannon. The titular character of *Hud* was written with Newman in mind by *Long Hot Summer* scribes Irving Ravetch and Harriet Frank, drawing on a minor subplot from Larry McMurtry's novel *Horseman, Pass By* (1961) (Oumano 92–93). The film's distributor, Paramount, certainly felt that the meshing between actor and character was strong, as they organized their marketing campaign around a provocative image of Newman and the slogan "Paul Newman is *Hud*." While this phrasing acknowledged Newman's star power and centrality to the film, it was also a bold risk given the despicability of its main character.

Hud is a morality play about a teenager pulled between two role models, his conservative cattle rancher grandfather and his unprincipled uncle. While the teenager, Lon, is enticed by the festive habits of his lively Uncle Hud, especially in comparison to the life of obligation led by his traditional grandfather, Homer, he slowly comes to realize that beneath Hud's charismatic exterior is a detestably selfish and morally bankrupt soul. Through actions that range from annoying (driving over a flowerbed) to distasteful (sleeping with married women) to unethical (wanting to unload possibly diseased cattle on unsuspecting ranchers) to reprehensible (attempting to rape the housekeeper), Hud is an unrepentant hedonist at nearly every moment in the film, and he was one of the biggest scoundrels that a star of Newman's caliber had ever played.

The screenwriters, director Martin Ritt, and Newman had intended to impart a lesson about the corruption of modern capitalism and the danger of admiring an individual for his personal magnetism without taking the measure of his character (Lax 105–07). In effect, these were roughly the same messages that Newman had frequently told the press he feared perpetuating as a popular star. However, youth audiences in particular read

Newman posing provocatively as Hud, too beautiful to be rotten. (Collection of the author)

Hud not as an objectionable scoundrel but as an admirable antihero, and they did indeed admire him for his personal magnetism without taking the measure of his character. As Newman later described, "The kids thought he was terrific. His amorality just went right over their heads; all they saw was this Western, heroic individual" (Lax 108).

Despite the filmmakers' best intentions to present an uncompromising portrait of a loathsome man, Hud was almost inevitably attractive due to Newman's star charisma. Legendary film critic Pauline Kael wrote a lengthy critique of the film that argued as such: "They could cast [Paul Newman] as a mean man and know that the audience would never believe in his meanness. For there are certain actors who have such extraordinary audience rapport that the audience does not believe in their villainy except to relish it, as with Brando; and there are others, like Newman, who in addition to this rapport, project such a traditional heroic frankness and sweetness that the audience dotes on them, seeks to protect them from harm or pain" ("Hud, Deep in the Divided Heart of Hollywood," *Film Quarterly*, Summer 1964, 16). While Newman had hoped that viewers would leave the theater understanding that an externally beautiful man could have a rotten core, few were apparently inclined to accept a favorite star, a beautiful star, as thoroughly rotten.

This determinant is best illustrated by the scene in which Hud demands to know why his father has such contempt for him. He assumes that their conflict stems from Homer's lingering resentment over Hud's responsibility for his brother's death in a drunk-driving accident, but Homer insists that his disdain for his son began long before that incident. Homer explains: "You don't give a damn. You don't care about people, Hud. You just don't give a damn about 'em. Oh, you got all that charm going for you, and it makes the youngsters want to be like you. That's the shame of it. Because you don't value nothing. You don't respect nothing. You keep no check on your appetites at all. You live just for yourself. And that makes you not fit to live with."

While the filmmakers' stated intention was for the audience to side with Homer and find the moral of the film within his words, one is hard-pressed not to sympathize instead with Hud. During Homer's rant, the anamorphic widescreen frame offers a rare close-up of Hud, which emotionally connects the viewer to him. Newman's intense stare belies Homer's claim of Hud's nonchalance, and an audience by now trained to read Method acting as a vehicle for themes of emotional repression could also easily dig beneath this glare to envision Hud's internal pain, a product of years of patriarchal rejection. Then, just as it seems that Homer's words might be cutting into him, Hud breaks into a wry smile, insolently affirming Homer's characterization, and exits after commenting, "My mama loved me, but she died."

For sixties audiences already inclined to align themselves with the young iconoclast over the aging authority figure, this is an inspired exit, not an ignominious one. Further, Newman's sheer beauty leaps off the screen during the close-up, simply making it difficult for the viewer to share in Homer's contempt. In that regard, Homer's comments about Hud's enviable charm echo the concept of star allure itself. What lingered in the audience's minds was not Hud's immorality but his confidence, his magnetism, his independence, and his individuality, all of which were traditional star qualities that Newman could relay so well. After Hud leaves, Homer implores Lon not to follow his uncle's example, lamenting, "Little by little, the look of the country changes because of the men we admire." This profound statement fittingly applies to the popularity of Newman's star image at this point in his career and in American culture. As dissatisfaction with traditional values and beliefs began to spread, audiences increasingly admired the antiheroic Newman screen image and the star's ability to imbue unsavory characters with seductive charisma.

The fact that his characters' rebellious motivations were frequently rooted in a resentment of the corrupt world that surrounds them resonated strongly with audiences, and no film illustrated this better than *Cool Hand Luke*. Newman plays Luke Jackson, a cynical, insolent loner whom the actor described as "the ultimate non-conformist and rebel" (Peter Bart, "A Newman Non-Interview," *New York Times*, 9 October 1966, X13). After committing the mindless, drunken infraction of sawing open city parking meters, Luke is disproportionately punished with a two-year sentence of hard labor on a prison chain gang. There he rebels against his captors and his fellow prisoners, eventually earning the respect and even the idolization of the latter due to his charismatic persistence in battling against the unforgiving brutality of the former. As with his original offense, much of Luke's defiance seems enacted for its own sake. When he is placed in solitary confinement after his mother's death because the guards expect prisoners to run off for funerals, Jackson does indeed escape, but he has no evident intention of heading off to mourn his mother. Instead, as Newman's trademark grin fills Luke's face when he flees, we understand that he is motivated by generalized insubordination in response to oppression, not by specific goals. Of course, every obstinate act ends in failure, and Luke's smile progressively fades into grim resignation as he continues to rebel as a matter of course. Because neither the law nor Luke will relent, the film inevitably ends with his death at the hands of prison authorities.

Luke Jackson was definitive of both Newman's filmic image and the late 1960s cultural milieu, resulting in an almost mythic creation. As a playfully arrogant and reckless outsider undeniably alienated by society's rules, Luke constituted a revealing progression from Newman's earlier antiheroes. Whereas Eddie Felson and Hud Bannon sought ways to opportunistically thrive within an unscrupulous society, Luke is so disillusioned with the inequitable world around him that he sees no value in even participating in it and is existentially driven toward defiance. One can understand how a significant segment of the American populace, with growing frustration over business, government, and military corruption, would follow a similar path, and Luke thus reflected a late 1960s sensibility of disenchantment with conformity and alienation from authority. Newman biographers Joe Morella and Edward Z. Epstein write: "When the film was released the country was in the midst of a social revolution. The flower children, the hippies, the discontented young of the day, were all looking for a hero like Luke, who would flout convention and take beatings, if necessary, to retain his integrity as a rebel" (130).

Warner Bros. perceptively targeted this audience and its mentality, as the film's marketing campaign featured such pithy taglines as "Paul Newman hits the establishment with everything he's got" and "When a man is as independent in spirit as Luke is, there is no form of discipline that can in any way be tolerated" (*Cool Hand Luke* pressbook, Warner Bros., 1967). The studio also developed a "hip radio campaign" directed to college students, pointing out to potential buyers that the "style and subject-matter of 'Luke' plus the unique place of Paul Newman as an interpreter of off-beat roles is a magical combination with particular appeal to the campus crowd" (*Cool Hand Luke* pressbook). It is also clear from the campaign, however, that this appeal was expected to reach well beyond flower children and the campus crowd. Declaring that college students were chosen as a target because of their status as a "top trend-setting sector of the population," the ad copy specifies that with "their 'in' social aspects and their youthful enthusiasm [students] can turn loose a huge wave of acceptance for 'Luke' among the rest of the movie-goers."

This indicates how readily mainstream culture would co-opt counterculture sensibilities as a signifier of hipness, and *Cool Hand Luke*'s image of rebellion was indeed easily absorbed into dominant culture. The brutality of the prison guards is so overwhelmingly dehumanizing that even a hardcore conservative wouldn't blame Luke for his ceaseless insurrection. The film is not truly about hitting the establishment, or about the fraudulence of America's prison system. It is an indictment of a group of criminally inhumane prison guards. Of course, one could interpret this group as an allegory for the absolute corruption of absolute power in the American government, and the flower children segment of the audience at the time likely did. But neither the film nor Newman's performance invites such an interpretation; instead, they invite viewers to revel in Luke's independent spirit, just as Warner Bros.' slick marketing campaign intended.

That independent spirit was also transmitted by Newman's performance, and as with Hud, Newman's star charisma makes Luke broadly appealing.

Newman as the iconic Luke Jackson. Newman's star charisma made Luke broadly appealing, an image of rebellion easily absorbed into the mainstream. (Collection of the author)

This is underscored in a heavy-handed way in the film's final sequence, a retrospective montage of shots featuring "that old Luke smile" that in effect supplies a happy ending to soften the otherwise harsh blow of Luke's death. The montage unspools shot after shot of Luke's charismatic smile, ultimately coming across more as a tribute to Newman as star than as a memorial for Luke. This and other elements, such as the frequent Christ symbolism,

lessen the true degree of subversion embodied by the film and the character. In the end, the establishment had nothing to fear from *Cool Hand Luke*.
Indeed, both the counterculture and the establishment could embrace
Newman's image as an antiheroic screen rebel. His most popular characters
embodied values of nonconformity and anti-authority, but particularly by
the time *Cool Hand Luke* was released, these values had been assimilated by
mainstream culture as signs of hipness. Newman's traditional star qualities,
from his close-up-ready looks to his charisma, also helped to make his
unconventional characters broadly appealing. Newman would come to
lament how these factors limited the range of roles in which audiences
would accept him, but his box office success would not have been possible
without them. An analogous dynamic operated within Newman's offscreen
publicity, which presented him as an idol to youth audiences without alienating older generations but also entrenched his image as the "super-cool"
iconoclast even more deeply.

★★★★★ The New Hollywood Life

In line with traditional modes of star publicity, coverage of
Paul Newman offscreen complemented his onscreen image, connecting
traits of his maverick characters to the star while deflecting their antisocial
connotations so as not to detract from the popular appeal of Newman's personality. For instance, the press often reported on Newman's boyish playfulness, from stories of the juvenile pranks he often played on colleagues,
which were all in good fun and never mean-spirited, to tales of his heavy
beer drinking, which was presented as a winsome addiction. While many of
Newman's characters displayed regressive behavior along these same lines
to the detriment of those around them, Newman's offscreen versions of
these activities were portrayed as positive evidence of his down-to-earth,
personably masculine ways. Most strikingly, Newman repeatedly played
arrogant, brash manipulators onscreen, yet publicity heavily stressed the
actor's humbleness. One profiler commented that Newman's "manner was
so unassuming and offhand he might have been just the boy next door"
(Kitty Hanson, "They Call Newman Rebel, But Look at Who's Talking,"
Daily News 4 April 1962, 44), and after remarking that "all my good roles
have been furthest from what I am," Newman self-deprecatingly told Sidney
Fields of the *New York Mirror*, "I'm as sexy as a piece of Canadian bacon"
("Newman: 'As Sexy as a Piece of Bacon,'" 12 June 1959).

Through reportage on his political activities, Newman was also separated
from the radical nihilism of characters like Eddie Felson and Hud Bannon

yet tied to their ideologies of nonconformity through his support of progressive social resistance. From civil rights to atomic energy education to antiwar protesting, Newman actively participated in numerous liberal causes. While stars traditionally kept quiet about their political inclinations so as not to alienate audiences, Newman said he refused to place his career above his conscience. He told *Show Business Illustrated*, "They keep telling me to shut up out in Hollywood. They keep saying if I sound off on controversial subjects I'll jeopardize a million-dollar investment by getting some pressure group mad. I frankly don't give a damn. I insist on my right to say what I think" (Al Morgan, "Paul Newman: New Breed of Screen Lover," February 1962, 22).

Rather than dismissing him as a naïve windbag, most critics praised Newman for his civic efforts, and the press frequently reported on his sincerity, intelligence, and dedication to causes beyond the film world. *Los Angeles Times* critic Charles Champlin lauded him as "one of the genuinely thoughtful actors around" ("No Blinkers on this Private Eye," 18 August 1965, D9), and Newman accordingly insisted that the frivolities of stardom were meaningless in light of the serious issues imperiling the country: "Who gives a damn about the Newmans, or anyone's trivial concerns, with civilization hanging in the balance? The only things that matter now are the real ones" (Kirtley Baskette, "Paul Newman: Fellow with a Fever," *Modern Screen*, October 1962, 58). Thus, audiences knew that Newman was actively committed to liberal causes, but he was driven by a genuine, educated concern for the country's welfare, not a subversive mentality.

While counterculture youth admired Newman's progressive political commitments, older audiences could appreciate his traditional domestic life. Profiles of Newman's marriage to Joanne Woodward portrayed the relationship as true love and even emphasized that, contrary to Newman's modern, libertarian screen image, the couple adhered to traditional gender roles at home, as Woodward often put her own career on hold in favor of motherhood and the advancement of her husband's career. One fan magazine described, "With grace and dignity, Joanne Woodward long ago adjusted her career and her ego to Paul Newman's. At the heart of their marriage, the things that are done are the things that are best for Paul. . . . At home Paul i a king. Everything is planned for his convenience" ("The Heaven and Hell o Living with the Most Attractive Man in the World!," ca. 1966). *Motion Pictur* magazine quoted Newman himself as saying, "I think the American woman is getting absolutely out of hand. With all the household chores a man i expected to do these days, it's very difficult for a child to tell his mother from his father" (Jim Hoffman, "Only Faintly Saintly," June 1965, 68).

These traditionalist connotations were bolstered by an associated image of the couple's nonconformity with Hollywood orthodoxy, which was framed as representative of a wholly positive new era in movie stardom. A 1963 *Los Angeles Times* profile of the pair's unpretentious life made this claim explicit: "If any couple in filmdom is typical of the New Hollywood, it is Paul Newman and Joanne Woodward. They don't ride in limousines or lead leopards down Hollywood Blvd. They wear slacks and don't go home in studio make-up. They don't fight in night clubs—on the rare occasions they go to such places. They disapprove of puffy publicity and they take their profession very seriously. This is the New Hollywood—the stark, studious life" (Art Ryon, "Paul Newman, Joanne Woodward Keep Down Pretenses," 6 January 1963, D6). The two were also geographically separated from Hollywood, as they chose to make a farmhouse in Connecticut and an apartment in Manhattan their primary homes, and they tried to keep the Hollywood press at a similar distance away from their private lives. Newman lamented, "In order to be a gold-plated success in this town, it's almost mandatory that an actor open his private life to public view, get himself trapped into making more and more money and become a yes-man to Hollywood brass. Not for me" (Baskette 57).

Newman and Woodward's image of folksy ordinariness was often explicitly tied to the presumption that they were not interested in the empty indulgences of movie stardom. In a newspaper article about how Newman and Woodward "live sensibly—and hence less glamorously" than past stars, Woodward insisted, "We're more interested in gratification in our work than the things money can buy" (Bob Thomas, "The Big Houses, The Big Money—Where Did They Go?" *Chicago Tribune*, 14 December 1958, F1). Newman even said that his desire to wear T-shirts and jeans and navigate the streets of New York in a scooter rather than dress and drive around Hollywood as a glamorous movie star was a moral choice: "Somehow the scooter bugs the Hollywood crowd more than anything else, even more than the way I dress. Don't think there aren't pressures on me to dress up, shut up and get off the scooter. I know I can jeopardize my position. I frankly don't give a damn. This is the way I am. It's my own business" (Morgan 22).

Fans young and old appreciated this image of personal integrity, especially because it was increasingly fashionable to criticize Hollywood in such way. In the wake of the arrival of television, the breakdown of the studio system's publicity machinery, and the rise of scandal magazines, a new generation of moviegoers had grown increasingly aware of the traditional manipulation of star images and appreciated actors who appeared to operate outside the Hollywood glamour machine. A Paul Newman fan club publication praised the actor for rejecting publicity coverage: "Could it be that Paul doesn't want to be recognized as someone the press creates through their sleek ability to discolor the truth and actually make millions of people believe their sometimes preposterous lies? If so, then Paul's intelligence deserves to be praised" (Sharen Berseth,"Paul's Unusual Technique," *Paul Newman Fan Club Newsletter*, August 1960, 9).

In a period of growing disillusionment with the artificiality of Hollywood's glamour machine, Newman's headstrong yet principled stances against the excesses of stardom came across as refreshingly genuine to many. To some Hollywood insiders, on the other hand, this made Newman an ungrateful interloper, which perhaps offers an explanation for why the star did not win an Academy Award in the decade despite receiving three nominations and giving numerous superior, original performances (Morella and Epstein 72). But at a time when Old Hollywood was crumbling and a new order was gathering in its aftermath, this impression was not detrimental to Newman's popular image. Kitty Hanson praised Newman's individuality as such in the *Daily News*: "To oldtimers frozen in the Hollywood mode, he's a nonconformist because he insists on doing things his way rather than the way someone has decided movie stars ought to do" (44).

★★★★★ Fighting the System

Newman also wished to break with Hollywood tradition by evading star typecasting, but in consistently professing that he insisted on doing things his own way, he only more deeply fortified his image as a benevolent dissident. He told *Modern Screen* in 1962, "I'm not a crusader. But the star system here is crippling artistically and it cheats the public of the great things Hollywood could give it" (Baskette 59). Newman wanted to truly revolt by essentially being an actor, not a star and not a sex symbol, and he was frequently lauded in the press for this stance, but he was bound by the traditional mechanisms of the star system nonetheless. For as much as Newman was labeled a Hollywood heretic and an "anti-star" (Douglas Brode, "The Superstar of the '60s," *Show*, February 1972, 23), it was only when his roles were aligned with his establishedstar persona, and thus the decades-long traditions of the star system, that he found his biggest box office successes.

Newman's struggles against and subsequent capitulation to the forces of stardom were evident throughout the 1960s. In *Sweet Bird of Youth* (1962 Newman played Chance Wayne, a swaggering gigolo trying desperately to scheme his way to movie stardom while still holding on to his hometow

Newman in *The Prize*, another role requiring him to take his shirt off. (Collection of the author)

sweetheart. Wayne had similarities with Newman's contemporaneous anti-heroes like Eddie Felson, as he is a cocky, ambitious charmer who manipulates people and receives his comeuppance in the end. But some critics complained that *Sweet Bird of Youth* relied too heavily on Newman's sex appeal, which both undermined Wayne's status as a pathetic loser and left the actor merely displaying his physique rather than his emotive skills. *The New Yorker*'s Brendan Gill wrote, "I hope to see Mr. Newman in a picture that doesn't require him to take his shirt off; here it is off most of the time. . . . An actor can't do much more than feel ticklish under such circumstances, and I think I detected an occasional looking of longing on Mr. Newman's face, as if he were thinking how nice it would be to be ugly and fat and middle-aged and allowed simply to *act*" ("The Current Cinema: Men in Trouble," 7 April 1962, 148). Here again emerges the impression that Hollywood custom was only holding Newman back artistically.

Of course, it was his traditional star charisma that enabled Newman to make a despicable character like Wayne so appealing in the first place, but Newman insisted on trying to douse that star appeal when he could. For instance, following *Sweet Bird of Youth*, Newman reprised an aging boxer character he had played on a 1950s television anthology drama for a cameo role in *Hemingway's Adventures of a Young Man* (1962). He told gossip columnist Hedda Hopper, "You might say I'm doing it as an exercise in acting. I want to run the old TV film and compare it with my present performance. I want to see if being a movie star has diluted my work as an actor" ("Paul Newman vs. the Bomb," *Chicago Sunday Tribune*, 7 January 1962, G26). This role also evaded his incessant star glamorization by letting him bury his face under bruises, scars, and cauliflower earsand dispense with his familiar dazzling smile in favor of the slack-jawed vacuity of a punch-drunk fighter. Director Arthur Penn later reflected on Newman's motivation: "You have to understand that he suffered a little bit from being so handsome—people doubted how well he could act" (Morella and Epstein 39). The very decision to take such a small part was unconventional for a thriving star, and critics praised him for the effort. *Variety* wrote, "Newman deserves credit for the fact that, as a top star, he's not above the undertaking of a small character role when it represents an artistic challenge" ("Review of *Hemingway's Adventures of a Young Man*," 20 July 1962).

Most of Newman's artistic challenges, or the films in which he departed from his intense rebel image, resulted in financial failure, including a string of five consecutive box office flops in the mid-sixties. Newman especially floundered when venturing into comedic roles. A pairing with Woodward in a frothy romantic comedy called *A New Kind of Love* (1963) was dismissed by *Variety*'s reviewer: "Mr. and Mrs. Newman are better at dramatic assignments than comedy, particularly the former" ("Review of *A New Kind of Love*," 28 August 1963). The lavish black comedy *What a Way to Go!* (1964) offered Newman a stunt casting cameo as one of the many husbands that Shirley MacLaine's jinxed bride survives, but critics complained that Newman played the role in such an over-the-top manner that his performance only detracted from the character. A 1967 *Photoplay* feature analyzed New man's difficulties with comedic performance, concluding that the studied, Method-inspired intellectual approach that worked so well for him dramatically was inappropriate for comedy. The article offered a perspective from *The Hustler*'s Jackie Gleason: "He doesn't study a character, he burrows into it, sniffs at it. Of course, that's what makes him such a fine dramatic actor—one of the best in my book. But it's the wrong approach for my racket" (Charlotte Dinter, March 1967, 98).

Newman also ran into problems with his dramatic acting in this period, though. *The Outrage* (1964) offered Newman a drastically offbeat role as a Mexican bandit and accused rapist in a western remake of the Japanese film *Rashomon* (1950). Newman, complete with a black wig, fake nose, darkened skin, and heavy Mexican accent, gave his most uncharacteristic portrayal of the 1960s, and few were willing to take it seriously. Biographer Daniel O'Brien succinctly states, "The paying public would not accept Newman as a Mexican rapist" (106). Of course, they had been willing to accept him as an American rapist in *Hud*, but the distance between Mexican identity and Newman's persona was too vast to reconcile. *Hombre* (1967) presented Newman in a similarly anachronistic role. Here he played John Sullivan, a white man raised by Apache Indians and an outcast among a group of stagecoach riders who reluctantly protects his fellow travelers, some less deserving than others, from attackers. While Sullivan shared traits with some of Newman's earlier incarnations, such as staunch individuality, the star played him with daring minimalism and stillness, completely jettisoning his usual glib smiles and energetic vitality. The result is an intensely underplayed performance, and while some critics dismissed this as contrary to what audiences wanted to see from Newman (Quirk 160), others lauded the actor for his ongoing quest to defy the rules of stardom. One profile ended with the following observation from the *Hombre* set: "The last I saw of him, he was arguing with director Martin Ritt. He was protesting explosively that a full close-up of him would spoil the mood of the scene and that the camera should be focused instead on Frederic March. It was obvious that in the war between the rebel's split personality, the dedicated actor was winning triumphantly over the Hollywood star" (Frank Rasky, "Movie Rebel with Those Sexy Eyes," *Toronto Star Weekly*, 10 September 1966, 19).

Box office results would soon tip the scales back to the Hollywood star. Newman himself acknowledged a problem: "I have a very American skin, and when I try to go out of my skin . . . I go wrong" (O'Brien 113). Newman would return to his own skin with a traditional genre film, the detective caper *Harper* (1966), which put him back among the top revenue-earning stars and reaffirmed his rebel cool status. This was Newman's first film at

Warner Bros. since departing his studio contract, and it was additionally a throwback to Warner Bros.' detective films of the 1940s, with the presence of Lauren Bacall added to ensure just such an impression. Accordingly, Newman was effectively channeling the spirit of Humphrey Bogart as a cynical, world-weary private eye who is devoted to justice, if only on his own terms. But in line with the *Hustler*- and *Hud*-defined Newman persona, Harper is more self-serving, more playful, and more of a sex symbol than Bogart ever was. Fittingly, after Bacall's character coyly responds to Harper's refusal of a drink with the comment, "I thought you were a detective," he quips, "New type."

This was really an old type for Newman, though, as Harper's air of casual toughness mixed with slick charm was familiar to him. Fittingly, Warners copied *Hud*'s marketing ploy by using the tagline, "Paul Newman is *Harper*." The studio also stressed the star's masculine allure with such poster slogans as "Excitement clings to him like a dame" and "Girls go for Harper" (*Harper* pressbook, Warner Bros., 1966). Such hackneyed ploys, plus the fact that *Harper* did not have nearly the intellectual depth of films like *The Hustler* and *Hud* nor the acting complexity of *Hombre*, must have been somewhat disappointing for Newman, but he was likely grateful for the film's success, given his lengthy box office drought. While Newman could try to push the boundaries of the star system, his fanbase had the power at the box office to rein him back in.

Newman's experiments with offcasting had helped to develop his skills as an actor, however. He had especially learned by the late 1960s how to moderate his characteristic Method acting quirks to more subtly grasp audience allegiance. *Variety*'s original review of *Sweet Bird of Youth* had observed that Newman tended to rely on "overly-mannered movements that distract," yet paradoxically, "these mannerisms, which tend to diminish his stature and versatility as an actor, serve to make him a star" (28 February 1962). Back then, Newman knew that every dynamic grin, icy glare, pursed lip, and bared chest would captivate audiences, if sometimes to the detriment of characterization. But in the wake of experiments like *Hombre*, he came to recognize that it did not take much for his glinting eyes and chiseled features to carry a great deal of expressiveness, leading him to exploit a more underplayed style in films like *Cool Hand Luke*. Even his most emotionally loaded scene in that film, when Luke sings in mourning of his mother's passing, is played mainly through stillness and a simple forlorn stare.

While *Cool Hand Luke* was a career and creative highpoint for Newman, it coincided with a string of articles in which Newman spoke of his insecurities about the future course of his career. He chiefly expressed frustration that his attempts to break from his star persona rarely succeeded with the public. Newman told *Playboy* in 1968, "I'm running out of steam. Wherever I look, I find parts that are reminiscent of Luke or Hud or Fast Eddie. Christ, I played those parts once and parts of them more than once. It's not only dangerous to repeat yourself, it's goddamned tiresome" (Richard Warren Lewis, "Paul Newman," July 1968, 68).

Fittingly, Newman's final film of the 1960s would be his biggest hit of the decade and a sign of the height of his star appeal, but it was not one of his more creatively ambitious efforts. *Butch Cassidy and the Sundance Kid* (1969) drew substantially on the charm and chemistry of its stars, veteran Newman and newcomer Robert Redford. The two play a pair of outlaws running from the authorities and from obsolescence. At times a revisionist debunking of western myths and at others a romanticized portrait of them, the film never stakes a deeply meaningful claim about the doomed protagonists and their ways. This did not deter audiences, however, who reveled in the adventuresome, inventive spirit of the outlaws and the considerable charisma of the stars who played them.

By now, Newman had mastered this character—the confident, independent, unruffled con artist with boyish charm—and he had developed an effectively underplayed comedic method to portray him, with no "burrowing" or "sniffing" in evidence. This seemingly effortless acting style helped to create a magnetic fusion of star, actor, and character. *Butch Cassidy and the Sundance Kid* was a prototypical star vehicle, and it performed like one at the box office, becoming the fifth highest grossing film of the decade, while Newman ended the sixties as the number-one box office star in a survey of movie exhibitors ("Paul Newman is No. 1," *Los Angeles Times*, 26 December 1969, E31). For as much as Newman had professed himself to be a Hollywood outsider throughout the 1960s, he ended it as the reigning symbol of the movie capital's still-powerful traditional ways.

★★★★★ Conclusion

Newman also ended the decade by more resolutely pulling himself out of the grind of the star system. He turned to directing with *Rachel, Rachel* (1968), a pet project of Woodward's that Newman helmed when the couple failed to find anyone else interested in the task. Newman had long talked of his desire to direct features, telling *Life*, "I've always wanted to direct because I've always enjoyed most the peripheral things about acting, the rehearsals and the field trips, the exploration of character and the whole intellectual exercise of the thing. I enjoy this more than actually getting up on a stage or in front of a camera. That has always been more painful to me than enjoyable" (Jane Wilson, "What If My Eyes Turn Brown?" 24 February 1968, 28). With his next film, Newman definitely reveled in the "peripheral things," when he appeared with Woodward in *Winning* (1969), a conventional action-romance set in the world of Indy car racing. Newman was developing a passion for auto racing at this point, which would quickly come to overtake his passion for acting. This production experience enabled him to obtain professional driving lessons and to perform his own racing scenes, and it also paid him more than any film ever had: $1.1 million in salary plus a profit percentage (Kerbel 117).

Newman similarly grew more detached from Hollywood offscreen. His political activism increased in this period, as he actively campaigned for Eugene McCarthy's presidential run, particularly because of McCarthy's staunch antiwar platform. Also, Newman and Woodward both stepped up their avoidance of the press in response to numerous salacious articles claiming that their marriage was in trouble. They even began refusing to sign autographs for fans in an effort to lay claim to their privacy (Felicia Lawrence, "Leave Us Alone!" *Screen Stars,* November 1969, 64–65). Overall, Newman repeatedly dismissed any allusions to his participation in the machinery of stardom, telling *Screen Stars* in late 1969: "In the early days of films, the movie star in this country replaced royalty. They've been demoted since, but they're still treated larger than life. Well, I don't want to be part of that fraud" (Lawrence 64). In countless interviews across the decade, Newman repeatedly told variations on the same lament: "People always come up to me, perfect strangers, and ask me to take off my dark glasses so they can look at my eyes. I simply answer: 'Is that all you think of me?' If blue eyes are what it's all about, and not the accumulation of my work as an actor, I may as well turn in my union card right now and become a gardener" (Joan Sand, "'I'm Not Afraid to Make Enemies,'" *Motion Picture,* June 1968, 30). With such comments and efforts, Newman carried forth an image of the Hollywood outsider, even as he could only be as popular as he was by being an insider.

It is also apparent that only when Newman played his broadly appealing rebel figure, which boiled his antihero rebellion down to a detached, youthful cool through which his star charisma shone, did he succeed. In a period that witnessed a burgeoning generation gap and ongoing cultural revolutions, Newman's image of righteous nonconformity resonated strongly. At the same time, the era's social polarization also could accommodate Newman's traditional image of masculinity and domesticity, especially as they were defined as genuine signifiers of a man with no pretensions. Newman was additionally representative of a period of turmoil in the Hollywood film industry. In both attempting to evade the star system but ultimately perpetuating it, Newman was a bridge between the classical Hollywood orthodoxy of rugged stars like Clark Gable and the New Hollywood iconoclasm represented by such actors as Dustin Hoffman and Robert De Niro. Finally, Newman's dynamic ability to translate a bevy of contradictions into Hollywood stardom also came by virtue of an ineffable quality of star charisma. Newman was a star because, as Eddie Felson's manager says of the pool shark in *The Hustler*, "He can charm anybody into anything."

2 ★★★★★★★★★★★

Elizabeth Taylor
The Biggest Star in the World

ALEXANDER DOTY

During the 1960s Elizabeth Taylor was one of the top box office attractions in the world, became the highest-paid female star, and won two Oscars. She was also involved in two major scandals with married men and began to garner bad press (and negative public opinion) for being "out of control" in various ways: sexual voracity, weight gains, constant illnesses, drug and alcohol use, and lavish spending. Until nearly the end of the 1960s, she was able to counterbalance "bad Liz" with "good Liz," by and large, by making certain she was in good trim for her films, using some of her illnesses to create public sympathy, not allowing her drinking or drug-taking to affect her filmmaking or public appearances, and being almost as generous as she was profligate. For a 1960s America that moved uneasily between valorizing conventional values and offering support for civil rights and counterculture movements, Taylor had it all. She out-mammaried Monroe, but with a touch of nurturing Earth Mother; she was a serious and hard-working actor who often appeared in trashy or (unintentionally) campy films; she was a conventional romantic who felt that she had to marry the men she fell in love with, although she had no qualms about falling in love with other women's husbands; she was a demanding, diamond-loving diva who also exhibited a raucous and self-critical sense of humor; and while her ongoing health and weight issues were frequently understood as the result of her frantic, indulgent "jet set" lifestyle, they also often made her a sympathetic (and even a heroic) figure—especially to other women and to queer men—in the vulnerability they exposed. Despite appearing on box office top-ten lists for most of the 1960s (she was number one in 1961), a series of critical and popular failures after *Who's Afraid of Virginia Woolf?* (1966) stripped Taylor of her career glory—so much so that by the latter half of the 1960s she became more noteworthy for her personal life and her besieged body than for her work as an actor.

Taylor entered the 1960s already having moved past her child star (*National Velvet* [1944]) and ingénue (*Father of the Bride* [1950]) periods via meaty roles as neurotics in such films as *Raintree County* (1957), *Cat on a Hot Tin Roof* (1958), and *Suddenly, Last Summer* (1959). Academy Award nominations for these films contributed to the industry and public perception of Taylor as a "serious actress," if one who was an untrained "natural" or "instinctive" performer. Mixed with this, however, were publicity campaigns that began to focus on Taylor's voluptuous body, in addition to her face and famous eyes: an image of the star lounging on a bed in a sheer slip advertised *Cat on a Hot Tin Roof* and one of her in a low-cut, white, skintight bathing suit garnered attention for *Suddenly, Last Summer*. Here was a star who had the body and, more important, the breasts of a Monroe, a Jane Russell, or a Jayne Mansfield combined with the acting talent of a Susan Hayward. Added to the mix around this time was a change in the way the press and public understood her personal life, particularly her romantic relationships.

By 1960, Taylor had racked up three husbands—Nicky Hilton, Michael Wilding, and Michael Todd. The press and public had been relatively benign about the first two marriages, chalking them up to youthful inexperience, while the star's marriage to Todd, a celebrated producer, was sanctified by his death in a plane crash. Taylor became the object of an outpouring of sympathy as the beautiful, grieving "Widow Todd." But the great public and industry goodwill Taylor amassed during most of the 1950s as a pretty, unpretentious "good girl" and a model, professional studio contract player who worked hard at her craft was troubled in the late 1950s and early

1960s by three things: her affair with the married Eddie Fisher, her resistance to working off her MGM contract by making *BUtterfield 8* (1960), and her part in the production of *Cleopatra* (1963), particularly her affair with married co-star Richard Burton. Press, public, and industry reactions to these films and these relationships, more than anything else, would construct the "Elizabeth Taylor" of the 1960s.

Initially, Taylor's post-Todd relationship with Fisher was understood as an extension of her and her husband's friendship with Fisher and wife Debbie Reynolds. Indeed, the quartet had been publicized as a young, happily married Hollywood foursome. The public, press, and industry shock and dismay at discovering that Taylor was, in fact, beginning an affair with Fisher during her mourning was compounded by feelings of having been tricked and betrayed. Taking up the imagined position of Reynolds, the press fed the public stories of a devious Taylor stealing her best friend's husband under cover of bereaved widowhood. Typical was the January 1959 issue of *Photoplay* that featured a picture of Reynolds, her children, and the family dog with the caption "Can't daddy be with us all the time?" (Walker, *Elizabeth* 206). In terms of her public image, Taylor's affair with Fisher squandered most of the good girl–as–young widow sympathy she garnered when Todd died. "Does God always punish?" asked *Photoplay* in its April 1960 cover story on the star (Walker, *Elizabeth* 224). Taylor only made things worse when, with her typical candor, she professed not to care about what other people thought, confessing "shamelessly" that she was "terribly happy" (Walker, *Elizabeth* 209).

Surprisingly, when the scandal broke, it didn't hurt the box office for *Cat on a Hot Tin Roof*. This was one of the first signs that, as far as Taylor was concerned, "the line between celebrity and notoriety, which had once been so strictly drawn, was ceasing to count in the public's view: now everything was becoming 'good publicity'" (Walker, *Elizabeth* 207). But this state of affairs wasn't fully apparent at the time, even though Taylor's next film, *Suddenly, Last Summer*, was also a box office success and would bring some of her best reviews. In part to counteract the supposedly bad publicity generated by the Fisher affair, director Joseph L. Mankiewicz and co-star Katharine Hepburn praised Taylor to the press for her professionalism and her development as an actor. Less publicized, but well known within the industry, was Taylor's on-set and off-set caretaking of longtime friend Montgomery Clift during the filming. In *Suddenly, Last Summer*, Taylor plays Catherine, the naïve cousin of a mother-dominated homosexual who uses her to lure young men when they are on vacation (his mother has become too old to perform this service). When her cousin Sebastian is killed and partially cannibalized on a trip to Mexico, Catherine goes into shock and is sent to an asylum, where Sebastian's mother wants her to have a lobotomy in order to keep the story a family secret. This heady melodrama was written by Tennessee Williams and marked the beginning of a long friendship between the writer and Taylor, who maintained close relationships with a number of queer (if largely closeted) men during her career, but particularly in the late 1950s and the 1960s (Roddy McDowell, Rock Hudson, James Dean, Noel Coward, Clift, Williams—even Richard Burton admitted to homosexual liaisons in his younger days). So, among other things, by the late 1950s and early 1960s, Taylor's status as what came to be known as a "fag hag" or "fairy queen" was already well established, if not just yet for the public at large then certainly within the industry.

Considering her public position as the femme fatale in the Taylor-Fisher-Reynolds triangle, maybe Taylor shouldn't have been surprised when MGM asked her to do *BUtterfield 8* (1960). Much of America already saw her as a wanton woman who slept around with married men, so why not capitalize on this public image by having Taylor play Gloria Wandrous, a high-class call girl who falls in love with one of her married clients? Whether this part was chosen by the studio in order to exploit current events or not, *BUtterfield 8*'s release marks the beginning of what would become a widespread practice by the press and public—and sometimes in film publicity campaigns—of connecting Taylor's roles to information and rumors about her "real life" personality and circumstances. (Within the industry, this practice of seeing some degree of [auto]biography in Taylor's films probably began with *Suddenly, Last Summer*, wherein gay-friendly Liz played the devoted cousin of a homosexual, while having a platonic relationship [onscreen and off] with co-star Montgomery Clift.) Even though he didn't play the part of the married man with the long-suffering wife, Taylor's insistence that husband Fisher join the cast further encouraged contemporary (auto)biographical readings of *BUtterfield 8*:

> It was no secret that a substantial part of the public perceived Elizabeth in a way that didn't differ much from O'Hara's heroine. . . . Elizabeth's disdain for public opinion reflected [Gloria's] disregard for her own reputation. Neither felt that she owed the public an explanation for her life-style, never mind an apology. (Walker, *Elizabeth* 216)

Kitty Kelley suggests that the star was well aware "that MGM was capitalizing on her notoriety by casting her as the call girl in John O'Hara's novel" (147). For her part, Taylor professed that she could see no similarities between herself and Gloria, and was very vocal at the time about her disdain

Liz and Eddie Fisher face off in *BUtterfield 8*, furtherconnecting Taylor's roles to information and rumors about her "real life" personality and circumstances. (Collection of the
author)

for the part: "I hate the girl I play. I don't like what she stands for—the men,
the sleeping around" (Kelley 150). But what appears to have incensed Taylor as much as her exploitative role in a "pornographic script" was that she
was being forced to do the film by her longtime studio for her standard
MGM salary (variously reported as $125,000 and $150,000) in order to
complete her contract so she would be free to accept a lucrative offer to play
Cleopatra at Twentieth Century-Fox (Amburn 121).

With *BUtterfield 8* and the end of her MGM contract, Taylor's reputation
within the industry as a savvy businessperson also begins to become known
to the general public through press accounts of her financial wheeling and
dealing. Agents rarely get mentioned in these accounts, leaving the star to
take all the glory or criticism for driving hard bargains. Her mother, and
then Mike Todd, taught her much about the economic end of the movie
business, knowledge that she would pass on to friends and co-workers
whom she felt were getting a raw deal. Reportedly, she "taught [Tennessee
Williams] how to negotiate for a percentage of the gross and burnish his
deals like a Hollywood pro" (Amburn 118). "I stepped in and tried to act as

his agent," she said later (Amburn 118). Taylor may have had to accept her standard salary for *BUtterfield 8*, but when she didn't show up to work for a week, the studio found itself giving in to a number of the star's demands, like casting Fisher, shooting the film on location in New York City, using Helen Rose for her wardrobe and Sidney Guilaroff for her hair, and hiring other crew members with whom Taylor had formed professional relationships (Sheppard 281).

Also beginning with *BUtterfield 8*, there was increasing press coverage constructing an "Elizabeth Taylor" who was capable of creating a rough shoot through her intransigence or illness, which were sometimes connected through suggestions that some of her illnesses may have been self-induced or psychosomatic, striking the star when she wasn't happy with what was happening in her life or on the set. Not surprisingly, questions about Taylor's heretofore vaunted professionalism come to the fore around this time, with people in the press and the industry both defending and criticizing the star on this count. Kitty Kelley's account of the *BUtterfield 8* shoot presents a Taylor who would become even more familiar to the public in press accounts of *Cleopatra*:

> Lashing out [at being forced to make the film], Elizabeth proceeded to punish everyone connected with [it]. She was hours late to location, hours late to makeup. "She was constantly sick and purposely late," said the producer [Pandro S. Berman]. "She made life miserable for the studio," said the assistant director. "Everyone suffered through the making of the film," said the costume designer [Helen Rose].   (151)

Director Daniel Mann says he felt compelled to lecture Taylor when she reported late once too often: "I told her she was part of a collaborative effort, and out of respect for her coworkers she owed it to herself—and to us—to comport herself professionally" (Heymann 212). On the other hand, there are many accounts of Taylor's initial resistance to the project being counteracted by her professional pride. Donald Spoto quotes playwright Mart Crowley, who worked on the film as a production assistant, as saying that while Taylor clearly "hated" making the film, she was "such a professional" that she would often ask for another take in order to make a scene better (Spoto 180). Alexander Walker also quotes producer Pandro S. Berman's assertion that he knew that, in spite of her threats to slow down the production, the star's "professionalism [would get] the better of her distaste for the film" (Walker, *Elizabeth* 221).

While *BUtterfield 8* was in production, some of the more negative accounts of Taylor's attitude toward, and work on, the film made it out to the public. Perhaps because it was the final MGM film on her contract, the studio's publicity department really didn't feel as compelled to protect her image as it otherwise might have—and she certainly felt little loyalty to a studio she believed was treating her shabbily. From MGM's point of view, stories about "bad Liz" could only make the studio look better and encourage the public to conflate Taylor with her role in the film. This situation becomes even more pronounced during the making of *Cleopatra*, an epic that took about two years to complete and that became the most expensive film ever made to that time. *Cleopatra* is also the project that could be said to cement one of the crucial aspects of the 1960s "Elizabeth Taylor," wherein press and public interest in her personal life becomes as important as—if not more important than—the film she is starring in. Perhaps part of the press's (and, therefore, the public's) intensified focus on the star's private life was the result of no Taylor film being released for almost three years. After *BUtterfield 8* in 1960 and before *Cleopatra* in 1963, entertainment journalists, studio publicists, and the public increasingly had to turn to the star's illnesses (including a near-fatal bout of pneumonia in 1960), her disintegrating marriage to Eddie Fisher, her adoption of a child with a hip deformity, her relationship with her other children, and her affair with Richard Burton to get their fill of news on Taylor. Initially, stories about the long and drawn-out production of *Cleopatra* did help fuel public interest in Taylor on and off the set, especially since the star was refusing to talk to the press (Maddox 161). Her often-fraught involvement in the chaotic production was covered in daily newspapers and popular magazines, as well as in trade papers and journals, and, after the filming was over, in a couple of "making of" books: producer Walter Wanger's *My Life with Cleopatra* (with Joe Hyams) and Jack Brodsky and Nathan Weiss's *The Cleopatra Papers: A Private Correspondence*. But what ultimately kept journalists and the public fascinated by the years-in-the-making *Cleopatra* was Taylor's glamorous, erotic, yet illness-wracked body and her affair with Richard Burton.

✰✰✰✰✰ Barging Up the Nile: The *Cleopatra* Years

Because no one was certain about its effects, there were some attempts by the stars and the studio to keep "le scandale," as Burton dubbed it, under wraps at first. Dick Sheppard notes that the late 1950s and early 1960s were a turning point for Hollywood, as the old studio system with its publicity machines that cleaned up or suppressed things was being pitted against a newly vigorous "tell all" style of tabloid entertainment journalism epitomized by *Confidential* magazine (326–27). It was also a period when the industry's self-censoring Production Code Administration was being challenged to become more sophisticated and "adult" in its judgments by the non-Code-approved release of American films like *The Moon Is Blue* (1953) and *The Man with the Golden Arm* (1955) and by racy foreign hits like *La Dolce Vita* (1960). This was but one sign that the industry was caught up in the same agitation and uncertainty about what constituted appropriate manners and morals as the rest of the country (and, indeed, a good part of the world). The Taylor-Burton affair became one of the more visible battle-grounds upon which forces of the "new morality" fought with the "estab-lishment." Although she was hailed and reviled at the time as representing either refreshing sexual freedom or immoral promiscuity, Taylor was provocative in the 1960s because she frequently straddled or blurred the line between "sexual revolution" (being unashamed about extramarital affairs) and old-fashioned values (devotion to her children, feeling that love/sex and marriage must always go together). In her first memoir, writ-ten in 1964, Taylor captures the "in between" position that made her such a compelling 1960s zeitgeist figure:

> According to the code of ethics today, I was, I suppose, behaving wrongly because I broke the conventions. But I didn't feel immoral then, though I knew what I was doing, loving Richard, was wrong. I never felt dirty, because it never was dirty. I felt terrible heartache because so many innocent people were involved. But I couldn't help loving Richard. I don't think that was without honor. I don't think that was dishonest. It was a fact I could not evade.   (*Elizabeth Taylor* 106)

When the press finally got wind of the Taylor-Burton liaison, there was a firestorm of publicity, with the affair consistently getting prominent, even front page, treatment in papers across the world beginning around 20 Feb-ruary 1962. As journalist Brenda Maddox noted at the time, "In 1962 there was more world interest in *Cleopatra* and its stars than in any other news event" (173). A later Taylor biography asserts: "In the spring of 1962, nuclear testing, disarmament, and the Berlin crisis were secondary news to what was happening between Elizabeth Taylor and Richard Burton in the Eternal City" (Kelley 184). In the middle of the press maelstrom, an exas-perated Burton reportedly exclaimed to *Cleopatra* publicist Jack Brodsky, "Jack, how did I know the woman was so fucking famous? She knocks Khrushchev off the front page" (Spoto 207). Initially, most of the press on the Taylor-Burton affair took on a critical tone, which seemed to confirm the studio's worst fears that this kind of publicity could only hurt *Cleopatra* at the box office. The Roman paper *Il Tempo* called Taylor "an intemperate vamp who destroys families and devours husbands," AP-UPI suggested that "Liz wants her bottom smacked" and that one of her husbands should have

Barging up the Nile: Taylor and Burton in *Cleopatra* share a look of love. (Collection of the author)

done it long ago, while Hearst columnist "Suzy" felt that Taylor was a "self-destructive" person who "flouts conventions, jeopardizes her career, wreck other people's lives, and flings herself headlong into folly" (Sheppard 383) Ed Sullivan was concerned that young people would find "the sanctity of marriage has been invalidated by the appalling example of Mrs. Taylor Fisher and married-man Burton" (Sheppard 383). There were even member of the House of Representatives (like Iris Blitch) who publicly denounce the pair, asking the U.S. attorney general to declare them "ineligible for re-entry into the United States on the grounds of undesirability" (Spoto 213).

But the public criticism that appears to have affected Taylor the most at this time came from the Vatican press, which attacked, among other things, her competency as a mother. An "Open Letter" in *L'Osservatore della Domenica* by someone signing as "XY" focused on Taylor's recent adoption (with Fisher) of a German girl with a deformed hip:

> Then, when you reached the point of adopting a baby girl, as if to make more stable this marriage which had no natural children, for a moment we really believed that things had changed. But children—whether they are natural or adopted—count little for illustrious ladies like you when there is nothing for them to hold together. . . . Where will you finish? In erotic vagrancy? And your poor children: those who are your true children and the one who was taken from an honest institution. . . . Was it not better to entrust this girl to an honest bricklayer and to a modest housewife rather than to you, my dear lady, and your fourth ex-husband?   (Sheppard 386)

Papers around the world picked up this open letter, which most readers assumed expressed the opinion not of (or not only of) "XY," but of the Vatican establishment, even of Pope John XXIII, who had already grumbled about Rome being in danger of becoming "a city of perversion" because of the presence of the *Cleopatra* production company and its stars (Taraborrelli 201). Reportedly, Taylor was so appalled by this attack on her maternal competence, particularly in relation to her recent adoption, that she asked if she could "sue the Vatican" (Sheppard 387).

As with her widowhood and her near-fatal illness, Taylor's adoption of a girl in 1962 who needed extensive surgery in order to repair a deformed hip initially won her a certain amount of admiration from the press and the public during those early, stormy days working on *Cleopatra*. For most of the 1950s Taylor had garnered positive press for being a concerned and attentive mother to her children, as she always had them nearby (if not actually on the set) when she was working and had often expressed her worries about the effects her hectic career might have upon the children. But early in her marriage to Fisher, articles like "Will Liz' Children Be Taken Away from Her?" and "Are Liz' Kids Ruining Her Marriage?" began to appear (Sheppard 328). After her affair with Burton became public knowledge, *Life* ran a photo feature in its 13 April 1962 issue titled "Please . . . who's my daddy now?" which suggested that Taylor's children, as well as those of Burton and his wife, were having an identity crisis because of Taylor's "headlong rush from one love to the next" (Walker, *Elizabeth* 253). The open letter in *L'Osservatore della Domenica* was only the most spectacular expression of the increasing invective that cast Taylor as a neglectful, self-ish, "bad mother," in spite of her adoption of a needy child. At the time, and with her usual candor, Taylor said in an interview, "I try to get as much time with [my children] as I can. I know I am doing a lousy job, but as God is my witness, I am trying to be as good a mother as Elizabeth Taylor can be" (Taraborrelli 209–10).

While most of the press corps were busy representing Taylor as a "bad woman" and a "bad mother," Fox's publicity department and a number of trade journals were encouraging the public to see Cleopatra as the role Tay-lor was "born to play," or, rather, the part that the star's life and experiences fully equipped her to play. Among other things, Taylor and Cleopatra were touted as "the most beautiful woman in the world." Both were also rich and powerful women whom the public saw as using their sexual allure to entice well-known, married men. It wasn't long before an entity that Andy Warhol dubbed "Liz Taylor-in-*Cleopatra*" was born. His 1964 silk-screen por-traits reproduce an image of Taylor combining a contemporary hairstyle with *Cleopatra* eye makeup—something the star herself affected for many years after filming was over. Regarding the effects of such (auto)biographical readings of Liz-in-*Cleopatra*, Francesca T. Royster notes:

> Taylor, like Cleopatra, was said to love too much. . . . Thanks to unprece-dented amounts of publicity about Taylor's love life and illnesses and the financial health of the studio, *Cleopatra*'s hyperinflated costs, production val-ues and even length (four hours) become conflated with Taylor's body and her hunger for love, food and the public eye. And Taylor's hunger, in turn, is further reinforced by the parallel construction of the historical Cleopatra as "enslaved by her appetites." (93–94)

Even her household staff got into the act when her butler, Fred Oates, interviewed in *Photoplay*, said that, at home, Taylor was "a dictatorial empress, a true-to-life Queen of the Nile who treated her husband [Fisher] like a virtual slave, rejected phone calls from her parents, invited guests for supper and then refused to dine with them" (Heymann 237). One of the most striking examples of the public conflation of star and role came while filming Cleopatra's triumphal entrance into Rome. Rather than chanting "Cleopatra!" as they had been directed, the extras screamed out "Leeez! Leeez! Baci! Baci!" when she appeared.

Shortly after filming was over, Taylor pronounced *Cleopatra* "the most bizarre piece of entertainment ever to be perpetrated" (Taylor, *Elizabeth Tay-lor* 101). However, some of her public pronouncements on the role of Cleopatra betray more than a touch of projection: "Cleopatra was more like a tigress than a sex kitten, even at nineteen, when she first met Caesar and had been queen for only two years. She was even more mature in her pas-sions and political feelings by the time she met Antony" (Kelley 170). Biog-rapher Walker speculates that while "it would be going too far to say that [writer-director Joseph L.] Mankiewicz saw the outlines of his *Cleopatra* screenplay in the recent events of Elizabeth's life. . . . As he watched Eliza-beth's marriage deteriorate, the role of a woman like Cleopatra who wants it all and receives the homage of two [married] lovers in rapid succession must have gained coloration and substance from contemporary events" (*Elizabeth* 227). Certainly, dialogue in the film like the following resonated with contemporary audiences who came to see the scandalous woman who had become the biggest, and best-paid, star in the world:

> *Caesar:* I seem to recall some obsession you have about your divinity. Isis, is it not?
>
> *Cleopatra:* I shall have to insist that you mind what you say. I am Isis. I am worshipped by millions who believe it.

Even more than on *BUtterfield 8*, when *Cleopatra* ran into production trouble, the studio was willing to allow the press to believe it was largely the result of the film's star—she was Cleopatra, after all. Typical for Taylor, much of the benevolence she had regained in the industry and with the public as a result of that near-fatal bout of pneumonia early in her involvement with *Cleopatra* (she even felt that she won the Oscar for *BUtterfield 8* because she almost died) eroded as allegations of costly production-delaying hijinks became a regular feature of *Cleopatra*'s press. Royster notes that

> repeatedly, in the narratives of the ensuing illness of Fox Studios, constructed in *The Cleopatra Papers* and *My Life with Cleopatra* . . . the excesses of Fox's pro-duction company get all mixed up with the sexual excesses of Taylor and, in turn, with that of Cleopatra. "I was a victim of *Cleopatra*," Darryl Zanuck claimed, after taking over as president of Fox Studios. . . . Taylor has been saddled with the brunt of the blame for Fox's troubles, which, in some hyper-bolic reports, extends to a responsibility for the fall of the studio system itself and the end of the Golden Age of film.   (105–06)

But there was already a tone in certain press reports of Taylor's initial deal to play the Queen of the Nile that heralded later, near-hysterical reports on the star's various excesses. Before she went into *BUtterfield 8*, the press, following the lead of Fox's publicity department, reported that the $1 mil-lion the star would receive for *Cleopatra* was a new record, and with it Tay-lor would become the highest-paid star in motion picture history. Actually, this wasn't quite true, as some male stars had preceded Taylor into the "mil-lion dollar club." What was true is that Taylor and her agent negotiated a number of financial perks in addition to her base salary—which was to be paid out in installments and into trust funds for her children, in any case—that would make Taylor's earnings for the film surpass those of any star before her for a single picture. The initial $125,000 a week for sixteen weeks' work was followed by $50,000 for each additional week (of which there were to be very, very many), $3,000 a week living expenses, and what has been reported as anywhere from 10 to 35 percent of the gross, as well as royalties for the use of Todd-AO to shoot the film. After the production shut down to allow Taylor to recover from pneumonia, it was restarted with a different director and leading men, and the star charged Fox another million to return to the production in Rome (it had been filming in England). All things considered, Taylor would earn about $7 million for playing Cleopatra. As Ellis Amburn notes, Taylor's *Cleopatra* deal "ushered in a new era of filmmaking, in which actors would call the shots" (160), which "brought home to the industry how precarious film investment had become once the studios no longer owned either the stars or the movie theaters" (Maddox 197).

Even though Fox studio heads attempted to keep their resentments to themselves, their displeasure with their "holding the studio hostage" star was picked up by journalists in Hollywood, New York, and on location. For its part, the studio appears to have tacitly encouraged the press to make uppity free-agent Taylor the scapegoat for the production's woes once filming started again in Rome, particularly when she began her affair with Burton. Sheppard quotes a representative piece of trade press criticism at the time: "The sympathy of the entire film industry can scarcely help going out to [Fox executive] Spyros Skouras and the 20th gang who have so patiently put up with Liz's antics and mishaps for so long" (380). But many people in the industry and the press also realized that studio mismanagement and bad luck combined to create most of the film's production woes—though they generally kept this to themselves. By the time the second company of *Cleopatra* began filming, studio heads seemed all too willing to let Taylor take the rap. In the absence of interviews with the reclusive star, the press was also ready to cast Taylor as the modern-day incarnation of the profligate queen of Egypt, thereby downplaying the studio's culpability.

After the film was released, this scapegoating reached its climax when Fox served Taylor and Burton with a much-publicized $50 million breach-of-contract suit in three parts, with $20 million brought against Taylor for a host of alleged misdeeds, including delaying shooting, "conspiring with others," and holding herself up to "scorn, ridicule, and unfavorable publicity" (Sheppard 416). Burton, by contrast, was sued only for $5 million individually, though $25 million was leveled against both for their disruptive adulterous behavior, among other things (Sheppard 417). Despite the fact that the studio dropped the lawsuit, publicly apologized to the stars, and gave them $2 million in restitution, just the fact of the lawsuit seemed to confirm for the public what the press had been reporting all along. As a result, Taylor's reputation as a reliable, untemperamental performer was seriously compromised. From this point on, "Elizabeth Taylor" would become one of those legendarily "difficult" actors both to people in show business and for the general public. Certainly Taylor did contribute to *Cleopatra*'s financial woes to some extent with her illnesses and the work-related effects of carousing with Burton (which added greater alcohol consumption to the "painkillers" and other prescription pills to which she was already addicted). But all this was a drop in the bucket compared to what studio mismanagement cost the production. In Taylor's own words:

> And what ballooned the unbelievably Wagnerian, insane quality of everything was the insanity going on at the *Cleopatra* set every day. They would actually misplace fifteen hundred spears. And when the expenses began mounting astronomically, suddenly the great way to save money was: "We've got to cut down on the number of paper cups used."
>
> (*Elizabeth Taylor* 106–07)

In spite of, or maybe because of, the press's year-long badmouthing of her personal and professional behavior on *Cleopatra*, Taylor emerged from the experience even more famous than she had been going into the project. According to Maddox, "What the popular press had been saying was true—that Elizabeth Taylor as Cleopatra had more power than the real Cleopatra ever had" (Maddox 167). Indeed, it was Taylor's celebrity notoriety that finally pushed the most expensive film ever made to the break-even point, if not to a nice profit (depending upon which account you read)—although this was not until a decade or so later, and as the result of re-releases in foreign markets, TV broadcast agreements, and video sales. Royster notes that "*Cleopatra* . . . appears at a historical point when the film celebrity emerges from the constraints of studio production and control," and that "Taylor's Cleopatra becomes synonymous with the increasingly outdated excess of the Hollywood epic, the death of the studio-made 'star' and the resurrection of the celebrity" (93–94). In other words, in many ways, "Liz Taylor-in-*Cleopatra*" could be understood as the apogee of Old Hollywood extravagance and glamour, as well as one of the signs of the end of that era. *Cleopatra* marks the point at which MGM's diligent, obedient, modest, popular glamour girl becomes one of the world's most outspoken, unrestrained, controversial, "famous-for-being-famous" personalities.

One indication of how Taylor's image had changed within the industry is that, after four successive Oscar nominations for Best Actress, she was denied one for *Cleopatra*, even though the film itself garnered nine nominations, including one for non-scandalous co-star Rex Harrison. One way to understand Taylor's non-nomination is as an attempt by the studio system's old guard to punish Taylor for what they saw as her taking advantage of Fox, as well as for her "they need me more than I need them" attitude toward studios and producers. Both Taylor and the studio chiefs knew that this particular star really didn't even need to make films anymore—just look at the three-year period between *BUtterfield 8* and *Cleopatra*, or the period right after *Cleopatra* when the press coverage of Taylor's private life became even more intense. Besides, now each new Taylor or Taylor-Burton film was being consumed as much for the insights it could provide into the life of its star(s) as it was for its value as entertainment or art.

★★★★★ Rich and Famous—and Fat and Vulgar

The only woman who was pretty enough to go without makeup was Elizabeth Taylor . . . and she wore a ton!

—Violet, *August: Osage County*, Act I

For Taylor, her *Cleopatra* and post-*Cleopatra* period as a celebrity-star—and as part of the world's most famous couple, "the Burtons"—included the constant critical monitoring of her physical appearance. Of course, comments on Taylor's looks was something that began during her ingénue period, but in the form of admiring comments on her hypnotic violet (or deep blue) eyes and maturing body, and continued in her early adult period with hyperbole about, again, her eyes, and her now voluptuous figure. But things began to turn nasty some time during the 1960s with increasing press and public remarks about her weight gains, or, less neutrally, her "fatness." During the filming of *Cleopatra*, even Burton contributed to the intensified critical focus on Taylor's body. While, reportedly, he was impressed by her famous eyes, he also began taking increasingly public potshots at her double chin and her "fat ass," besides calling her "Miss Tits," all of which Taylor graciously laughed off. "He's such a perverse tease," she says in her 1964 autobiography. "Nothing delights him more than to call me, in front of some reporter, 'A comfy, nice little girl,' and then throw in something about a double chin and stumpy legs" (Taylor, *Elizabeth Taylor* 130). On the other hand, Taylor sued the *Daily Mail* for libel when it suggested her extended absence from the public eye at the start of *Cleopatra*'s filming in London was because she was "too fat" and was trying to reduce (Maddox 162). A number of *Cleopatra* reviews also made a point of alluding to Taylor's weight as part of their damning the film. "Miss Taylor is a plump, young American matron in a number of Egyptian costumes and make-ups," the *New Republic* critic noted, while TV critic David Susskind called the star "overweight, overbosomed, overpaid, and undertalented" (Kelley 191). John Simon, somewhat more tactfully, described Taylor-as-Cleopatra as being "rather overripe" (Simon 93).

But it wasn't just Taylor's weight that the press and the public began making fun of, or being appalled by, when *Cleopatra* was released. That high, thin voice that had been fine with most critics and audiences when she was a child star, an ingénue, and when playing neurotic young women suddenly became a problem when Taylor played Cleopatra. "When she plays Cleopatra as a political animal, she screeches like a ward heeler's wife at a block party," was *Time* magazine's opinion (Kelley 191). Along the same lines, Judith Crist in the *New York Herald Tribune* found that Taylor, as the queen of the Nile, had "no modulation in her voice that too often rises to fishwife levels" (Kelley 191). Continuing in this vein, Simon found the star's "speech" to be "unpleasantly commonplace" (Simon 93). Pitting Taylor against her theatrically trained British co-stars, *Cue* magazine, unsurprisingly, found that she "simply does not possess the emotional range—in voice control or movement—to match consistently the professional perfection of Rex Harrison, superb as Caesar . . . or Richard Burton as the tempestuous, passionate and utterly tragic Antony" (Kelley 191). Attacking Taylor's weight and her voice became a commonplace for the remainder of the 1960s—and it continued in the 1970s and 1980s, tapering off somewhat when she became an AIDS advocate in the late 1980s and wrote her second autobiography, *Elizabeth Takes Off: On Weight Gain, Weight Loss, Self-Image, and Self-Esteem* (1987). The only respite from all this during the 1960s came with *Who's Afraid of Virginia Woolf?* when Taylor lowered the pitch of her voice, and where her weight gain was seen as necessary and appropriate in order for the star to essay the role of middle-aged, boozy Martha.

Behind all the criticism (and apparent in the comments about her voice) is a class bias that uses the star's "shrill" and "loud" voice and her increasing size to construct an "Elizabeth Taylor" who had become undisciplined and crassly nouveau riche to much of the press and public during the latter half of the 1960s. Even worse, many saw her as dragging down the "classy" and classically trained Richard Burton (when, in fact, he had been born into a working-class family), even while she tried to gain some sophistication-by-association through her relationship with him. If truth be told, Burton was even more eager to gain international fame from

Diamonds—and caftans—are a girl's best friend. (Collection of the author)

his association with Taylor. As much as her voice and weight, the star's steady acquisition of some of the most famous jewels in the world in the late 1960s and early 1970s (the Krupp diamond, the "La Peregrina" pearl, and what came to be known as the "Cartier-Burton" diamond, among others) clinched Taylor's position as a figure of outrageous, tacky excess. To some extent, Taylor took the harsh and sometimes cruel press and public judgments about her body and her spending habits in stride. A *New York Times* editorial took her and Burton to task for being proud standard bearers "in this Age of Vulgarity." "I know I am vulgar," Taylor reportedly responded, "but would you have me any other way?" (Spoto 250–51).

More and more after *Cleopatra*, it seems that producers, following press and public opinion of the star, did want a "vulgar" Taylor—or at least to have her play outrageous characters. This didn't happen right away, as Taylor quickly jumped into the role of a socialite in *The V.I.P.s* (1963) in order to co-star with Burton again and reap the financial rewards of the pair's notoriety. There followed a nearly two-year hiatus from filmmaking during which Taylor—amid much press coverage—played the devoted girlfriend and wife, following Burton to New York when he starred in *Hamlet* onstage in 1964 and to Mexico when he was cast in *The Night of the Iguana* (1964). She also wrote her first autobiography during this time, which, if nothing else, performed some degree of damage control on her public image as it reinforced her reputation for unpretentiousness and openness. At the end of the autobiography, however, Taylor turns her candor on the press and public, implicating them in the current state of her star image:

> I don't think because you are an actor or actress you have any special responsibility to the public just because they want to pry via the press into your private life, make conjectures and decide what kind of person you are. . . . Everything that I have done in my life that is a mistake I will admit is a mistake and answer for it. But I am not going to answer for an image created by hundreds of people who do not know what's true or false. . . . I know that I will never be able to be really and truly dignified in the eyes of the public. I shall not be allowed to be. . . . The public seems to revel in the imperfections of the famous . . . which I guess makes them feel a bit superior. So I should have delighted lots of fans throughout the world. If anybody had given them an opportunity to feel superior, I have.   (*Elizabeth Taylor* 174–75)

While Taylor suggests that she possesses a "dignity" the public doesn't see because of the current press coverage of her life, most of the films she appears in during the last half of the 1960s seem to conform to, and to reinforce, the image of an indulgent, raucous, immoral or amoral, and appetitive (in many senses of the word) "Elizabeth Taylor." There are exceptions to the rule, or, rather, an exception to the rule besides *The V.I.P.s*: in the adaptation of Graham Greene's novel *The Comedians* (1967), Taylor takes what is essentially a supporting role as the wife of the German ambassador to Haiti. However, even when cast as socialite or as ambassador's wife, audiences were still able to connect Taylor's characters to "Elizabeth Taylor," as these characters took on lovers to satisfy sexual desires that exceeded the bounds of matrimony. In addition, the former film has her character returning to an alcoholic husband, played by Burton, and the latter film has her engaging in a torrid affair with a character played by Burton. Between them, *The V.I.P.s* and *The Comedians* (and, later, *The Sandpiper* [1965] and *Who's Afraid of Virginia Woolf?*) offered "Liz and Dick" in both the "adulterous affair" and the "married couple" stages of their relationship to a public that was primed to read press-constructed images of "the Burtons"—individually and as a couple—into each of their seven co-starring films.

As for Taylor's other mid- to late 1960s and early 1970s films, she was cast as a free-spirited, bohemian artist who has an affair with a married minister (Burton) in *The Sandpiper*; as the blowsy and abrasive wife, Martha (opposite Burton as husband George), in *Who's Afraid of Virginia Woolf?*; as a loud and vulgar Katharina in *The Taming of the Shrew* (1967) (with Burton as Petruchio), a film *Playboy* called "[a] news event—another colorful episode in the lives of Elizabeth Taylor and Richard Burton, whose supposed follies happen to fit into a comedy from the first folio" (Maddox 190–91); as the angry, "sex starved" wife of a homosexual army officer in *Reflections in a Golden Eye* (1967); as the eccentric, much-married, chronically ill, "richest woman in the world," Flora ("Sissy") Goforth, in *Boom!* (1968, with Burton as an "Angel of Death"-as-gigolo character); as an over-the-hill prostitute who begins a quasi-maternal, quasi-incestuous relationship with a rich young woman in *Secret Ceremony* (1968); as an aging chorus girl stranded in Las Vegas who has an affair with a younger man in *The Only Game in Town* (1970); and as an aggressive and abusive wife who decides to seduce her husband's mistress in *X, Y, and Zee* (1972, also known as *Zee and Co.*).

At the time, each of these films had elements of "prestige" associated with them and seemed to be part of a strategy by Taylor and Burton to become the film equivalent of the theater's legendary acting couple Alfred Lunt and Lynn Fontanne. *Reflections in a Golden Eye* was based on a Carson McCullers novel, with John Huston directing and Marlon Brando co-starring; *The Comedians* was based on a Graham Greene novel; *Boom!* was the result of combining a Tennessee Williams play called *The Milk Train Doesn't Stop Here Anymore* with his short story "Man Bring This Up the Road," and with Joseph Losey directing; *Secret Ceremony* again had Losey directing and Robert Mitchum co-starring; *The Only Game in Town* was based on a Frank Gilroy play and had George Stevens directing; while *X, Y, and Zee* boasted a screenplay by Edna O'Brien with Michael Caine and Susannah York co-starring. With the exception of *The Only Game in Town*, however, there were also elements of heavy-handed pretentiousness in these films that, when combined with the increasingly harsh publicity about the Burtons' lavish, jet-setting, supposedly hedonistic lifestyle, and the increasingly visible onscreen evidence of Taylor's bouts with pill and alcohol addiction and weight gain (the latter insistently emphasized in reviews), turned most of the public decisively against Taylor, the Burtons, and their films by the early 1970s.

By the late 1960s Taylor (with or without Burton) was beginning to seem somewhat behind the curve as the "Youth Movement" began to have an explosive impact on Hollywood and the popular imagination with films like *The Graduate* (1967), *Bonnie and Clyde* (1967), *Easy Rider* (1968), and *Midnight Cowboy* (1969), and new stars like Dustin Hoffman, Faye Dunaway, Jack Nicholson, Ali McGraw, Donald Sutherland, Jane Fonda, and Julie Christie. Big budgets, old-style glamour, and romantic excess were on their way out; small-scale productions, new style realism, graphic sexuality, and violent excess were coming in, and becoming "in." Maddox suggests that Taylor had become a sexual "anachronism": "By 1968 the image of Woman projected by Taylor had gone out of style. There she was in *The Comedians* in *haute couture* and teased hair, reeking doom, just as Vanessa Redgrave was removing her plain checked shirt and baring a bony chest to the camera in *Blow-Up*" (200).

During the late 1960s and early 1970s, however, Taylor held on gamely, still commanding a large salary and plenty of press coverage, though, in retrospect, *Who's Afraid of Virginia Woolf?* was the apex of her late 1960s career as she was able to translate all the negatives that had been building up around her star image (marital woes, illnesses, weight gains, signs of aging, voice issues, questions about her maternal abilities, boozing and pill-popping, sexual voracity, and a general sense of excess) and turn them into positives by playing Martha. "People liked Taylor for playing" this character, Maddox notes, and adds:

> In her press coverage, Taylor made another major jump: off the editorial pages and onto the women's pages. The Chicago *Sun-Times* lady readers were treated to a friendly cartoon of Taylor, bulging out of toreador pants, in among the recipes for sour cream coffee cake. There was a poem, too:
>
> > Elizabeth Taylor, we give you our hearts,
> > Our hot fudge sundaes and cherry tarts.
> > For "Virginia Woolf" you've earned our prizes
> > By bringing glamour to half-sizes.   (194–95)

At the same time, there were intimations of the decline to come, as *Who's Afraid of Virginia Woolf?* was also Taylor's "debut as Medusa, the monster-woman," a role she was to play variations upon in succeeding years in such critically and financially unsuccessful films as *Reflections in a Golden Eye*, *Boom!*, *Secret Ceremony*, and *X, Y, and Zee* (Maddox 195). But, if these bitchy, blowsy characters made Taylor increasingly less popular with the general public, they helped clinch her place as a gay camp-cult icon—a position Taylor laid the groundwork for with Cleopatra's drag queen-ready makeup, hairstyles, and accessories. More than one commentator found it telling that Taylor, aided and abetted by Burton, began the period of her most conspicuous, jewel-centered consumption—and bolstered her press coverage—about the time she began to lose her luster at the box office and with critics. "By the late 1960s," Spoto notes, "Elizabeth Taylor no longer had to have great starring roles: she had only to live like a star" (249).

3 ★★★★★★★★★★

Dustin Hoffman
As Artistic as Possible

DANIEL SMITH-ROWSEY

For its first forty-six years, *Time*, America's newsweekly of record, invariably presented cover illustrations of important people or events. The very first *Time* cover photograph, dated 7 February 1969, featured not a world leader, astronaut, or international conflict, but Dustin Hoffman and Mia Farrow: "The Young Actors: Stars and Anti-Stars." The article talked about how their recent movies have spun "a new myth of lost innocence, of the individual against the wicked system." And the magazine aligned the meaning of the actors with the meanings of the films:

> The new young actors themselves represent the death of many movie myths—among them, the one of the movie star. The big press build up, the house in Beverly Hills baroque, the ostentation and the seven-picture commitment are giving way to a stubborn kind of performer who is as suspicious of the Hollywood system as a student rebel is of the university trustees.

Time explained that "anti-stars" like Hoffman were in fact a response to recent changes in the culture:

> As comedy grew steadily blacker and as audiences grew steadily younger, hipper and more draftable, the old concepts began to erode. The invulnerables like Peck and Holden and Wayne seemed lost in a country full of people whose destinies were not in their own hands. The nation of cities needed new images, and suddenly Hoffman became an archetype.
>
> (Stefan Kanfer, Jay Cocks, and Carey Winfrey, "The Moonchild and the Fifth Beatle," *Time*, 7 February 1969, 51)

America's discontent now had a genuine Hollywood face, a star image.

In July of the same year, the cover of *Life* trumpeted: "Dusty and the Duke: A Choice of Heroes." At the peak of a summer of bitter Vietnam discontent, Woodstock, and a manned trip to the moon, *Life* chose to compare Dustin Hoffman and John Wayne, then appearing onscreen in *Midnight Cowboy* and *True Grit*, respectively. Throughout the article, Wayne is the "he-man," Hoffman the "everyman." Wayne's image is "strong, decisive, moral, and nearly always a winner." Hoffman's "characters . . . are conspicuously short on these traditional qualities. His people are uncertain, alienated, complex, and, by any familiar standard, losers." Wayne's Old Hollywood performance wisdom—"I don't act, I react"—gets aired near a caption that reads: "Every role Dustin Hoffman has played so far has been unique." In direct contrast to Wayne, Hoffman reveals that he's still seeing an analyst, that it's not "particularly courageous for an actor to speak out politically" as he (Hoffman) had about Eugene McCarthy, and that an actor shouldn't do at fifty what he did at thirty. Wayne blames irresponsible professors for current student unrest, while Hoffman says, "The youth outburst in this country is a good thing. The kids are angry because the American leaders have made mistakes and refuse to admit it" (Ralph Graves, *Life*, 11 July 1969, 3). Again and again during the 1960s, and unlike today, journalists referred to a younger generation with new values; here, *Life* positioned Hoffman as an innovative, incorruptible avatar. (This Wayne-Hoffman competition arguably continued until that year's Oscars, where Wayne's performance beat Hoffman's, but Hoffman's film won Best Picture.)

For contemporary mainstream sources, Dustin Hoffman represented the 1960s' break from the past. Hoffman symbolized both radical transformation and a certain familiarity, both of which the studio system was quick to incorporate. Marsha Kinder suggested as much when she wrote that films of "the new American humanistic realism"—she named only *The Graduate* (1967), *Midnight Cowboy* (1969), *Easy Rider* (1969), and *Five Easy Pieces* (1970)—"render suspect their own 'revolutionary' perspectives by easing back into the values they appear to be questioning" partly because "the value of several of them depends largely upon performances, such as Dustin Hoffman's in *Midnight Cowboy*" (Kinder 221). Kinder suggests that star performance transforms, or obviates, any sort of true challenge to the system, like the more avant-garde films she details.

This essay examines contemporary media sources to determine how Hoffman was understood and contextualized during the 1960s, particularly in the discourse surrounding his two major films of the period, *The Graduate* and *Midnight Cowboy*. Hoffman was not simply a great actor whose talent would have assured his stardom at any time in the twentieth century. Hoffman's star image was also mobilized to represent the rebellious spirit of contemporary young adults. This essay asks: What was gained and lost when Dustin Hoffman became a (perhaps *the*) representative of the "anti-star" movement? How did Hoffman, on and offscreen, both give voice to and stifle the most radical aspects of the counterculture? Many historians have credited young auteur directors with the "New Hollywood" or "Hollywood Renaissance" flowering of creativity that happened at this time. How did a non-directing actor like Hoffman influence it, for better and worse? One reason that these questions merit attention is that, to a considerable degree, Hoffman established the paradigm of formal "ordinariness" and thematic alienation for the 1970s "anti-stars"—like Jack Nicholson, Elliott Gould, Gene Hackman, Al Pacino, and Robert De Niro, to name a few—that succeeded him. And we are still living with their standards of quality and authenticity.

While the term "anti-star" may have been new, the concept was old, as Hoffman well knew. In "Dustin Hoffman Savors the Bittersweet Taste of Success," Hoffman asked, "Wasn't Bogart, even Tracy, off the conventional line—for their time? Isn't the anti-hero simply the alienated man?" (Judy Michaelson, *Pageant*, June 1968, 48). The apparent difference had to do with studio disarray, the attendant rising power of stars (exemplified by talent agency MCA's takeover of Universal Pictures), and the more anti-establishment attitudes of the 1960s. It seemed that people were enjoying star-actors with the same amount of simple voyeuristic pleasure with which they enjoyed stars of the past, but with their guilt (about star worship and corporate art) vitiated by their knowledge of these stars' "authenticity" and their "real" actor chops. The press flattered people who were apparently smart and tasteful enough to see Hoffman as successfully both subverting and playing the Hollywood game.

Gilles Deleuze implicitly agrees with *Time*'s judgment regarding men whose destinies were not in their own hands." Deleuze wrote that much

American cinema of the late 1960s and early 1970s exemplified the same "crisis of the action-image"—the gap between perception and action—that dominated Italian neorealism, but the difference in America was that the gap/crisis was a traumatic event that always led to the same conclusion: the hero's realization of his utter powerlessness (19–20). In a similar vein, Thomas Elsaesser writes,

> What the heroes bring to such films is an almost physical sense of inconse-
> quential action, of pointlessness and uselessness: stances which are not only
> interpretable psychologically, but speak of a radical scepticism about Ameri-
> can virtues of ambition, vision, drive: themselves the unacknowledged,
> because firmly underpinning architecture of the classical Hollywood action
> genres.   (Elsaesser 282)

Time and *Life* and other contemporary sources aligned this alienation with the young student protestors. But as with so many protestors, alienation, as presented by Hollywood, was never a direct challenge to America's capitalist system. Hoffman spearheaded the new authenticity even as his status as a rising star curtailed its most radical impulses. In this, he shared—and, crucially, established—many of the traits of the films that were eventually named as part of the Hollywood Renaissance.

Alexander Horwath claims that the era's most celebrated films "pushed back the boundaries" of industry possibilities. Yet at the same time, the movies were "internalizing these boundaries" by cinematic allegory (12). Like its characters, politically, aesthetically, and economically, it failed to develop viable alternatives. Elsaesser finds that the Hollywood Renaissance films rehearsed their own futility profilmically, either with a despairing shrug or a fatalist laugh. Hoffman turned out to be an expert at both.

The *Life* article was actually something of a retread. Fifteen years before, John Wayne had already been used as a counterpoint to an emergent wave of "torn T-shirt types." Figures like Marlon Brando, James Dean and Montgomery Clift personified rebellion, not only on the filmic level even in the very titles of the films—*The Wild One, Rebel Without a Cause*—but also on the extra-filmic level, with their anti-establishment lifestyles and adherence to a new more "authentic" style of acting dubbed the Method (Cohan 33). So, was Hoffman's star image no more than a reiteration of a bygone cycle of films and actors (one might also include Elvis Presley and Sidney Poitier here) that gave America the word "teenager," and that articulated postwar adolescent angst? Were *Time* and *Life* and others wrong in 1969 to hail a new sort of anti-star?

One difference might be that Brando, Dean, Clift, Presley, and Poitier were never seen or marketed as ugly or even ordinary-looking. Hoffman met this requirement; he did not have matinee-idol looks, a point that comes up in contemporary periodicals again and again. Of course, he was not the first (he was wise to note Bogart and Tracy), but he may have been the first to be filmed with non-bright color stock, generous crowd shots, eye-level split focus, and other aspects of contemporary realism. Hoffman's formal "ordinariness" is also inevitably tied to his ethnicity; he's an every-man because of his non-WASP—read: ethnic—appearance.

The Graduate and *Midnight Cowboy* were Hoffman's two major films of the time, and they were both hailed as formal and thematic challenges to the old Hollywood, with more in common than most critics realized. Both films feature a surfeit of folk-pop music as supposed internal monologue. Both use camera "tricks," such as rack focus pulls, four-frame nudity flashes, and discordant memory flashes. Both have extreme long shots of their leads, seen from 45 degrees up, alone and lost in a crowd. And both films end with Hoffman and friend/lover on a bus, heading into an uncertain future. This was the time when Ken Kesey had announced to potential acid-trippers "you're either on the bus or off the bus," and busing was becoming the new and most contentious battlefield in civil rights (already some school districts were mandating it). Hoffman's one-two punch of mordant musings on the American Dream was right in step with the most celebrated transgressions of the time.

★★★★★ The Graduate

During the mid-1960s, Hollywood casting agents and producers were mining the New York stage for new talent. This fact, often neglected in film histories, was at least as powerful an antecedent to the Hollywood Renaissance as, say, the evanescence of censorship. The New York dramatic stage of the 1960s privileged the work and style of Tennessee Williams, Eugene O'Neill, Arthur Miller, and Edward Albee above all others. The "best" actors would be the ones that had proved themselves in this sort of gray, American Dream–questioning, pessimistic material. These actors would almost certainly have at least acquainted themselves with Stanislavsky's Method—in very reductive terms, the recourse to "affective memory," by which one recalls a childhood trauma to find the emotional truth of a given scene or character. One of these actors, who piled up gushing accolades for his Broadway roles, was Dustin Hoffman. Mike Nichols, then piling up his own gushing accolades for the film based on the cynical play *Who's Afraid of Virginia Woolf?* saw Hoffman in the play *Eh?* at the end of 1966. Somehow Nichols saw the possibility for existential disaffection in an excellent Jewish performer doing (for *Eh?*) a sort of Buster Keaton impression.

Mike Nichols's casting of Hoffman as the lead in *The Graduate* opened the floodgates; it was the moment that empowered an unexpected phenomenon (the film's blockbuster success) that in turn led to a surfeit of lead roles for men who in years past would have been relegated to character roles. Nichols is not, however, James Marshall at Sutter's Mill in 1848, discovering gold in a virgin wilderness. His decision was based at least partly on increasing cultural validity of ethnicity and alienation. Nichols well knew that American audiences had warmed to lead unknowns in recent European films, and he perhaps needed some sort of zest lest the film seem unbearably pat or smarmy. If anything, Nichols's decision was almost a defensive maneuver, a way to stay in front of market trends.

Of course, Nichols could have gone many ways with the title role of *The Graduate*. Robert Redford was, according to many writers, the logical choice to play Benjamin Braddock. Redford did test to play Benjamin for Nichols, and, as one critic eventually said, Redford wound up playing a "straight surfer that year in *Barefoot in the Park* anyway" (Ella Taylor, "Boomer Reunion: *The Graduate* Turns 30," *L.A. Weekly*, 7 March 1997, 57). Even in 1967, in "Tales of Hoffman in *The Graduate*," Hoffman said,"I thought I was wrong for the part. The character suggested to me a young, conventional, square jawed, *Time* Magazine Man of the Year type" (Michael Williams, *Los Angeles Times*, 31 December 1967, C3). Four years later, he told another reporter that after finishing Charles Webb's novel, he put it next to his copy of *Time*'s Man of the Year for 1966,"25 and Under," with just that sort of clean-cut WASPy caricature on the cover. Even if this story is apocryphal, it is instructive, because the *Time* "25 and Under" cover represented a sort of saturation point for the then-obsessively covered story of the generation gap that had people shouting, "Don't trust anyone over thirty." Auditions for *The Graduate* took place a few weeks after the issue of *Time*. According to "How to Fail and Yet Win," Hoffman told Nichols: "Clearly, the character, the graduate, 'Ben Braddock,' wasn't Jewish." Nichols replied: "No, but he's Jewish inside" (Earl Wilson, *Los Angeles Herald Examiner*, 29 January 1968, 19). Nichols's bold statement predicted that a Bob Dylan–like Jew (whose internal thoughts were articulated in song by a sort of Dylan-lite Paul Simon) would represent student alienation as well as, and perhaps better than, the Robert Redford type now officially minted by *Time*. Nichols's decision to turn Braddock's nervous alienation in a "Jewish inside" direction was either brilliantly attuned to the zeitgeist or borderline antisemitic, or perhaps both.

Describing Ben Braddock in "I Plummeted to Stardom," Hoffman told *Newsweek*, "The whole character is one moment out of my life, me at 21 years old in a drugstore trying to ask for prophylactics, sweating, and walking out as soon as the druggist's wife started to wait on me" (22 January 1968, 45). Nichols had told Hoffman to keep using that. Hoffman was apparently far more respectful of Mike Nichols than he was of some of his theater directors. "In New York I blow my top when things aren't going right," Hoffman reportedly told Nichols. "But here I go to the other extreme." Nichols told him to go ahead and tell him to go to hell, but Hoffman internalized instead, particularly as the filming went badly. The results "delighted" Nichols. In "A Homely Non-Hero . . . ," Nichols told *Life*: "On screen, Dusty appears to be simply living his life without pretending" (24 November 1967, 10).

Life began the positioning of Hoffman as a subversive yet authentic star-actor, even an antihero. The headline said, "A homely non-hero, Dustin Hoffman gets an unlikely role in Mike Nichols' *The Graduate*." The sub-headline read, "A swarthy Pinocchio makes a wooden role real." The article read:

> If Dustin Hoffman's face were his fortune, he'd be committed to a life of poverty. With a schnoz that looks like a directional signal, skittish black-beady eyes and a raggedy hair-cap, he stands a slight 5-foot-6, weighs a mere 131 pounds and slouches like a puppet dangling from a string. . . . Nichols gambled that Dusty's talents would triumph over his appearance. He has won his gamble. . . . Dusty is one of the few new leading men in Hollywood who look like people rather than profiles in celluloid.
>
> ("A Homely Non-Hero . . . ," *Life*, 24 November 1967, 11)

While *Life* demonstrated classic antisemitic coding, the film codified a new ordinary-man star as a daring casting choice.

For critics, the performative significance of Dustin Hoffman in *The Graduate* was not one of technique. No review (in the twenty-plus researched sources) ever used the word "innovative" or "revolutionary" or even "Method." The significance was one of persona and looks. America had learned this before, but based on the press it seemed to be relearning it all over again. Or as Mel Gussow had it, "He's given hope to hordes of homely men" ("Dustin," *McCall's*, September 1968, 35). In "Dustin Hoffman Savors the Bittersweet Taste of Success," Hoffman said: "I am the boy next door, only the boy next door is not supposed to have pimples" (Judy Michaelson, *Pageant*, June 1968, 47).

Nor did writers ever name Hoffman as Jewish. The everyman persona was the crucial keystone of reviews even while its ethnic origins remained

Dustin Hoffman and Anne Bancroft in *The Graduate*. Hoffman as unlikely love interest, the boy next door with pimples. (Collection of the author)

unmentionable. Michael Williams was among many critics who echoed *Life*'s assessment of casting unconventionality: "Dustin Hoffman is not exactly your average Hollywooden romantic lead. For one thing, he looks like the original Thurber model for the male animal—he's 5 feet 5 inches, about 130 pounds, has definitely beady, brown eyes, a more than adequate chin; and a nose, my friends, what a nose" ("Tales of Hoffman"). In "*The Graduate* to Open," Charles Champlin agreed:"Dustin Hoffman may not be everybody's conception of the graduate, visually or intellectually (there are moments when both the ladies seemed daft to give him a second thought)" (*Los Angeles Times*, 18 December 1967, C1). But then they rushed to say that the movie surprisingly worked. As one wrote, "With deadpan style, Dustin Hoffman moulds an original character and never falls back on to stereotype" (David Austen, *Films and Filming*, October 1968, B2). In "Little Big Man Clings to Life" *Esquire* summed up the prevailing sentiment, referring to the actress who played Benjamin's eventual love interest in the film: "America is after all a nation full of men to whom girls like Katharine Ross never paid any attention in high school, and of women who long to prove that, unlike those other girls, those beautiful nasty girls, they have great stores of love to give to a deserving young man, however short, if he be only as charming as Dustin Hoffman" (Sally Kempton, *Esquire*, July 1970, 78). Gussow ended his article by predicting that "rejected producers will start asking for *a* Dustin Hoffman. . . . 'But there'll come a day,' predicts the original Dustin Hoffman, 'when a face like mine will not be able to get work. Ten years from now, they'll say, "I'll give half my kingdom for a walking surfboard."' But for the next ten years—watch out" (Gussow 42). As things turned out, this was quite prescient.

Later historians gave Hoffman the credit for a persona revolution. In "An Advanced Degree of Influence on Modern Film," Susan King wrote, "Hoffman heralded the arrival of the non-traditional leading man in movies. He perfectly captured the fear, clumsiness, and ambivalence of Benjamin" (*Los Angeles Times*, 1 May 2005, C5). An article entitled "In the 1960s, Dustin Hoffman Rewrote the Rules of Who Could Be a Star. Now He's Ready to Enjoy Himself" was more to the point: "With *The Graduate*'s success in 1967, life for Hoffman changed for ever, as it did for Al Pacino and a host of other ethnic actors, ushering in an era of unconventional leads and outstanding film-making" (Jeff Dawson, *Sunday Times* [London], 9 January 2005, P1). Even as early as 1971, in "Dustin Hoffman—He's Not Really Part of Any Scene," the *Los Angeles Times* said that Hoffman had "changed a nation's aesthetic tastes" (Joyce Haber, 27 June 1971, 21). In a time of social ferment, Hollywood had proved itself pluralistic and inclusive, with headlines like "He's the kind of person you pass without seeing— even though he's Hollywood's hottest property" (Peer J. Oppenheimer, "Dustin Hoffman: From Odd Jobs to Superstar," *Hollywood Citizen-News*, 29 March 1970, 10).

Many in the press positioned the film and Hoffman as a force of the counterculture, or at least of youth rebellion. Said one, "Dustin Hoffman, a major talent find, brings off a weird characterization as the hapless fellow battling his environment. . . . In style as well as content, the film is a clarion call to youth" (*Cue*, 23 December 1967, 13). Similarly, Bosley Crowther described Hoffman as having "the ironic and pathetic immaturity of a mere baccalaureate scholar turned loose in an immature society. He is a character very much reminiscent of Holden Caulfield" (*New York Times*, 22 December 1967, D2). A year later, in "Beware the Baron," *Newsweek* said that Hoffman had come "to be regarded as the very soul, catatonic and rebellious at the same time, of contemporary American youth" (16 December 1968, 33). *Newsweek*'s parsing was accurate: at once, Hoffman symbolized, even performed, the revolutionary potential and fatalist viscosity of the new generation.

Of course, *The Graduate* was hardly as subversive as, say, *The Battle of Algiers* (1966). David Brinkley, Renata Adler, Hollis Alpert, and many other writers quite rightly took the Nichols film to task at the time. But marketing as in the *Life* article encouraged people to "get it," to position the joke, the film, and the off-beatness of Hoffman as a way to freak the squares. Adopting Hoffman as a cultural symbol became a way for a potent generation to prove it knew better than their parents. When it came to Hoffmans of the late 1960s, baby boomers' tastes proved closer to Dustin than Abbie. Clever alienation resounded louder than liberal activism.

Like a lot of the movement films to come, *The Graduate* picks up on the restlessness of novels like Jack Kerouac's *On the Road* by emphasizing Benjamin Braddock's frantic driving all over California, particularly in the second half of the film. Wherever Hoffman goes he looks lost, whether drifting around the Berkeley campus or running down a sidewalk in Santa Barbara. The film eventually demonizes Mrs. Robinson, while her daughter's best trait seems to be the fact that Benjamin barely knows her. The film, led by Hoffman's performance, is a mostly lighthearted, perhaps even satirical, characterization of disillusionment, but it still aligns well with the more whimsical Beat novels and Dylan songs to present an unrooted, disaffected narcissism that never tries too hard to understand women. And critics and audiences wanted more.

By the end of 1968, *The Graduate* had earned about $40 million (on a budget of about $3 million), making it the third highest grossing film of all time. Hoffman was telling anyone who would listen that he wanted to play Malamud's Raskolnikov, Brecht's Arturo Ui, *Catch-22*'s Milo, Holden Caulfield, Malcolm X, Che Guevara, and especially Adolf Hitler. (He would never play any of these roles.) He also said that he was almost done with acting and ready to direct. (He never has.) In "The Graduate Turns Bum," in September 1968, he said, "Now I can articulate the feelings of those who aren't in a position to talk" (Daniel Chapman, *Look*, 17 September 1968, 33). Indeed, as long as the marginalized could have their story presented in a classically made Hollywood film with a straight white male in the lead, he could.

★★★★★ *Midnight Cowboy*

The story of how Hoffman went from *The Graduate* to *Midnight Cowboy* is frequently misremembered. Did he commit to playing Ratso Rizzo before or after the Nichols film became a hit? The answer is both. Director John Schlesinger and producer Monte Hellman had seen Hoffman onstage before *The Graduate* and told him he'd be great in the role of Ratso Rizzo. Hoffman had told them he'd do it but signed nothing. By March 1968, *The Graduate* was a phenomenon, yet the person who needed reconvincing was not Hoffman but Schlesinger. (Of course, now the production would have to pay Hoffman a lot more—$250,000, more than ten times what he'd earned on *The Graduate*.) According to Peter Biskind in "Midnight Revolution," Schlesinger said he couldn't visualize Hoffman in the role anymore. Hoffman met the director in Times Square, dressed and looking for all the world like the most indigent sort of bum. Schlesinger apparently said, "Oh, you'll do quite well." On 11 March 1968, Hoffman signed the contract to play Ratso Rizzo, promising to lose weight and stay out of the sun (*Vanity Fair*, March 2005, 314).

Hoffman later recalled that Mike Nichols, upon hearing about the casting of Rizzo, told him: "I made you a star, and you're going to throw it all away? You're a leading man and now you're going to play this? *The Graduate* was so clean, and this is so dirty." That was exactly the point for Hoffman, and he made sure that the media knew it: "I had become troubled, to say the least, by the reviews that I had read of *The Graduate*." He did not like being called Nichols's creation, and he did not like "a kind of disguised anti-Semitism. . . . I was determined to show them, in big letters, THEM, that I was an actor. Revenge is always a good motive in creativity" (Biskind, *Vanity Fair*, March 2005, 315). This 2005 interview is the first piece in the mainstream media in which anyone mentions antisemitism as applied to Hoffman, and it's he himself who does so. During the 1960s, in many, many, press interviews, he at least appeared to be happy to represent the "ordinary" (and thus, not explicitly Jewish) man.

How much did Hoffman's infamous ego matter? One of his biographers explains Hoffman's on-set approach this way:

> Throughout his career, Dustin has been an advocate of his own theories of movie-making. He was unafraid to speak his piece with directors or provide input into writers' screenplays, preferring to control the situation; that way, the character was really his. Some directors have complained about Dustin's infringement on their own creativity, but the vast majority of directors encouraged it. In interjecting his own ideas into a specific character or scene, Hoffman was following not only the example of other actors but also his own intuition, since he seemed to know his own ability best.   (Lenburg 27)

Industry history tells us that actors (who weren't also directors/producers) in previous eras could not exercise such agency. Hoffman, accounts suggest, broke the mold, even while he signaled a new alienated everyman mold for other actors to use. He declared, "I will no longer accept anything unless the character is rich, the story important, and the director acceptable" (Oppen-heimer, *Hollywood Citizen-News*, 29 March 1970, 10). He said to another source, "Art has never been for the masses, but now people seem to see what's good. The least I can do is try to make what I do as artistic as pos-sible" (Lenburg 78). Some scholars ask if stars weren't merely in the right place at the right time. That may be, but Hoffman was canny about making his time and place suit his abilities and taste quite rightly.

Unlike most of the more famous roles of the Hollywood Renaissance, Hoffman's Ratso Rizzo (and arguably the film's lead, Jon Voight's Joe Buck) was, at least, genuinely lower class. To some degree, then, *Midnight Cowboy* expanded everyman alienation beyond the middle class. Yet Rizzo was still being played by someone who had just appeared on the cover of *Time*, someone who worked toward institutional solutions. That February 1969 *Time* article noted: "The anti-star attitude itself threatens to become a new pose or convention in which the Hollywood swimming pool is replaced by the interesting East Side pad, the Valley ranch by a Martha's Vineyard retreat, the antic table-hopping by frantic political activism" (Stefan Kanfer, Jay Cocks, and Carey Winfrey, "The Moonchild and the Fifth Beatle," 53). This last part referenced Hoffman's campaigning for Eugene McCarthy in the 1968 presidential primaries. In a year when activist parties proliferated, Hoffman found himself supporting the relatively safe Democrat. This was Hoffman's level of deviance. When push came to shove, he flattered the earnest liberal, not the embittered radical. And so would his roles and his films.

In May, *Midnight Cowboy* and Hoffman's role in it were greeted with thunderous applause. John Simon found Hoffman "able to turn scrounging into a gallant, Robin-Hoodish activity" ("Rape upon Rape," *New Leader*, 7 July 1969, 31). Hollis Alpert spoke of a "totally surprising tenderness" (*Saturday Review*, June 1969, C1). *Glamour* magazine attributed "a kind of tawdry panache" to Hoffman's Rizzo (August 1969, 10). *Films and Filming* enthused, "Ratso's crippled pathos and sleazy humour are not exploited for their obvi-ous entertainment value, but contained superbly as contributive factors in the character development of Joe Buck" (Gordon Gow, October 1969, 16).

As Hoffman had surmised, critics could not stop comparing Ratso to Benjamin. The star image of "Dustin Hoffman" had been so radically shifted as to force a reconfiguration of meaning. One critic began a review by say-ing, "*Midnight Cowboy* seems to be this summer's *The Graduate*; the kids who loved Dustin Hoffman sweet and clean are just as happy to love him dirty and sweet" (John Simon, *New Leader*, 7 July 1969, 31). Another: "Dustin Hoffman, as the ratty Ratso Rizzo, turns in a tour de force performance that

Hoffman's Ratso Rizzo, a marked change from the clean-cut Benjamin in *The Graduate*. Hoffman's Rizzo is dirty, pathetic, sleazy—everything a character actor could want to play. (Collection of the author)

will surprise no one who saw him Off-Broadway in *Journey of the Fifth Horse*, but may unnerve the fans who knew him only as the clean-cut nebbish of *The Graduate*. His performance is anti-romantic, detailed, and for a young man with matinee idol pretensions, highly courageous: his makeup is truly repulsive, from the ever growing limp to the bad teeth to the overall greasiness. Some of his teenybopper fans may never get over it" (Neal Weaver,

After Dark, July 1969, B3). Another, from an absolute rave: "Dustin Hoffman, on the other hand, brings to bear on his role a talent of astounding power and versatility. The contrast with his part in *The Graduate* is total, for here, instead of a youth just out of college, he is a healthless, scrounging worm from a lower-depths level of society. And he gives it not only its proper loathsome aspects, but a heart as well. It is a performance that, like Voight's, sticks in the mind as if embossed" (Archer Winsten, *New York Post*, 26 May 1969, 72). Finally, from Andrew Sarris in the *Village Voice*: "By following up the glamorous *Graduate* with the dregsiest drop-out imaginable, Dustin Hoffman has achieved his aim of not becoming the Andy Hardy of the '60s and '70s. With a dragging limp, a perpetually preserved five o'clock shadow, a fungus-like fever of expression, and a way of smoking a squashed cigarette as if he were inhaling oxygen underwater, Hoffman will not only preserve all his old following of adoring females but should add a few more masochistic maidens to his fan base" (29 May 1969, 12). Hoffman, as the only actor working in Hollywood in 1969 who could point to a phalanx of reviews like these, surely provided a model to all the other younger star-actors then emerging—Jack Nicholson, Gene Hackman, Elliott Gould, and many more.

Sarris's comment about "masochistic maidens" is telling. Later historians (but no critic at the time) would credit *Midnight Cowboy, Easy Rider*, and *Butch Cassidy and the Sundance Kid*, all released during the summer of 1969, with the inauguration of the buddy film genre and/or the road movie, where the two leads, echoing Sal and Dean (of *On the Road*), would look for answers on the road and find everything but. The restless alienation and grungy appearance were inevitably attenuated with exclusion or dismissal of females. (Homosexuality was generally suppressed.) The New Hollywood built its reputation on the backs of women, and Hoffman represented that as well as anyone, on-and offscreen. Hoffman said in 1969's *Life* cover story that "film acting [seems] to me to be more of a female profession. The director, who has all the creative power, really uses the actor. I don't know many actors who enjoy the work of acting" (Ralph Graves, 11 July 1969, 8). But perhaps this failure to countenance women is part and parcel of the lionization of "character." Claire Johnston found that historical Hollywood male stereotyping went against the notion of character, but dominant ideology kept women eternal and unchanging (Johnston 184).

Hoffman's tastes were the press's version of anti-establishment—even when they weren't. Hoffman refused to find fault with actors that do commercials, even though he hadn't: "Get what you can! Certainly. But at the same time shrewdness, quite apart from any kind of artistic integrity thing, tells me that I will have more longevity, and more respect, the straighter I play it" (Jane Wilson, "Dustin Hoffman [Superstars: Will *Midnight Cowboy* Spawn Another?]" *West*, 11 July 1969, 23). Already his positioning as an artist was merely a careful business decision. Hoffman made it clear to older Hollywood producers that they didn't have to fear any kind of radical agitation from him. The same article said:

> His manager thinks that the fans want him back as he was in *The Graduate*—more or less. Hoffman may, in fact, have a better instinct about this. The film industry is in a state of some confusion about the box office success of movies without stars, such as *The Graduate, Goodbye, Columbus,* and *If. . . .* What these films have are the new faces of good young actors rather than the expensive presence of familiar stars, who come to each new role trailing clouds of old associations from previous appearances. To be durable now it may be necessary to positively avoid acquiring any of the old "star quality"—to become Promethean in aspect, in fact to take on character roles.   (22)

This was written next to a photo of Hoffman inside a star-shaped frame, apparently without irony, even in an article that calls Hoffman "small, too small certainly for hero or lover." The validation of character roles is validation for the Method and Stanislavsky, for whom the character actor is supreme. But what would happen when the "clouds of old associations from previous appearances" started building around these new everyman character actor stars? Hoffman had already told Mel Gussow that he was ready for that day of the return of the "walking surfboard," and to some extent he was almost precipitating it ("Dustin," *McCall's,* September 1968).

★★★★★ Conclusion

Hoffman remained a challenge to the old ways for quite some time, and a way for Hollywood to say that it had changed, something it would use for successive anti-stars. One article in the July 1970 *Esquire* summarized Hoffman's newly minted star image well:

> The publicist was upset by the very idea of Dustin Hoffman. "The most unlikely star ever to come down the pike," he would write in an exclusive to Rona Barrett. "Clark Gable must be turning in his grave." Or, "Dusty's new bride will just have to learn to live with her husband's hordes of lady fans, although why the girls go so strong for the five-foot-six-inch actor has old Hollywood hands shaking their heads." . . . In fact, Dustin read those releases and groaned a little, for surely that unlikely-star routine is dead by now. . . . Dustin Hoffman is, after all, an authentic star. . . . Contemporary stars differ from the stars of the past in that their star quality is involuntary: when the

spotlight first hits them they are nearly always doing something else. . . . Hoffman (had) had to rent a tuxedo for [*The Graduate's*] opening. It was (the) first brick in the construction of Dusty's anti-star image.

(Sally Kempton, "Little Big Man Clings to Life," *Esquire*, July 1970, 42)

Once again, Hoffman is positioned as unlikely, even doing "something else." His "involuntary" stardom is tended by Hollywood, the press, and fans, who maintain a shared interest in keeping his (anti)stardom alive. Over and over, Hoffman is positioned as David versus the entrenched Goliath of the old system. He gains "authentic" stardom by building and rebuilding his anti-star image.

4 ☆☆☆☆☆☆☆☆☆☆☆

Steve McQueen
Cool, Combative, and Disconnected

INA RAE HARK

Steve McQueen was cool. Few star images crystallize around just one word, but his certainly does. What's more, he was "the King of Cool." The first entry for the phrase in the online *Urban Dictionary* reads: "Nickname for actor Steve McQueen. No one has ever owned the screen like Steve McQueen. He was the King of Cool" (www.urbandictionary .com). This soubriquet forms the title of two books about McQueen: *Steve McQueen, King of Cool: Tales of a Lurid Life* by Darwin Porter and *Steve McQueen: A Tribute to the King of Cool* by Marshall Terrill, as well as a 1998 documentary film by Robert Katz, *Steve McQueen: The King of Cool*. It is the heading for the Life.com picture gallery devoted to him. "King of Cool: The Films of Steve McQueen" is the name of a ten-movie retrospective that ran from January through March 2010 at the Seattle Art Museum. The majority of biographical sketches of the actor begin with formulations similar to "Steve McQueen, nicknamed 'The King of Cool' . . ."[1]

Cool has many connotations, and the McQueen star image fits several of them. Most of the characters he plays are "not excited; calm; composed; under control" and "calmly audacious or impudent" (dictionary.reference .com). Moreover, both on- and offscreen, McQueen, the master of motorbikes and racing cars and wearer of clothing and accessories that became iconic, reflected the more generalized approbation of the term that originated in jazz culture to designate a style and personal presentation that was "fashionable," a 1933 coinage "said to have been popularized in jazz circles by tenor saxophonist Lester Young" (www.etymonline.com). The hipster and Beat designation of the "cool cat" could have well applied to the McQueen who pursued an acting career in the mid-fifties while living in Greenwich Village in New York City. Throughout his life he peppered his conversation with "man" and "baby," and he referred to his first wife, Neile, as "my old lady." A 12 July 1963 article on him in *Life*, "The Bad Boy Breaks Out," reports, "He talks the lingo of the rough world that spawned him, a world of hipsters, racing car drivers, beach boys, drifters and carnival barkers" (68), a patois Neile described as "part musician talk, part jive talk, part street talk, and part Steve talk" (Toffel 79). His friend, photographer William Claxton, says, "He was street smart, animal-like, nonintellectual, and hip. In fact he brought new meaning to the word hip; he was superhip" (qtd. in Terrill, *Life* 205).

As his cool image solidified in the latter part of the 1960s, Steve McQueen's films begin to have jazzy scores, from the New Orleans beats of *The Cincinnati Kid* (1965) to Lalo Schifrin's work on *Bullitt* (1968), Michel LeGrand's on *The Thomas Crown Affair* (1968), and Quincy Jones's on *The Getaway* (1972). The musical work that best epitomizes the King of Cool, however, may be "Cool" from *West Side Story*, which the McQueens saw on Broadway while on vacation in New York with Frank Sinatra in 1959. While Leonard Bernstein's jazzy melody and Jerome Robbins's finger-snapping dance rhythms represent the McQueen film persona, Stephen Sondheim's lyrics, which caution the members of the Jets to throttle back their engines, so to speak, give advice that the real McQueen should have heeded but rarely did.

The essential paradox of this particular star was that although his public life and the details of his biography frequently appear interchangeable with those of the men he played onscreen, the chief variation between image and actuality was that, in temperament, McQueen was anything but cool. As Matt Feeney observes in one of the most perceptive meditations on

the actor, "Watching the laconic, slow-to-react title characters in *The Cincinnati Kid* (1965) and *Bullitt* (1968), it's easy to imagine that the performance
is just Steve McQueen showing up and acting like himself. But when Steve
McQueen showed up and really acted like himself, it wasn't pretty: He was
a hothead and a paranoid, a grimly compulsive womanizer and a prolific
druggie far ahead of his time" ("An Extremely Macho Elf: Reconsidering
Steve McQueen," *Slate*, 16 June 2005). Notoriously "difficult" on set, he
caused writers to quit and scripts to be adapted to his liking even early in
his career. Once he had the authority of the established star to approve all
aspects of production, his whims often "resulted in someone losing out
because Steve felt threatened. It may have been a director being kicked off
a set because he did not placate McQueen's ego, [or] an actor or actress who
was too tall and lost a part" (Terrill, *Life* 202). However, McQueen "har-
nessed his inner demons" in support of creating a persona that he was content to represent him to the world (Whitmer vii). An amalgam of many
attributes that derived from McQueen's own experiences and enthusiasms,
the King of Cool additionally manifested all the calm self-control he would
never master anywhere but in his movies.

☆☆★★★ The McQueen Narrative

On the brink of stardom in 1959, the actor's two most significant roles of that year presaged the star image he would establish for two-
thirds of the 1960s. He was midway through the three-season run of the
television series "Wanted: Dead or Alive" (1958–61), in which he starred as
bounty hunter Josh Randall. Since bounty hunters inhabit the border
between criminality and law enforcement, Randall inspires distrust and
resentment wherever he goes and lets his holstered sawed-off shotgun, the
"mare's laig," do most of his talking. During his hiatus from the series he had
appeared in a featured role in his first A-picture, *Never So Few*, a World War
II combat film set in Burma, in which Frank Sinatra's Captain Tom Reynolds
and a few Allied troops lead a native guerrila force against the Japanese.

McQueen plays Bill Ringa, the driver assigned to Reynolds and his
second-in-command when they report back to base for new orders and
some leave time. A veteran of "combat" in the toughest neighborhoods of
New York City, Ringa maneuvers his jeep expertly but at harrowing speeds.
Cheerfully insubordinate, eminently resourceful, and never afraid to skirt
regulations, he so impresses Reynolds that the captain has him assigned to
his squad when he returns to the guerrillas in the mountains. Eventually
Ringa earns a battlefield commission to second lieutenant and marvels at

his elevation from working-class enlisted man to officer and gentleman. Ringa's reaction to a Japanese ambush during the squad's Christmas banquet provides an early example of McQueen cool. He is at the table holding a huge piece of watermelon, out of which he has just taken a bite, when the shelling begins. He freezes for just a split second, then drops under the table in one fluid motion. After assessing his position, he runs low to the ground, locates a mortar, and begins firing back at the enemy. As Neile McQueen Toffel observes in her memoir, "The Western series had established a character that was heroic, courageous, and monosyllabic all at the same time, and the role of Bill Ringa launched a screen character who was both off-center and daring. With the passage of time, the two characters would be taken further and further along so that all the qualities came together in one person" (87).

Never So Few's director, John Sturges, was obviously impressed, since he subsequently gave McQueen his two breakout roles, as Vin Tanner in *The Magnificent Seven* (1960) and as Virgil Hilts in *The Great Escape* (1963). Those two films share with their 1959 predecessors two types of men whom McQueen would play repeatedly: a cowboy and a member of the military. His subsequent western roles were more spread out over his entire career— in *Nevada Smith* (1966), *Junior Bonner* (1972), and *Tom Horn* (1980). At the same time, he played six soldiers, sailors, or airmen between 1961 and 1966, with five films in a row putting him in uniform (*The Honeymoon Machine* [1961], *Hell Is for Heroes* [1962], *The War Lover* [1962], *The Great Escape*, and *Soldier in the Rain* [both 1963]). The absence of military roles in his later films is probably due to the increasing antiwar sentiment of the late 1960s and 1970s, although scripts that cast McQueen as a soldier never stopped being sent to him, right up to his death.

Cowboys and soldiers share a certain rootlessness. Neither career keeps a man in one place for long or prioritizes his domestic stability. The difference, of course, is that the military man goes where he's ordered, whereas the itinerant gunslinger, bounty hunter, or rodeo rider can choose the direction in which he wanders. Nevertheless, an unsettled, wandering life characterizes the most iconic McQueen characters in the first phase of his career. Even if the character isn't always on the move, this meme expands to roles like the Cincinnati Kid and Rocky Papasano in *Love with the Proper Stranger* (1963), both men who are averse to commitment and who lack strong ties to people from their pasts. In short, the McQueen persona is usually that of a loner who doesn't relate well to authority, social networks, or peer-group norms. From this sense of disconnection it is not far to the impudent, insubordinate rebel, the scamming con artist, or the defiant prisoner he often played.

In *The Great Escape*, McQueen breaks out of a German POW camp—and as a star. (Digital frame enlargement)

A second cluster of attributes revolves around the risk-taking, performative activities the McQueen character engages in. Although playing high-stakes poker is central to the plot of *The Cincinnati Kid*, the daring behavior is often more a grace note than an important theme in itself. Yet it is the grace notes that always counted for the star. Ask almost anyone to name *the* iconic McQueen sequence and they will probably cite either the motorcycle pursuit in *The Great Escape* or the car chase from *Bullitt*. Leerom Medevoi says, "McQueen's special appeal, what made him 'cool,' was that he was a passionate motorcycle and drag car racer" in real life. "To race like McQueen was to gain accolades for taking risks, ignoring social opinions, and insisting on speed over stasis, ensuring that one moved forward, as McQueen did when he cashed out his race winnings to become a successful Hollywood player." Archer Winsten's *New York Post* review of *Bullitt* confirms Medevoi's assertion: "McQueen keeps his cool as only he can, now that Bogart's long gone. The best, most exciting car chase the movies have ever put on film. McQueen, motorcycle and auto racer, knew what he was doing and what had to be done" (qtd. in Terrill, *Portrait* 171). Many publicity photos of McQueen place him on a motorcycle, whether with Neile holding on behind him for his *Life* cover in 1963, or bare-chested at full throttle in a 1971 *Sports Illustrated* cover, or in photographs taken at a dirt-bike race in the pages of a 1965 issue of *Silver Screen*. The actor bankrupted his Solar Productions by going to all lengths to realize his long-time desire to make a film about auto racing, *Le Mans* (1971).[2] He failed to realize that audiences who thrilled to a great car chase in a dramatic context did not want to sit through endless racing scenes that lacked one. A number of fan magazines also speculated that McQueen's daredevil racing might indicate a death wish, another complication in a star-image so linked to speed.

Mastering speeding metal vehicles is highly cinematic, but the less kinetic activities of gambling or game-playing also mark the McQueen characters in many films. And since these often attract an audience, we might also include the musicians he portrayed in *Love with the Proper Stranger* and *Baby, the Rain Must Fall* (1965). Far and away the role that incorporates the most of these "player" identities is Thomas Crown. Unlike most of the McQueen protagonists, Crown is extremely wealthy and so has the resources to indulge his every whim. Since he is the ultimate thrill seeker, he designs elaborate bank heists just for the kick of it, even telling the insurance investigator who is on to him (Faye Dunaway) that he is going to pull another job and daring her to stop him. He plays polo, drives a dune buggy at full blast down the beach, and flies a glider. Even his seduction of said investigator occurs over a chessboard; he describes taking her to his bed as merely playing a different game.

The iconic McQueen narratives find a way to place these rebellious, thrill-seeking, loner antiheroes in situations where they produce conflict with others while simultaneously proving indispensable to a perilous, long-shot undertaking they share with the very people whom their personalities grate upon. At the same time, whether the larger group succeeds or fails, the McQueen protagonist rarely enjoys unqualified triumph. When Chris (Yul Brynner) says at the end of *The Magnificent Seven* that while the farmers have won, gunslingers like himself and Vin "always lose," he could be pronouncing judgment on the 1960s McQueen. Hilts does not retain his freedom in *The Great Escape* and most of the other escapees are executed by the Germans. His character Reese dies in battle in *Hell Is for Heroes*, as does Jake Holman in *The Sand Pebbles* (1966). Henry Thomas "fails at becoming Elvis Presley" (Terrill, *Portrait* 102) in *Baby, the Rain Must Fall*. Frank Bullitt manages to kill a double-crossing mobster but not before an innocent couple has died. The inability to take the man alive sinks the hoped-for testimony that would bring down his confederates, leaving Bullitt even more in dutch with the San Francisco political establishment. His girlfriend Cathy (Jacqueline Bisset) is appalled that the carnage his job exposes him to no longer raises any emotional response: "I thought I knew you but I'm not so sure anymore. Do you let anything reach you, really reach you? Or are you so used to it by now that nothing really touches you. . . . How can you be part of it without becoming more and more callous?" McQueen's Crown does jet off to reunite with his stolen millions beyond U.S. extradition but cannot convince Vicky to put love for him above her job for the insurance company.

While it deemphasizes some other prominent McQueen memes, *The Cincinnati Kid* foregrounds this tendency for his star image to be linked to failure far more than is the case with many other macho stars. The film presents itself as a classic Oedipal struggle, with the young stud poker virtuoso Eric Stoner, "the Kid" (McQueen), challenging the aging, reigning champion Lancey Howard (Edward G. Robinson), known as "the Man." But in the end the Kid's too-supreme self-confidence and competitive zeal cost him the game and the woman he loves. Even the young shoeshine boy who aspires to beat him one day at penny-pitching succeeds.

With these elements of the McQueen narrative in mind, an examination of the actor's early life reveals just how closely screen success paralleled his life. As co-star James Coburn remarks, other actors "would always base their character on what the character would do, whereas Steve would base his character on what Steve McQueen would do" (Terrill, *Portrait* 84). Born in the Indianapolis suburb of Beech Grove in 1930, Terrence Steven McQueen had very poor luck as to his parents. His mother, Julia Ann Crawford, known as Julian, was a teenage runaway who would be addicted to alcohol and unsuitable men for her entire life. His father, William Terrence McQueen, an itinerant stunt flyer, did the "right thing" by marrying Julian but left the family when his son was only six months old. When he was three, his mother left him with her parents, Lillian and Victor Crawford. Bankrupted by the Depression, the Crawfords sent Lillian and Steve to live on the farm of her brother Claude Thomson in Missouri. The next six years were the only stable ones of McQueen's childhood. His great-uncle was a strict but fair disciplinarian and a caring, if distant, guardian.

The boy's orderly farm-boy life ended abruptly when a remarried Julian returned and took him with her to Indianapolis. The nine-year-old soon got into trouble by thieving with other street kids, and his mother sent him back to the farm. She attempted another reconciliation when he was twelve, but with the same result. At fourteen, Steve decided to strike out on his own and take up with a traveling circus. After spending several months on the road, he finally turned up in California, where his mother was living with a particularly nasty man named Berri, who physically abused him. Once again he joined a gang and got in trouble with the law for more serious thefts and other offenses. His mother declared him incorrigible and had him committed to a reform school, the California Boys Republic in Chino.

At first, McQueen was defiant, a loner whom the other boys distrusted because his breaking of rules affected their own privileges. He tried to run away but was caught. One of the staff finally succeeded in getting through to him and he shaped up, even going on to be elected to the governing council. Although he would hardly be a model citizen after serving his fourteen-month sentence, McQueen insisted in later years that the Boys Republic had turned his life around. After he was a star, he often visited, corresponded with, and gave advice to current students, and he left a large bequest to the facility in his will. Released from the school in 1946, he had the last of his formal education—completion of the ninth grade—behind him. An uncertain future was ahead of him as he rejoined his mother, now living in Greenwich Village.

Once more McQueen could not tolerate his mother's lifestyle and he ran away again. Soon he was tricked into joining the merchant marine but jumped ship in Cuba. After months of wandering and working odd jobs from the Dominican Republic to Texas, he decided to enlist in the Marine Corps in 1947. According to Marshall Terrill's researches, by doing this he unwittingly joined a long line of McQueen ancestors who had served in the armed forces since the Revolutionary War (*Life* 2). His experience there was eerily similar to his experience at Boys Republic. He went AWOL to be with a girl and spent forty-one days in the brig. Yet he finally settled in, completing his three-year stint with an honorable discharge in 1950.

McQueen made his way from South Carolina, where he broke off with the sweetheart he had left behind there, up the East Coast, and finally returned to Greenwich Village (though not to his mother). There he made the fateful decision to apply his G.I. Bill education benefits to acting school rather than to a training program for tile setters. (Acting was where the girls were, he later said.) Accepted into Sanford Meisner's Neighborhood Playhouse, he subsequently applied to the Actors Studio and was one of two admitted from among two thousand candidates (the other was Martin Landau). He supplemented his scholarship money with poker winnings and prizes from motorcycle races. As with his stints at Boys Republic and in the marines, McQueen's acting career had its ups and downs, some due to his own volatile personality. But, in the end, he obtained the role of Josh Randall and went on to success in the movies, this time of a magnitude the lonely, hustling street kid could never have imagined.

The role that most mimics the "whole man" of McQueen's pre-stardom real life is Jake Holman, the China sailor and machinist's mate in *The Sand Pebbles*, for which he received his only Academy Award nomination. Set in 1926 aboard a U.S. Navy gunboat, the *San Pablo*, the film is one of those bloated prestige roadshow epics that followed in the wake of David Lean's success in the genre. It wants to say something about the American role in Vietnam and Western imperialism in Asia generally, but it doesn't quite know what. This overload of message, as well as sluggish pacing, means that the film has not aged well, which is probably one reason we do not think of Jake Holman as an iconic McQueen performance. Yet there is no doubt that the facts of Jake's life and McQueen's life are very similar. The

actor and the character's love of machinery, for instance, dovetailed so precisely that, as director Robert Wise reported, McQueen knew the ship's systems backward and forward and could easily have operated it on his own.
(When in the marines, McQueen was assigned to a tank brigade.) As the
Variety reviewer noted: "Steve McQueen looks and acts the part he plays
so well—that of a machinist's mate with nine years of navy service" (31
December 1965).

Like McQueen, Jake had a troubled youth. He joined the navy as an
alternative to reform school after an altercation with his high school principal cost that man an eye. China sailors are men who enjoy being rootless
and far from home: missionary Jameson (Larry Gates) explains, "They
reduce life to a very simple point or no point at all. As long as they obey
orders, the navy takes care of them. It's a way of life that appeals to a certain kind of man." But Jake is an extreme case even among his fellows. He
has transferred from a larger ship because he wants to get away from "all
that military crap" and people telling him what to do. He has chosen the
engine room as his base because it gives him virtual autonomy: "They leave
you alone."

Nevertheless, he immediately gets on the wrong side of the other men
on the *San Pablo* because he disapproves of their dependence on Chinese
coolies. When Jake is insubordinate, the audience feels him to be in the
right, yet his refusal to go along with the status quo repeatedly leads to
tragedy. Relations with his crewmates become so strained that they are
willing to turn him over to the Chinese, who have framed him for a murder he did not commit, and they almost mutiny when the captain refuses
to do so. He does fall in love with American teacher Shirley Eckert (Can-
dice Bergen), but both times that he is ready to desert to join her, the navy
reclaims him. Of course, when the chips are down, Jake proves a hero. He
is crucial to freeing the ship from a blockade and sacrifices his life so that
several crewmates can escape an ambush and bring Shirley to safety. Had
McQueen reenlisted in the marines and gone to Korea, his life might have
ended much as Jake's does.

After *The Sand Pebbles*, the McQueen narrative underwent a shift.
Because that film had gone substantially over its scheduled shooting schedule, the star was left without a follow-up project. His wife and his agent
Hillard Elkins thought he should expand his range by going after the lead
in *The Thomas Crown Affair*, in pre-production with *Cincinnati Kid* director
Norman Jewison. Since McQueen had never played a rich and cultivated
businessman, or an outright thief, for that matter, he had little interest in
doing it. To persuade him to pursue it, Neile and Elkins used the fact that

Thrill-seeking, stylish criminal mastermind Thomas Crown in *The Thomas Crown Affair*. (Digital frame enlargement)

he had not been sent the script; they knew his intense competitiveness with fellow actors—to the extent that he was a "dog-in-the-manger" (Toffel 157) as far as others succeeding in roles he had declined—would kindle his desire for the part. Perfect as the super-cool criminal mastermind (if still out of his element as the society playboy), McQueen enjoyed great success in the film and considered it one of his favorites.

Of particular importance is the contemporary setting of *Thomas Crown*. McQueen's previous signature roles had all found him somewhere in the past. Now he would commit decisively to the present. From *Thomas Crown* through his last major hit, *The Towering Inferno* (1974), only *The Reivers* (1969) and *Papillon* (1973) would have historical settings.[3] Although the McQueen character remains an insubordinate individualist often swimming against the tide, when he works for a social organization, such as the police or the fire department, he is serving and protecting on the American audience's current home turf, rather than defending the country's interests on foreign soil. And when he is the antiheroic loner, he goes all the way to making criminal success his overriding goal. (Even though Henri in *Papillon* is innocent of the murder charge that sent him to Devil's Island, he is an admitted thief, unlike Hilts in *The Great Escape*, whose only crime is trying to escape in order to fight for his country again.)

The Getaway intrigues because it turns the McQueen narrative on its head. We meet Doc McCoy in the penitentiary after the parole board has turned him down for early release. Rather than being cocky and defiant, he meekly complies with all the commands issued to him as his days of incar-

ceration wear on. With scarcely any dialogue, McQueen conveys how desperate Doc is becoming. It is as if he were Hilts's pal Ives, who goes stir crazy
and lets the guards shoot him as he tries to scale the fence in full view. To
preserve his sanity, Doc finally agrees to commit whatever crime the corrupt parole board member Benyon (Ben Johnson) wants him to. Rather
than being a Thomas Crown effortlessly in charge and impossible to thwart,
he is more like the operatives Crown hires, pays off, and dispenses with.
Only when Doc realizes he has been double-crossed by Benyon, as well as
by one of his accomplices and his wife, Carol (Ali McGraw), does he begin
to show the combative finesse we expect. In the improbable denouement,
he gets to keep the money, reconcile with Carol, and make it to freedom in
Mexico.

★★★★★ A Man among Men

Steve McQueen was the foremost American male star to
emerge in the 1960s and achieve the hallmarks of that stardom within the
decade. The twenty-first-century magazine devoted to films of the 1960s
and 1970s, *Cinema Retro*, confirmed his centrality to the era by giving him
the cover of its inaugural issue (January 2005). He was also among the first
television series leads to make the jump to film superstardom. With most
of his signature roles positioning him as a man both working with and
competing against other men, he became an icon for a new sort of masculinity. Much of the discourse about him then and now has to do with
trying to position that masculinity within the broader spectrum of male
star-images. Feeney states: "McQueen defined a fleeting moment in Hollywood's depiction of manhood, standing between the '50s kitsch of Sinatra,
John Wayne, and Elvis and the post-Vietnam second-guessing of the
pathological Eastwood, the sensitive New Age Redford, and Burt Reynolds.
He was the first and maybe the last action hero to be neither absurd nor
ironic." Richard Luck also views him through the lens of the action star:
"So, while he will forever appear in lists of great Hollywood action heroes,
Steve McQueen on camera wasn't quite like the other boys. He was a mix-
ture of made man and misfit, ice-cool loner and lukewarm companion"
(7). During the 1960s, however, it was much more common for observers
to see him in the context of other Method-trained actors, and I think we
can get a better sense of his uniqueness in the company of Dean, Brando,
Hoffman, and De Niro than by comparing him with Wayne and Reynolds
(although Eastwood, his fellow western television star who made it big in
the movies, is a closer analogue).

During his early career, McQueen saw Dean and Brando as the contemporaries he was trying to join. In his uncredited part as Fidel in *Somebody Up There Likes Me* (1956) and in "The Defender" episode of "Studio One" (1957) that convinced Elkins to sign him on as a client, he is all mumbles and twitches. "At that point, he was not sure whether he was Marlon Brando or James Dean, so he wound up imitating both of them and showed none of himself," Neile reflected (Toffel 42). By the time he played Josh Randall in "Wanted," however, he had perfected the McQueen cool, although comparisons to Brando would persist in reviews of his films.

The male star of the 1960s who makes for the most accurate comparison with McQueen is Paul Newman. Both were conventionally handsome sex symbols who often played rebels and possessed between them the bluest blue eyes in Hollywood. Because McQueen's first, small film role (in *Somebody Up There Likes Me*) was in the film that made Newman a star, he always felt a sense of particular rivalry with him, even though they often socialized together. McQueen resented Newman's inauthenticity in playing the social outsider because he hadn't lived that life as Steve had; McQueen saw him as a *poseur* because of his well-to-do, "frat boy" upbringing. They seemed destined to share the screen once again after both were on top, and Newman offered McQueen the role of Sundance in *Butch Cassidy and the Sundance Kid* (1969). But McQueen balked over not being guaranteed first billing. When they finally paired up for *The Towering Inferno*, McQueen did receive first billing, the largest salary as yet paid to an actor ($5 million), and better reviews, despite opting out of the lead role of the architect to play the fire chief who comes to the rescue. In the end, Newman's well-educated and wealthy builder admits he should have deferred to the working stiffs who understand how to keep such skyscrapers safe.

As the decade came to a close, and McQueen was one of the most popular and highest-paid stars in the world, a new sort of Method actor emerged to take movie stardom in a different direction. Upon first seeing Dustin Hoffman in *The Graduate* (1967) McQueen said to Neile, "What's gonna happen to us, do you suppose?" He was referring to the many handsome leading men in Hollywood in an era when "a good actor" but "one homely cat" could be a movie star (Toffel 172). Nevertheless, when he and Hoffman shared the screen six years later, in *Papillon*, McQueen was still top-billed and the main box office draw.

Watching McQueen emerge from the pack in the large male ensemble of *The Magnificent Seven* provides a tutorial on his brand of masculinity. Despite establishing himself in the film's opening sequence as a man whom the Seven's leader, Chris, can count on and so recruits as his second-in-command, Vin suffers from the disadvantage of having no distinguishing character arc or traits among otherwise very individualized comrades. Narratively, the true second lead is Chico (Horst Buchholz), as he abandons his peasant roots to become a gunfighter but then embraces them for the love of a woman in the village they are protecting. Britt (James Coburn) has his extraordinary skill as knife thrower and marksman, Bernardo O'Reilly (Charles Bronson) bonds with three village boys, Lee's (Robert Vaughn) nerves are shot, and Harry (Brad Dexter) schemes to make a profit from the Seven's "pro bono" heroism. So how did McQueen become the breakout star?

Partly it was because he set out to be noticed and to steal focus from the other actors. He inserted bits of physical business everywhere, especially involving his constant fiddling with his sweat-stained cowboy hat. Such behavior infuriated his foreign-born co-stars, Brynner and Buchholz. In an interview taped decades later (which is part of the DVD), Buchholz seems as angry with McQueen as he was when the film was in production. But none of these shenanigans would have paid off if McQueen didn't stand out for his authenticity. He had been the man Vin was, an Anglo-American guy drifting around the West. By contrast, the film asks us to believe that the Russian-Swiss Brynner is a Cajun; that the German Buchholz and first-generation Americans of Eastern European ancestry Bronson and Eli Wallach are Mexicans; and that New York City–born Vaughn is a southerner. Moreover, in a film with a fair amount of speechifying, Vin Tanner's aphoristic style and sparse dialogue make a spectator listen when he does speak. His "No Prospects" monologue has him wearily explaining that a gunslinger has nothing an ordinary man might treasure, in contrast to the others in the group who emphasize that lack can also be freedom from constraining authority or personal entanglements: "Home—none. Wife—none. Kids . . . none. Prospects—zero." The extended pause McQueen inserts between "kids" and "none" tells us all we need to know about the life of a man who, never having stayed with a woman long enough to know whether he has impregnated her, now feels the poignant regret that he isn't the sort that wants to find out.

Saying so much with so little was the key to McQueen's performance style. Feeney reports, "Filming a scene with Dustin Hoffman for *Papillon*, McQueen interrupted his co-star: 'Less, man, less!'" Frequent co-star Don Gordon remembers the same mantra ("Steve McQueen: The Essence of Cool" documentary [2005]). An integral part of the McQueen cool was his avoidance of any excess. Brando, Dean, and Newman have classic cinematic moments of intense emotional or physical anguish: the cry of "Stella!" in *A Streetcar Named Desire* (1951) and the terrible beating of *On the Waterfront*

(1954); the "You're killing me!" scene with the parents in *Rebel Without a Cause* (1955); the thumb-breaking scene in *The Hustler* (1961). Although McQueen's characters sometimes receive physical injury, they scarcely appear to feel pain. When Hilts's motorcycle crashes into the barbed wire in *The Great Escape*, his difficult extrication of himself concludes as he reveals the American military insignia he retained inside his shirt collar, preventing him from being executed as a spy as many of the other escapees were because they could not self-identify as soldiers. So impudent and pleased with himself is he, despite his capture, that his injuries hardly seem in need of even a Band-aid.

Emotional excess occurs rarely as well. McQueen is in fact not very good at conveying intense surprise, joy, or sadness. He tends to mug. One of the false notes in his *Thomas Crown* performance comes when the caper has succeeded and Crown, alone at home, surveys himself in a mirror with narcissistic satisfaction, then laughs uproariously and does a little dance. Not cool, and definitely not Steve McQueen. *The Sand Pebbles* resolves his difficulty by using Jake's Chinese assistant Po-Han (Mako) as a sort of external correlative for the suffering Jake may feel but cannot express. It is Po-Han who takes a beating in a fight so that Jake can win a bet to help a friend. When the communists seize and horribly torture Po-Han, Jake defies orders in order to accommodate the man's pleas to shoot him and end his torment. This latter series of events does cause Jake to break down, but McQueen significantly plays his sobs with his back toward the camera so that we know he is crying only because his shoulders are heaving. (According to Steven Spielberg, McQueen gave as a reason for turning down the proffered lead in *Close Encounters of the Third Kind* [1977] the fact that he couldn't cry on cue.) If one looks for a full-on McQueen breakdown in the face of severe injury or an emotional punch to the gut, the most one will get is the image of him slowly backing up to a wall and sliding down it into a sitting position as his eyes go hollow, a scene that repeats from *The Great Escape* to *The Cincinnati Kid* to *The Sand Pebbles*.

Besides turning down his emotional affect, McQueen also advocated for less dialogue. Several directors and co-stars refer to his desire to cut lines or foist them off on other characters. Alan Trustman, who wrote the screenplays for *The Thomas Crown Affair* and *Bullitt*, offered McQueen an insightful précis of his strengths and weaknesses as a performer that pinpoints why less was more as far as dialogue was concerned: "You are shy, you don't talk too much. . . . You never deliver a sentence with more than five or ten words . . . because paragraphs make you lose interest or something goes wrong with your delivery" (qtd. in Terrill, *Portrait* 147). The important corollary to

Reacting in close-up: Frank Bullitt spots the hitman's vehicle and begins the famous car chase. (Digital frame enlargement)

this laconic persona, however, was the necessity that the camera stay focused on McQueen while others did the talking. His acting, he liked to say, was more about reacting.

More accurately, his acting was bodily rather than vocal, in motion in long shot and in stillness in close-up. The wiry, athletic McQueen doesn't need the big, speeding machine props to transfix an audience as he gets from place to place. He has a loose-limbed, loping stride and almost balletic grace, shown off in the flight through the train yards in *Cincinnati Kid* or the sequence in *The Magnificent Seven* in which Vin twirls around to shoot at enemies on all sides, takes a bullet to the leg, ties off the wound, and seeks cover inside a building all in one continuous motion. Even more mesmerizing was his face. A *Newsweek* profile on 6 January 1964 remarks upon "Steve McQueen's splendid amalgam of blinks, furrowed brows, smirks, quick smiles, pursed lips." Feeney rhapsodizes:

> He had one of the greatest of all movie faces, even though he wasn't perfectly handsome. The broad masculine nose and deep leathery creases around his taut mouth didn't connect to those scary blue eyes. What brought his features alive on-screen were his wide cheekbones and a narrow tapering chin—the kind of triangular bonework more commonly associated with female beauty. Shot from certain high angles, McQueen could resemble an extremely macho elf.

When she first encountered Steve, Neile remembers noticing his "adorable smile and wonderfully piercing blue, blue eyes" (31). Onscreen

McQueen bestowed his smiles less frequently, so that the effect when he did was striking. That perfect poker face, with its intense, steel-blue stare, which suited the Kid's profession so well, would crinkle up in an instant to express mischievous amusement or affection. Trustman describes the trademark McQueen grin perfectly: "You have a tight smile, you don't show your teeth, but it's a small smile around your mouth" (Terrill, *Portrait* 147). If the grin tended to be the same grin always, the stare could modulate itself with a much greater range of expressions. Sam Peckinpah, according to Terrill, "would always tell people, 'If you really want to learn about acting for the screen, watch McQueen's eyes'" (*Portrait* 237).

This minimalist performance style was at the heart of McQueen's cool masculinity, whose appeal lay in large part in how it tamed and controlled any hint of melodramatic—read feminine—emotion. A 27 January 1970 *Look* magazine profile dubbed him "Mr. Manmanship." And his decision to construct his star image in this way may spring from fears he expressed throughout his career that acting as a profession was emasculating. Neile quotes him as saying that it was "women's work" (Toffel 102). (The guy who took up the stage to meet girls ironically came to consider his life's work too girly.) Biographer Christopher Sandford identifies a fear of being thought a "candy ass" as an overriding factor in McQueen's life. (It probably didn't help that his name was Mc*Queen*.) When an anonymous caller in 1968 said that an underground book would name him as one of Hollywood's many closeted homosexuals, he was furious and shaken. His habit of spending so much offscreen time either hanging out with tough guys or bedding women supposedly stemmed in part from this fear. Perhaps it also motivated his insistent homophobia and proud declarations of male chauvinism.

Taken altogether, this behavior raises the question of whether McQueen felt insecure in his own masculinity rather than simply being worried about the opinions of others. When he first became involved with Neile, and for several years after they married, she was an up-and-coming dancer and singer who supported him with an income ten times what he was bringing in; he would probably never have been signed by a Hollywood agent had she not urged her own to give him a chance. Moreover, given his unsettled childhood, his abandonment by his father, and the absence of positive influences from adult males during his adolescence, constructing a coherent masculine identity must have been difficult. It is of course quite a leap to infer, as the tabloid-esque Porter book does, that McQueen was sexually abused as a boy and just as promiscuous sleeping with men as with women during his Hollywood years. There is a long continuum from full-on bisexuality to the occasional unacted-upon same-sex desire; suspicions linger in the discourse about McQueen as to whether his compulsive womanizing and heterosexist proclamations might not have been compensation for his falling somewhere within that continuum. It is certainly true that for all his professed concerns about being feminized, McQueen actively sought to burnish his star image in ways that might have earned him a "metrosexual" designation in later decades.

★★★★★ The Style of Steve

McQueen had a sophisticated awareness of how the right costuming could make a performance stand out. He was very concerned that the ribbed white turtleneck sweater James Garner's character sported in *The Great Escape* would draw all eyes to him and so he selected as his own costume the short-sleeved sweatshirt, khaki pants, and leather bomber jacket that he believed flattered his own physique. Given the number of period pictures he made, as well as the flamboyance of style in the later 1960s and early 1970s for films set in the present, McQueen manages to look timelessly contemporary. The other characters in *The Cincinnati Kid* and the disguised escapees in *The Great Escape* look every bit as if they are living in the 1930s and 1940s. With an array of jackets worn over crewneck or turtleneck sweaters in the former and a simple black pea coat in the latter, McQueen looks right for 1930, 1970, or 2010. And there is no better way to sum up his minimalist cool masculinity than with the iconic image from the *Bullitt* poster in which he leans pensively against a wall clothed in a black sweater and black pants, the only contrast provided by his shoulder holster. Attesting to his timeless look is a feature from *Esquire* showing a model in a McQueen mask "wearing ten classic pieces of American sportswear, each as iconic and cool this spring as in the days when McQueen wore them" (March 2008).

Neile writes that offscreen, in any style, he preferred form-fitting clothes that displayed his body to best advantage. (He also encouraged photographers to shoot him with his shirt off, and in the *Life* feature he appears totally naked from behind as he emerges from the family swimming pool.) He was "a fashionable man" who during the last half of the 1960s "was featured in all the fashion magazines—men's and women's—modeling the latest sportswear and also the Cardin and Brioni suits he favored at that time" (Toffel 159). In February 1965 he would be the first male ever to grace the cover of *Harper's Bazaar*. McQueen was also known for his distinctive, layered haircut; he was one of the first male Hollywood stars on whose hair his stylist, Jay Sebring—also one of McQueen's closest friends—used a blow dryer. These fashion innovations have retained their "cool-as-crushed-ice" cachet, as demonstrated by a story in *Time* twenty-five years later. When the magazine reviewed celebrity trends for the week of 24 October 1993, it discovered that "the fashion world's newest paragon of cool seems to be Steve McQueen in *The Thomas Crown Affair*," citing "fashion-world hanger-on" Sofia Coppola's statement that "whoever's doing what they want is cool. Steve McQueen in *The Thomas Crown Affair* was cool," and Paul Cavaco, fashion director at *Harper's Bazaar*, explaining his haircut as "I'm Steve McQueen in *The Thomas Crown Affair*."

This dual star image of daredevil rebel racer and trend-setting fashionista still defines McQueen decades later. Although after his death in 1980 he receded from public discourse for the next couple of decades, he began to regain his iconic status in the twenty-first century, not as much in the world of cinephiles as in the world of advertisers. In a 2007 *Forbes* magazine article, "The McQueen Resurrection," Elisabeth Eaves notes how the "old king of cool" has become the "new king of cool," debuting in the tenth spot on the publication's list of highest-earning dead celebrities. Among several factors powering this resurrection, she singles out the use of his image in a 2005 television commercial for the Ford Mustang: "There may be no better match than McQueen and a Mustang. The television ad scored on multiple levels—McQueen's *Bullitt* character, Frank Bullitt, actually drove one during a high-speed car chase. In the ad, McQueen hopped into the retro-styled 2005 Mustang and took it for a spin." She also cites a campaign that watchmaker Tag Heuer built around the timepiece the McQueen character wore in *Le Mans*. A 29 April 2010 article in *GQ* displayed photos of ten contemporary items that might help the consumer "get the look" of Steve McQueen, with the following advice: "Steve McQueen favoured clothing with purpose: when he wasn't dressed for car or motorbike racing, he'd be seen on set in his favourite sport coat and black rollneck. McQueen's style was all about clear-cut masculinity, so invest in pieces that look better with a bit of dirt such as a leather jacket or a denim shirt. Man up." Thus, despite his anxieties, McQueen's star image manages to project untroubled masculinity even while serving as a primer in fashion magazines.

Although all superstars have images that exceed the characters they play in any one film, McQueen represents an extreme case. There is often at least one perfect match between star image and filmic role that captures the essence of the performer and elevates what might have been a forgettable film into a classic. Bogart's Rick in *Casablanca* fills the bill precisely. Even though McQueen's star image has parallels to Bogart's, there is no Rick in his repertoire, and no *Casablanca* either. Had he played the part, we would remember a guy who looked really sharp in white dinner jackets, tailored trench coats, fedoras (and fog) and was cool while helping his ex-girlfriend make the flight out of town—and of course who expertly undertook a fast and harrowing drive to get to the airport on time. McQueen, thus, is almost abstracted from his films, merely an image and a signifier of a certain sort of rebelliousness and masculinity.

Medevoi theorizes: "Steve McQueen's stardom rests in his role in celebrating the mobile youth as an icon of political freedom, and more specifically in instantiating the relationship of the suburbs, anti-communism, and teenage speed." On a less cerebral note, the 2000 film *The Tao of Steve* distills the essence of three iconic Steves of the 1960s and 1970s, Steve McGarrett (Jack Lord) of "Hawaii Five-O," Steve Austin (Lee Majors) of "The Six-Million Dollar Man," and especially Steve McQueen, to provide a Tao that allows a schlumpy-looking kindergarten teacher to become a successful ladies' man. In an essay on the film, Steven C. Combs explains that "this is a metaphor for the ideal male—a blend of elements of Eastern wisdom with the on-screen persona of Steve McQueen, especially noted for his unflappable bravery and motorcycle riding in *The Great Escape*. McQueen never tries to impress women, but 'he always gets the girl'" (120). That the first two Steves are characters while the third is an "on-screen persona" of an actor reinforces my point about the relative unimportance of any particular role in creating the "Steveness" of McQueen.

This tendency is perhaps responsible for the fact that, in retrospect, McQueen made mostly mediocre movies. "The actor appeared in only three or four films—'The Magnificent Seven,' 'The Great Escape,' 'The Getaway,' and, perhaps 'Bullitt' and 'Papillon' at a stretch—that are seen and well regarded today," says *Variety*'s Todd McCarthy in a 30 March 1998 review of the "King of Cool" documentary. McQueen aficionados, bemoaning this fact, often point to the many better-regarded films that McQueen passed on for one reason or another. Thus he appears in *Love with a Proper Stranger* but not *Breakfast at Tiffany's* (1961), *The Sand Pebbles* but not *Apocalypse Now* (1979), *The Towering Inferno* but not *Butch Cassidy and the Sundance Kid*. I would counter that these latter films might not have turned out as well as they did had McQueen appeared in them, given his tendency to battle with directors, antagonize castmates, and insist on changes to his roles so that they conformed to what he considered the limits of his acting ability and reflected what Steve McQueen (or rather the idealized version of Steve McQueen that the actor nurtured) would do.

The function of the Virgil Hilts character in *The Great Escape* provides a micro-illustration of the relationship of the McQueen star image to the

McQueen cinematic corpus. Because he is repeatedly serving solitary time in the cooler, Hilts is absent from most of the sequences that involve the planning and execution of the escape. He provides intelligence about the surrounding terrain by making a solo escape and then letting himself be recaptured, then helps the escapees negotiate the gap between the tunnel's opening and the shelter of the woods. Otherwise he's on his own. The end credits reflect his isolation from the group effort; while every other POW has a nickname associated with his role in the escape—"The Scrounger," "The Forger"—Hilts is "The Cooler King," most important for being himself while by himself. Similarly, McQueen's star image breaks free from the adventures of Hilts or Vin Tanner or Frank Bullitt or Thomas Crown to become only itself alone: Steve McQueen, the King of Cool.

NOTES

1. I haven't been able to pin down a first citation of the "King of Cool" nickname. Porter claims that it was coined after *The Cincinnati Kid*'s release but does not document his assertion. It seems likely that it was a play on McQueen's breakout role as "The Cooler King" in *The Great Escape*, but there's no evidence of it getting into general use that early. The adjective "cool" to describe McQueen is there almost from the beginning, however, as in Louella Parson's piece in the December 1962 issue of *Seventeen*, "Keep It Cool."

2. McQueen's first attempt to do a racing movie failed when Warner Bros. cancelled his project with John Sturges, titled *Day of the Champion*, because shooting delays on *The Sand Pebbles* meant that it would not beat a competing racing film, John Frankenheimer's *Grand Prix*, into theaters. Ironically, Frankenheimer first offered McQueen the lead in his film but McQueen turned it down because he "hadn't felt good vibrations from either Frankenheimer or his producer Ed Lewis" (Toffel 121). He was furious with James Garner for many years for taking the role—part of his dog-in-the-manger behavior.

3. Two of the last three films McQueen made—*An Enemy of the People* (1978), *Tom Horn* and *The Hunter* (1980)—return to the past but they are footnotes to a career that essentially ends with *Towering Inferno*. He stepped away from the cameras for five years and only agreed to do the Ibsen adaptation because he was contractually obligated to make another film for the First Artists production company. Although he seemed ready for a comeback when he made the other two, he was already ill with the mesothelioma that killed him at age fifty in 1980.

5 ★★★★★★★★★★★★
Mia Farrow
Categorically Intangible

LESLIE H. ABRAMSON

Amid the intoxication of metamorphosis, the magnetizing struggles of cultural transformation that constituted the 1960s, Mia Farrow emerged as an icon of mutability, a resonant emblem of the intangible. Transliterated into the mass-circulated domains of celebrity profiles, gossip columns, interviews, fashion shoots, and reviews, her image was, in large part, that of a figure of free-spirited changeability, a captivating cipher. Farrow's attraction activated in Hollywood discourse the infatuation with permutation and indeterminancy as well as a converse urge toward circumscription, engaging the fascination and problematics of definition. In essence, Farrow's celebrity conjugated the epistemology of stardom with the dynamism of the modern decade.

Consistently characterized as ethereal, indefinable, and otherworldly, considerable measure of Farrow's allure was located in her status as a personality graspable only in the abstract, the embodiment of the transitional, indefinite, and unbound. The remarkable nature of such mesmeric typecasting was that Farrow's elusiveness, her celebrated intangibility, was a shared illusion, a fantasy in which the performer, press, and public manifestly conspired. This exemplar of modernity was, ironically, a figure whose materialization as a star and continued notoriety was entirely indebted to her status as an individual firmly bound to the industry and cultural milieu of the Hollywood Establishment by genealogical cords as well as through the professional and personal attachments she formed in the course of the decade. In a historical moment during which rebellion against the System defined youth culture, Farrow simultaneously represented compelling individualism and the institution of American cinema.

In the conjunction between her highly publicized offscreen life and onscreen performances, Farrow became a marker of the decade's tensions, a nexus of the competing rhetoric of classical stardom, Establishment values, and liberation discourses. Emerging as a celebrity in 1964, when, at age nineteen, she starred as a virginal, illegitimate teenager in "Peyton Place," a hugely controversial new television soap opera depicting small town licentiousness, Farrow was best known for her strong associations with Hollywood studio culture and moral conservatism as the Catholic school–educated daughter of 1930s movie star Maureen O'Sullivan and film director John Farrow. By the end of the decade, when her fifth feature film was released, Farrow had become a contract actress, wife and divorcée of middle-aged singer and veteran film star Frank Sinatra, celebrated nonconformist, established magazine cover image, modern fashion icon, devotee of Transcendental Meditation, temporary ashram resident, and paramour of conductor and film composer Andre Previn, by whom the unwed Farrow was pregnant in 1969. Farrow's sphere of intimates and acquaintances, with whom her associations were followed by the media with considerably more interest than her screen work, included 1940s and 1950s studio stars, aged surrealist painter Salvador Dali, the Maharishi Yogi, and such contemporary performers as the Beatles. Taken together with her handful of film roles exploring untethered and delimited femininity, including the pregnant housewife victimized by devil worshippers in *Rosemary's Baby* (1968), her sole box office hit, Farrow's almost universally agreed-upon charming image attracted intensely debated issues of the Generation Gap, the sexual revolution, gender roles, experimental spirituality, and shifting moral codes.

At the same time, Farrow was a critical figure of suture, linking the Establishment and youth culture, the studio system and New American Cinema, domestic and foreign aesthetics, classical art and modern media.

matrimony and liberated womanhood, and traditional, folk, and contemporary spiritualism. In the process, Farrow reinvigorated public fascination with celebrity in a fashion that both hearkened back to studio culture's longed-for Golden Age and celebrated the new. During a decade of hemorrhaging box office returns, when no less than the industry of American cinema itself seemed to be at stake, the immense stardom of Mia Farrow constituted one of the few affirmative ways of resolving the question, "Can Hollywood survive the 1960s?"

☆★★★★ Cover Girl

Though her image was mass distributed on no fewer than sixty magazine covers in the course of the 1960s, issues of apprehension were foremost in media discourse dedicated to the representation of Mia Farrow as a star.[1] A figure whose inhabitance of the celebrity sphere not only predated but almost consistently overshadowed her display of talent as a screen performer, one of a contemporary breed of star defined by historian Daniel Boorstin in 1961 as those "notorious for their notoriety," Farrow seemed to both invite and elude definition. From 1964 through the end of the decade, Farrow's image in the popular press was that of the inexplicable, unattached, and extramundane: a "waif," a "sprite," "almost unearthly," an "airborne colleen," a "merry little mystery, a misunderstood visitor from the future, or the occult past." This incarnation as the ineffable, a shape shifter, was evoked by Farrow herself, who, in one of her earliest interviews, suggested, "I'm like a kaleidoscope . . . I see a different person every time I look in a mirror" (S. Gordon, "Mia Farrow: An Actress in Search of a Character," *Look*, 1 December 1964, 72–76). Voted among the top ten "Most Promising New Faces of 1966" in a *Motion Picture Herald* poll of theater owners, her visage conveyed infinite changeability. The following year, a reporter observed, "She is Mia Superstar as the camera focuses on her, smiling, laughing, flirting, looking innocent, looking sexy. Completely in charge. She's everybody at once—a duke's daughter, Peter Pan, Joan of Arc, the Constant Nymph. Instant quicksilver" (Suzy Knickerbocker, "Mia," *McCall's*, May 1967, 144–45). By the end of the decade, Farrow's classification as the indeterminate incarnate, albeit critiqued as shopworn by some, remained a dominant trope in media texts. As late as 1969, *Time* included among its compilation of quotes about the young star from fellow celebrities—an epistemological strategy frequently employed in what the press characterized as the difficult attempt to define Farrow—an observation by actor Roddy McDowell: "Trying to describe Mia is like trying to describe dust in a shaft of sunlight. There are all those particles" (Stefan Kanfer, Jay Cocks, and Carey Winfrey, "The Moonchild and the Fifth Beatle," *Time*, 7 February 1969, 52). As McDowell's remark suggested, in measuring the appeal of Farrow, star discourse became manifestly suffused with issues of knowing. Attempting to grasp her allure, *Newsweek* observed, "Mia's uniqueness may yet make her into a movie star. People are interested in her, and it can't simply be because of the acting she's displayed up to now. . . . There is something about her—that lost sparrow look, her kooky comments in the columns, not to mention her marriage to, and estrangement from, Frank Sinatra, that makes her talked about" ("Faye Dunaway: Star, Symbol, Style," 4 March 1968, 43).

Among the facets of her Otherness, Farrow's screen work was markedly Europeanized. Three of her five studio releases of the 1960s—*Guns at Batasi* (1964), *A Dandy in Aspic* (1968), and *Secret Ceremony* (1968)—were British-made and feature Farrow as English characters, while *Rosemary's Baby* was invested by its director, Polish émigré Roman Polanski, with a foreign art-cinema aesthetic.[2] Taken together with the reportage of her British heritage, childhood in Beverly Hills, England, and Spain, ecumenical education, temporary residences in London for filming, much-publicized association with the Spaniard Dali, and her 1968 pilgrimage to India, Farrow's persona and work were inflected with tropes of geographic, psychic, and cultural dissociation.[3]

Amid Farrow's literally and aesthetically foreign films, the works of modern Americana, "Peyton Place," the romance, *John and Mary* (1969), and the image constructed in celebrity texts, McDowell's "particles" assumed a particular shape. Farrow's aura was one of familiarity and estrangement, a figure both affixed to and unmoored from the lineages of nationality, family, Establishment culture, and conventional femininity. Both as screen persona and media figure, Farrow was largely a cultural traveler, engaging the thematics of investigation, as both inquisitor and subject of inquisition, through which the decade interrogated the nature and limits of its own metamorphoses.

Farrow's Otherness with regard to the spheres of Establishment studio and fan culture with which she was nonetheless closely allied constituted a distinct component of her image in the 1960s. She was perceived as a new, anti-Hollywood female star, a figure of sexuality who at the same time possessed a body antithetical to Marilyn Monroe's, endowed, according to *Time*, with "measurements . . . closely akin to a newel post's," and sporting a coiffure the opposite of Rita Hayworth's, with boyishly cropped hair (Kanfer et al., "The Moonchild and the Fifth Beatle," 52).[4] Summing up her enigmatic appeal, *Look* noted, "Mia represents the new breed, the talented in-depth actress who has displaced, at least temporarily, the sexy starlets of yesteryear. This year [1964], say the Hollywood pros, 'those cute, round, bouncy, all-American girls can't even get arrested here anymore'" (Gordon, "An Actress in Search of a Character," 76).

In her essay "Icons of Popular Fashion," Valerie Carnes observes, "Our female icons were switching from *femme fatale* to nymphet. . . . The new Sixties girl was not only childlike; she was kinky, kooky, adventurous, spirited" (229). A central figure in ushering in this updated image of femininity, the wide-eyed and delicate boned Farrow cut a subtle alternate facet in the newly emerging surfaces of young femininity onscreen. Farrow's roles and her popular persona combined innocence and juvenility with worldly sophistication; desire with cool, almost matter-of-fact sexuality; shelteredness and pure spirituality with exploration and experimentation. Her physical body and body of texts repressed the erotic, which played a significant part in her screen roles and gossip culture.[5]

An ironically compelling figure of vulnerability at the cusp of the women's liberation movement, as some have observed (see Derry), one of Farrow's central attractions was her precariously delicate physique and nature. Repeatedly using a single descriptor, media texts characterized the actress on- and offscreen as "looking infinitely fragile," "hopelessly fragile," "enchanting in her fragility." However, in one of the numerous binary oppositions encompassed by her persona, Farrow's celebrated delicacy was counterbalanced by reported toughness and manifest ambition. Pointing to this conjugation of qualities—quite unlike, for example, the unmitigatingly brazen Bette Davis of decades past—*Ladies' Home Journal* recognized Farrow as a "seemingly fragile but deceptively strong young woman," reporting that she had once informed gossip columnist Hedda Hopper "'I want a big career . . . a big man and a big life. You have to think big—that's the only way to get it'" (Vernon Scott, "Mia Farrow's Swinging Life with Frank Sinatra," May 1967, 86).

In the course of the mid-to-late 1960s, Farrow imported this captivating "fragility" to the screen and celebrity text as a figure of purity and innocence informed, stained, or threatened by cultural, erotic, and psychic knowledge and violation. Onscreen, she permutated among daughter-figures in "Peyton Place," the outset of *Dandy in Aspic, Johnny Belinda,* and *Secret Ceremony* to seductive and worldly, often cosmopolitan, independent social and sexual adventurers—an alluring secretary in the British occupation drama *Guns at Batasi,* a globetrotting photographer in the spy film *Dandy in Aspic,* and a Manhattan art gallery assistant and proponent of free love in *John and Mary*—to figures of the violated maternal, particularly in *Rosemary's Baby*, the apotheosis of the Farrow character as a woman at risk. Such representations of the feminine engaged in a constant dialectic with Farrow's offscreen life as her initial figuration as a daughter gave way to incarnations as a spouse and a liberated social, sexual, and spiritual quester who remained simultaneously attached to and disengaged from Establishment culture. In effect, Farrow's delicate physique became a screen onto which the decade's tensions and fantasies of reconciliation were projected, embodying cultural contradictions and abridgments key to the 1960s.

☆★★★★ *Tarzan* **Meets Peyton Place**

The attraction of Farrow's "particulate" image, as a figure of constant shift and ungraspability, was a central irony of her early career insofar as it belied an equally well publicized, countervailing facet of her stardom: an absolute groundedness in traditional cinema culture. Integral to the construction and comprehension of the young Farrow as a celebrity was her status as a scion of Hollywood's Golden Age, evoking an aura of stardom, glamour, elite social circles, the studio system, and colonialism. It is nearly impossible to find an article on Farrow written in the mid-1960s that does not reference her ancestry as a second-generation cinema star, one in effect born into the industry and raised within the rarefied atmosphere of celebrity culture. This star whom Pauline Kael and others referred to as a "waif" ("Gloria, The Girl without Hope," *New Yorker*, 20 December 1969, 62) was invested with lineages of the cinema Establishment coupled with a British heritage as the daughter of often-described Hollywood "royalty": actress Maureen O'Sullivan and director and writer John Farrow, émigrés from Ireland and Australia. They appointed as her godparents fixtures of studio culture and its dissemination, MGM director George Cukor and Hearst newspapers gossip columnist Louella Parsons, a prescient dual ancestry insofar as Farrow's celebrity in the 1960s became a convergence of screen work and media fixation.

O'Sullivan's screen persona and position of cultural notoriety as the plucky Jane Parker in the *Tarzan* series of the 1930s and early 1940s prefigured her daughter's first feature film appearance in the 1960s and her star image. In O'Sullivan's role as a young woman of proper English background who travels alone to Africa to become reunited with her father, an ivory trader, and ends up forsaking British culture for the lure of the wild, Jane bridges the Empire and the untamed. As a smitten Englishman observes in the second film of the series, *Tarzan and His Mate* (1934), "She's priceless. A woman who's learned the abandon of the savage, yet she'd be at home in Mayfair." The figure of the female as embodiment of both the Establishment and its relinquishment, a cultural adventurer who harbors the transformative agency to dually retain and shed an aura of colonialism—in Jane's case, by not only abdicating British life for the erotic and social freedoms of the jungle, but transporting English culture into tree house living—informed Farrow's persona as a young woman conjoining both the known and exotic liberation, a nonconformist sustaining an approach-avoidance association with figures and structurations of patriarchy.

Farrow's first credited feature film appearance, in *Guns at Batasi*, echoed the Jane Parker role insofar as she was also cast as a Britisher in Africa who abandons English culture, albeit temporarily in this case, as a secretary who has accompanied a team of UN observers to the continent and, after the mission, "stayed on for a little holiday."[6] In Farrow's minor role as a quiet young woman caught in a British Army command post during a military coup by African rebels, she is a figure associated with diplomacy who, like Jane, coalesces innocence, eroticism, and liberation, bridging Establishment culture and the unbound in Africa. Attired in desexualized commonwealth khaki, Farrow, characterized by one of the English soldiers as an alluring "crumpet," uninhibitedly acts upon her erotic desires, seducing a private who readily reciprocates. Yet binary oppositions contained in Farrow's decidedly lower-wattage embodiment of sensuality were recognized; in the wake of *Guns'* release, a *Look* interview reported: "'I played a seductress,' [Farrow] giggles. 'It's marvelous playing a seductress.' But when she posed in sheer lingerie for a full-page picture in a fashion magazine, somebody said she looked exactly as if she were in church" (Gordon, "An Actress in Search of a Character," 76).

★★★★★ Life as a Soap Opera

Farrow catapulted to celebrity as a figure of dual progenitor, occupying the roles of both fictive and empirical daughter upon her debut in the immensely popular new television series "Peyton Place," groundbreaking both in its status as the first evening soap opera and, in accords with the sensationalist 1956 novel and 1957 film from which the program was adapted, in its forthright treatment of the lurid undercurrents of American communities.[7] In the series, which premiered on 15 September 1964 (nine days before the Warren Commission Report was issued in an attempt to quell the eruption of conspiracy theories that surfaced in the wake of the Kennedy assassination), the locus of rumors, assignations, scandals, and shock were displaced onto the circumscribed site of a small New England town. Farrow played a central role as a figure of notorious lineage and problematic innocence: Allison Mackenzie, the shy, illegitimate seventeen-year-old daughter of an unwed bookstore owner, "a romantic who believes in good and purity and is disturbed by anything contrary to that," according to the network's press release (Leo Litwak, "Visit to the Town of the Mind," *New York Times*, 4 April 1965, 46).

In opposition to youth rejections of the parental constituting the widening "generation gap" in the mid-1960s, Farrow's character conducts a search for the progenitor. Likened by the *New York Times* to "some girl Oedipus . . . on the brink of discovery," Allison becomes a traveler through her own community, engaging in a journey to locate her father's identity (Litwak, "Visit to the Town of the Mind," 47). In the wake of the program's numerous transgressive erotic and social entanglements, she is a victim of another illicit sexual coupling when her wealthy boyfriend is forced to marry the deviously alluring lower-class woman whom he has impregnated.

By the end of October, "Peyton Place" was ranked sixth in the Nielsen ratings and had caused its own scandal as a Kinsey-unleashed site of prurient interest and moral violation contested by forces of repression and clandestinism. As sexual liberation discourses of the 1960s were surging in the wake of such works as *Sex and the Single Girl* (1962), "Peyton Place" inspired a heated debate—played out in the media through articles, reviews, and letters to the editor—about contemporary sexuality, ethics, commercialism, and spectatorial desire. Specifically, the dialectic centered on whether the program stooped to new lows in sensationalism or, as its executive producer claimed, "reflect[ed] the moral revolution in America" (Gordon, "An Actress in Search of a Character," 76).

Farrow initially figured into this discourse as a celebrity whose off-screen life both mirrored and constituted an antidote to Alison's biography and Peyton Place culture. The actress who played the fictive daughter of an infamous soap opera coupling was also introduced to the American public in 1964 as the child of parental notoriety; yet Farrow's progenitors were prominent Hollywood figures, one upon whom had been conferred familial and cultural legitimacy. Amplifying her character's innocence and purity in opposition to the lurid immorality of Peyton Place, the press foregrounded Farrow's devout spirituality. Periodicals recounted her sheltered education in a series of foreign and domestic Catholic institutions, including a convent boarding school in England (in the wake of which, it was reported, she had briefly planned to become a nun). In this respect, as in numerous others, the Farrow who emerged from these early portraits was again a figure of oppositions and their reconciliation. Embodying the decade's tensions between traditional and alternate spiritualism, she was often profiled as not only a strictly raised Catholic, but one with a polymorphic affinity for the Irish legends of her ancestry, palm readers, and the newly popularized Zen Buddhism.

Cultivating Farrow's image as a figure of mass appeal, one who resolved rather than stirred cultural tensions, the media initially celebrated Farrow as a transitional emblem of alternative femininity, one who shifted from ecumenically sheltered ingénue to free soul without representing the threat of radical liberation. Shortly after the debut of "Peyton Place," *TV Guide* described the actress as one who, like the innocent Allison, "lives in her own special world," in Farrow's case, personally delimited. A figure of self-containment of the nonconformist, autonomous feminine, this actress with a "highly independent spirit" reportedly constructed her own site of circumscription: "I think of my life as a garden . . . I rarely go out of that garden" (Marian Dern, "The Third of the Seven Little Farrows," 9 October 1964, 16–17). Yet the Victorian-inflected iconography of the once-sickly Farrow's life (at age nine, she suffered from polio) within a "protective garden," a figure of "girlish abstraction," was contravened by her self-professed ambitious pursuit of stardom and masterful manipulation of the discursive levers of classical celebrity culture. In another 1964 interview, she declared, "I can't stand being anonymous. I didn't want to be just 'one of the Farrows'" (Gordon, "An Actress in Search of a Character," 75).[8] This feminine ambition, too, was confined within classical masculine culture. As the last vestiges of the studio era were disappearing with the elimination of long-term contracts for performers, Farrow committed herself to the cinema establishment through a five-film contract with Twentieth Century–Fox and a romance with a Hollywood star.[9]

Farrow's celebrity status was not only guaranteed but also launched into stratospheric heights shortly after her soap opera debut, when she embarked on what became a highly publicized love affair with the forty-nine-year-old Frank Sinatra, thirty years her senior. In an actualization of what Molly Haskell has referred to as the decade's "Lolita cult" (345), Farrow's image alchemized from ingénue to nymphet. In the process, the press transliterated her private life into the genre of real-life soap opera through accounts of a liaison so publicly riveting that it overshadowed the fictive scandals of "Peyton Place."

In the course of the relationship, which began in the fall of 1964 and extended through their two-year marriage, from 1966 to 1968, Farrow's association with Sinatra became a nexus of the decade's central tensions

The twenty-year-old Farrow's image underwent a sea change when fan magazines and the mainstream press fixated on her two-week cruise with the forty-nine-year-old Frank Sinatra in August 1965. Farrow, who was then starring as the innocent Allison Mackenzie in the television series "Peyton Place," became the subject of a scandal that manifested the limits of American culture's shifting moral codes. Typical of fan magazine reportage was the cover story in *Screen Stories*, published in November 1965. (Collection of the author)

and fantasies of reconciliation. The romance became an intensely controversial index of the sexual revolution, hedonism, the generation gap, cultural conservatism, female gender roles, normative moral and social codes,
and the association between classical and contemporary visual culture. In
response to gossip columnist Sheila Graham's early reports of the relationship, "Irate women's groups, even the PTA, began petitioning the studio
and the sponsors regarding Mia's behavior," according to a Farrow biography (Epstein and Morella 83). The romance transmogrified into one of
the mid-decade's most publicized scandals when mainstream media and fan
texts fixated on a private cruise taken by Farrow and Sinatra during the
summer of 1965. Reports of the vacation metamorphosed her image from
one of innocence to nubile eroticism with shocking velocity, chronicling
Farrow's literal embodiment of the cultural sea-changes represented by
"Peyton Place."

The cruise generated a spate of journey-narrative tropes attesting to
mid-1960s culture's intense curiosity about the nature of its own passage
and the limits of its shifting moral codes. According to *Time*, "The ensuing
voyage was probably the most closely watched since Cleopatra floated down
the Nile to meet Mark Antony" ("Triple Jeopardy," 20 August 1965, 65).
Photoplay reported that the trip constituted "one of the world's most bally-
hooed adventures since Homer's 'Odyssey'" (George Carpozi Jr., "Voyage of
the Southern Breeze," November 1965, 19). The fictive infamy shading
Allison Mackenzie's background became stitched to Farrow insofar as the
overriding preoccupation with the cruise centered on issues of sexual liberation and legitimacy. Indexing the dramatic possibilities of the voyage,
Photoplay, which discerned Farrow to be situated at a "plateau of prominence—and predominance in reflecting the moral revolution of America,"
suggested that the excursion "held infinite promises of relaxation, rounds
of pleasure, romance and, conceivably, even marriage" (Carpozi, "Voyage of
the Southern Breeze," 18).

As the controversy associated with "Peyton Place" was thus ratcheted
higher (according to *Time*, the soap opera's executive producer "needed
Mia Farrow's cruise like a hole in the hull" ["Triple Jeopardy," 20 August
1965, 65]), Allison bore the marks of the offscreen scandal. A victim not
only of Farrow's infamy but of displaced anxiety, ironically, about legitimation and its consequences—the prospect of Farrow's marriage to Sinatra and,
by extension, her potential withdrawal from the soap opera as she assumed
a conventional spousal role—Allison solved the "problem" of Farrow's
absence during the shooting schedule by lapsing into an indefinite coma.
Through this symbolic co-option of Farrow's body, too unruly even for the

producers of "Peyton Place," fantasies of immobilizing the modern protean feminine surfaced at the site of sexual revolution.

One year before the foundation of NOW, forces of classical cultural authorization remained critical to rescuing Farrow for mass consumption from both daunting independence and one of the strongest remaining social taboos. As narrativized by celebrity discourse, the "old-time Hollywood establishment," 1940s studio stars Rosalind Russell, Claudette Colbert, and Merle Oberon, who, with their spouses, accompanied Farrow and Sinatra on the cruise, represented the film community's endorsement and regulation of Farrow, both embracing the new television star and acting as the Lolitaesque figure's "chaperones" (T. Thompson, "Mia," *Life*, 5 May 1967, 79). *Screen Stories*, among other magazines, worked just as hard to suture Farrow's troubling abridgment of the generation gap as it had to scandalize the relationship: "His closest friends . . . had never seen the seagoing, going-on-50 Sinatra look younger," and "As for Mia . . . what could be better for her than the stabilizing influence of a man like The Leader." Repressing cultural anxieties through an excess of normalizing narratives, the article erroneously noted, "Mia's mother . . . had been practically a child bride herself," reporting that significant age gaps were both traditional in O'Sullivan's native Ireland and typical of Hollywood's numerous "May-September marriages" (Mike Connolly, "The Untold Story of Mia's Weird Love Cruise," *Screen Stories*, November 1965, 47, 56).

Most commonly, the thematics of the loss of, and search for, the father central to Farrow's soap opera character were projected onto the actress' offscreen romance as it was to other relationships in a spate of pop Freudian diagnoses that would endure throughout the 1960s. Farrow was designated as the empirical child of paternal absence insofar as her father had died in 1963, the year before her television debut. Her relationship with Sinatra, subsequent association with Maharishi Yogi, also in his fifties, and oft-mentioned friendship with sexagenarian Salvador Dali were typically interpreted as quests for a father figure in the wake of John Farrow's death. *Screen Stories*, for example, reported that one of Farrow's friends observed, "Mia has a built-in father complex" (Connolly, "The Untold Story of Mia's Weird Love Cruise," 57). Farrow herself tended to articulate such affiliations quite differently. During a decade when repudiation of the older generation was normative, Farrow fashioned her image as one of embracement: "I haven't been in touch with my own generation much. Most of my friends have been older people, like Salvador Dali" (Gordon, "An Actress in Search of a Character," 73, 76). Moreover, Farrow was commonly depicted as a figure that embodied both youth and old age. Bette Davis observed, "She was born with an old soul" (Knickerbocker, "Mia," 145). Shirley MacLaine described Farrow as "a child . . . [but] from the neck up, she's 80" (Kanfer et al., "The Moonchild and the Fifth Beatle," 52).

If Farrow was to be celebrated as an emblem of contemporaneity, such oppositions would have to be reconciled for mainstream consumption in the literature of the New. In *Vogue*'s 1966 "Who's a Breakaway?" photo spread, Farrow was described as a contemporary "It" girl: "They're the girls who look like the Generation as opposed to the Establishment." Yet, at the same time, struggling to accommodate her ties to the older generation, the magazine cited an unnamed source: "She has the wonderful looks of the modern girl but not all the tiresome talk of youth" (April 1966, 72). Farrow's image was inflected by other problematizations of her modernity as well. The haircut that was key to her reputation as a fashion icon—and became an international sensation—was represented as a mark not only of contemporaneity, freedom, and nonconformism, but also of the wounds of classical masculinity. Dali famously characterized the cut as "a mythical suicide" insofar as, according to rumor, Farrow initially sheared her long hair in anger at not being invited to Sinatra's fiftieth birthday party (Thompson, "Mia," 79). With regard to her dramatic artistry, in an era when modern performance was allied with the Actors Studio, Farrow commented, "I hate starlets who spout off about the Method. . . . Acting is simply telling the truth under different sets of circumstances," eschewing contemporary technique for classic naturalism (Knickerbocker, "Mia," 145).

Of most intense fascination was Farrow's embodiment of hugely competing tensions between modern femininity and womanhood committed to the traditional ideals of domesticity informing the "feminine mystique." Following her wedding in 1966, the media's interrogation of Farrow's metamorphic persona fixated on her inscrutably retrograde shift to matrimonial attachment to a figure of orthodox masculinity. A subject of particular inquisition was the degree to which Farrow's spousal status entailed the abandonment of a spate of liberation narratives (and, by implication, the eschewal of the burgeoning feminist movement), including the temporary relinquishment of careerism. In a 1967 cover story subtitled "The gifted, wide-eyed sprite who is Mrs. Sinatra," *Life* celebrated "her shapeless world—a place of surmise so fascinatingly complex and maddeningly naive that Sinatra could fathom it only by marrying into it" (Thompson, "Mia," 75). Yet, conversely, *Life* among other publications took Farrow's measure as a woman circumscribed by patriarchal culture. Cataloguing her new signs of domesticity, *Life* noted that "there are evenings when Mia functions as the proud wife [watching Sinatra perform]," quoting Farrow's self-abnegating confession: "'Nothing I could ever do in films would make me as proud as I am of him'" (81).

Farrow's constitution as a figure of modernity nonetheless intimately attached to the Establishment—the elusive Other in both contexts—informed much of her screen work during the later 1960s. *A Dandy in Aspic*, *Rosemary's Baby*, and *Secret Ceremony* contain relationships between younger women and representatives of patriarchy, investigating through Farrow's roles the allure and acute dangers of containment insofar as her characters are both attracted to and grapple with the monstrous flaws of the older generation. The imprimatur of her relationship with Sinatra, and the suggestion of personal risk, was central to Farrow's return to the screen after a post-marital hiatus, in her first 1968 release, *Dandy*. This spy film, starring forty-year-old Laurence Harvey as a world-weary Russian double agent who becomes romantically involved with the twenty-three-year-old Farrow, reflexively references the latter's offscreen life, commodifying and interrogating her empirical condition. Not only are the leads figures of intergenerational ligature, but Sinatra's endorsement was implied both by Farrow's appearance in a film starring his former castmate (from *The Manchurian Candidate* [1962]) and friend as the leading man as well as by his graphic presence in one of her initial scenes, when Farrow's character picks up a camera next to a book titled *Frank Sinatra*, featuring a photograph of her real-life husband on the cover.

Dandy couples 1950s Cold War subterfuge with contemporary 1960s culture, imported by Farrow into the film in the role of Caroline, a young, stylish, globe-trotting British photographer whose cosmopolitan presence foregrounds issues of liberated sexuality, modern fashion, identity, and media notoriety. In her first starring film role, Farrow reenacts the arc from daughter to lover of an older man insofar as she is introduced into the plot as the child of a socialite who alchemizes into a figure of eroticism and romantic attachment as she enters into a relationship with a spy, Eberlin. In essence, Caroline encounters patriarchy at risk. Not only does Eberlin's status as a Russian double agent who works for British intelligence threaten western culture, but his midlife enervation and longing to extricate himself from his profession is a menace to the spy establishment internationally. Farrow's character counterbalances the literal and figurative exhaustion of this middle-aged man tethered to the dated world of Cold War tensions and archaic patriarchal establishments devoted to dramatic production in the form of spy plots. She also constitutes the attractive enigma of the untethered modern woman and new aestheticism, offering the promise of youthful revitalization, erotic escapism, and the graphic invigoration of

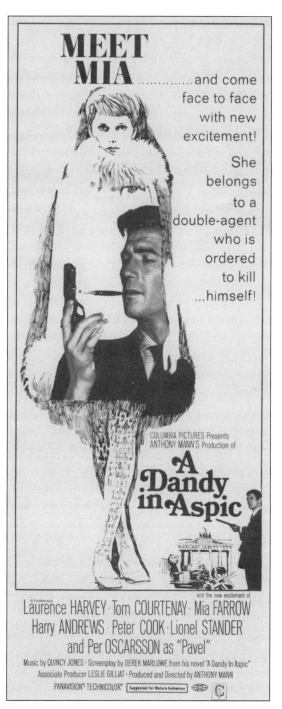

Ads for *A Dandy in Aspic* tended to privilege Farrow—and her status as newly emerged celebrity and fashion icon—rather than its established star, Laurence Harvey, who commanded significantly more screen time. (Collection of the author)

contemporary photography and fashion. At the same time, Caroline, like Farrow, constitutes a figure of vulnerability and retrograde desire. In a world of disequilibrium represented by crumbling Cold War culture and modernity's constant shift—in the wake of which, referencing Farrow's persona, Caroline admits, "I just seem to drift endlessly half the time"—she is willing to forfeit her independence and free-spiritedness for the constancy of the older man's love and a stable attachment.

Amidst *Dandy*'s numerous extradiegetic references to the biographical Farrow, most central is the film's meditation on issues of identity and notoriety. In its reflexive world of constant surveillance and infamy—cameras, photographs, film, slide shows, passport pictures, photo booths, constant stalking—one of the most acute dangers is the image. *Dandy* is preoccupied with the predicament of the fabricated persona: Eberlin not only longs to shed his public identity but is forced to take on an assignment to execute an elusive Russian agent—who is, in actuality, himself—in a mandate that amounts to the assassination of his true character. Through the figure of the photographer, who embodies her own reflexive double agency, coalescing subject and object positions by continually shifting between the focus and bearer of the investigative and desiring gaze, the film repeatedly references Farrow's offscreen cultural status as alternately beneficiary and victim of the image. In an early exchange, after Caroline gazes at herself in a mirror, Eberlin advises, "Oh, I wouldn't be too unsettled about your reflection. . . . I haven't found one yet that has interpreted my image correctly." This counsel constitutes a manifest commentary on Farrow's condition of stardom insofar as, by her own description, in the wake of her romance and marriage she was beleaguered by the press as an object of intrusive scrutiny. Yet, ultimately a cautionary tale, in *Dandy* the malignancy of the public image eventually kills Eberlin.

According to the *New York Times* review, "[Farrow] represents youth, mischief, innocence—everything that would draw Harvey into life again" (Renata Adler and Vincent Canby, "Screen: Harvey Plays a Deadpan 'Dandy in Aspic,'" *New York Times*, 3 April 1968).

Yet she is represented as an individual defined in part by lack. If the Farrow figure disengages herself from the familial at the outset of the film to become a liberated woman, she quickly reconstitutes herself as one desirous of the security of masculine attachment. Whereas in *Dandy*, the older man ultimately rejects this commitment, protecting Farrow's character from imprisonment in dying male culture, in her next film, *Rosemary's Baby*, patriarchy seizes upon Farrow as one whose presence is absolutely requisite for its continued reproduction.

The pinnacle of Farrow's film career in the 1960s, *Rosemary's Baby* constituted both the mainstreaming of the horror genre in American cinema and the professional legitimation of Farrow. As typified by a *Newsweek* reviewer's comment, Farrow was generally perceived, prior to the film's release, to be one "whose achievements to date have been outstripped by her publicity" (Paul Zimmerman, "Devil Child," 17 June 1968, 92). While validating her habitation of the celebrity sphere, paradoxically, Farrow's celebrated performance in this seventh highest grossing film of 1968—which earned her a Golden Globe nomination for Best Actress—emerged in a work that not only problematized the feminine condition within Establishment culture but allied its dangers with the threat of classical Hollywood, implying the joint menace posed by her personal and professional associations.

A reply to *Dandy*'s representation of the Farrow figure as an untethered, yet attachment-seeking cultural traveler, *Rosemary* constructs multiple spheres of containment for the actress's title character. Conferring upon Rosemary the conditions of Caroline's wish fulfillment, the Farrow character is not a figure of drift but a married child-bearer. Simultaneously, the film fully engages the thematics of the at-risk Farrow. In a commentary on what is at stake for the modern woman, released during a year in which feminists protested outside the Miss America pageant, the consequences for one whose desire remains shaped by the feminine mystique of fulfillment in traditional domesticity is the horrific of regulation, imprisonment, and violation by patriarchal culture.

In the film, Rosemary and her husband, Guy, a struggling actor, rent an apartment in the Bramford, a gothic Manhattan apartment building that has, in decades past, harbored practitioners of witchcraft and a series of strange fatalities. As Rosemary becomes pregnant and increasingly suffers, oddly monitored and controlled by her nosy elderly neighbors and an aged physician, she begins to suspect a conspiracy, but only when it is too late. Rosemary eventually discovers that the Bramford is inhabited by a satanic cult run by her neighbors, who have surreptitiously enlisted Guy in their scheme to impregnate her with the devil in exchange for professional success. Powerless against them, she ultimately, much to her horror, gives birth to Satan's offspring.

Typically considered a child of 1960s gender, familial, and social anxieties, *Rosemary's Baby* has been diagnosed variously as the "gynecological gothic," the "Maternal Macabre," and a "demon child film," born of the cultural traumas of pregnancy and domesticity and haunted by the specter of the juvenile delinquent (see Fischer; Heffernan; and Penelope Gilliatt,

A publicity still from *Rosemary's Baby* (1968). Rosemary embodies a feminist critique of the consequences for one whose desire remains shaped by the feminine mystique of fulfillment in traditional domesticity. (Collection of the author)

"Anguish under the Skin," *New Yorker*, 15 June 1968, 87). According to these pathologies, Rosemary occupies an intensely charged space in the warp of modernity, a chamber of procreative horrors in which contemporary feminine experience remains demonically institutionalized by patriarchal culture. Ratcheting up the menaces extant in "Peyton Place," *Dandy*, and *Johnny Belinda*, the community surrounding Farrow's character in *Rosemary* constitutes an even more terrifying site of clandestine evil, threat to legitimacy, and endangerment.

Albeit a figure of traditional desire insofar as she yearns for domesticity, in accordance with the actress's celebrity persona, Farrow—literally a shape shifter in her role as mother-to-be—again constitutes a figuration of the Other. "As Rosemary's pregnancy progresses," Lucy Fischer points out, "[the film's] baroque narrative constructs a distorted projection of quotidian experience" (9). Farrow's character becomes estranged from, and an inquisitor into, her own cultural context as she experiences childbearing as victimization and increasing imprisonment by Establishment figures who challenge her independent powers of perception: the elderly physician who counsels against reading contemporary books on pregnancy and taking vitamins, her husband, who tries to shield Rosemary from the advice of her female friends, the elderly couple next door (clandestine coven leaders) who take growing charge of the young couple. Farrow's Otherness constitutes the problematic of modernity—the interest in reading new medical literature, the fashionably short-cropped hair that disturbs Guy, and the European aesthetic she bears into the film through a series of surreal, stream-of-consciousness subjective images that violate both the Establishment's demonic plot and classic continuity editing.

Yet, as Fischer notes, that which marked the renascence of the horror film in 1968 through the occasion of the harrowing birth narrative constituted another order of propagative struggle as well. *Rosemary* is haunted by the lineage of institutionalized production that is classical cinema. In this work, through which Polanski reconceived terror for the mainstream release and which marked Farrow's apotheosis as a star, the demonic is no less than Hollywood itself. From the moment Rosemary enters the Bramford, a decades-old site of notoriety, she steps into an edifice of celebrity culture. The building is introduced to the couple as a structure "very popular with actors." In fact, the diegesis is rife with figures from the studio era, including Ralph Bellamy, Elisha Cook Jr., Ruth Gordon, and Sidney Blackmer, who haunt both the diegetic and nondiegetic cultures of contemporary performance and genre production that Polanski and Farrow were commissioned to revive. Through these actors of the 1930s and 1940s, classical cinema undertakes, via Farrow, to replicate an archaic production system in the landscape of the modern spectacle, one in which the Establishment is equated with the studio system, whose habitués constitute a coven. Reinterpreted as Satanists, the vestiges of the studio era malevolently seize upon the bearers of contemporary culture through apparitions of Hollywood's Golden Age and antiquated genre plots. The result of consorting with denizens of the classical cinema establishment results not only in the struggling actor sacrificing his (re)productivity for the promise of stardom, but the harrowing appropriation of Farrow/Rosemary's body for its own revitalization through the procreation of the ultimate figure of classical infamy; which, in this film about the menace of the star system, is reinterpreted as satanic.

Accompanying this film that burnished Farrow's image as an actress while problematizing the archaic context in which she had become firmly affixed, media texts were suffused with discourses of the young star's jeopardy via the specter of Old Hollywood. Foregrounding the tensions between homemaking and careerism, writers rumored the offscreen Farrow to be a figure of troubled domesticity insofar as her film work was reportedly imperiling her marriage. According to an article in *Ladies' Home Journal* published during the year *Rosemary* was in production, "Most of her friends know that Mia does not want to give up her acting career. On the other hand, Sinatra once said that he would never again marry a career woman, especially an actress [after divorcing Ava Gardner]. . . . Sinatra might be happier if Mia became a full-time wife instead of making movies" (Scott, "Farrow's Swinging Life with Sinatra," 168).

If Farrow's screen character relinquishes herself to her husband's acting career in satanic domesticity—according to a *Newsweek* review, "sacrificed on the black altar of her husband's ambition" (Zimmerman, "Devil Child," 92)—the actress herself was of course not so self-renunciating. She had recognized the crucial importance of taking on the role of Rosemary to advance her film career, initiating a marital struggle. In her autobiography, Farrow recounts how, upon reading the script, Sinatra's "only comment was that he couldn't picture me in the part." Suggesting her own dangerous proximity to Rosemary's condition—the perilous vulnerability of female spousal perception to a dominant masculine vision—Farrow recalls, "Suddenly, I couldn't picture myself in it either" (Farrow 118). Paradoxically, although Farrow's independent discernment ultimately prevailed, her acceptance of the role of screen homemaker resulted in her disengagement from the sphere of domesticity. In the course of the film's production—as it was widely reported—she was delivered divorce papers on the set, marking the power of patriarchy and her liberation from it.

☆☆☆☆★ Spiritual Mia

As *Rosemary's Baby* entered its final stages of gestation, an alternative facet of Farrow's persona emerged: the ecumenically raised actress, who would soon become most celebrated for playing a violated Catholic, resurfaced in the headlines in conjunction with yet another metamorphosis, that of the spiritual journey. Months before the summer release of the film that would be the target of censorship efforts by the National Catholic Office of Motion Pictures, Farrow became a figure of renewed fascination as a seeker of alternative spiritualism, when the press widely reported on her trip to India to meditate with the Maharishi Mahesh Yogi. Associated with yet another figure of older masculine guidance, ironically, Farrow's connection with the Maharishi constituted her most unmitigated embracement of youth culture to date. Transformed into an emblem of the younger generation's psychic quest, Farrow was at last allied largely with contemporaries, including fellow ashram visitors the Beatles. At the same time, her earlier obsession with celebrity shifted to a rejection of fame and those who, she observed in an ashram interview with *Saturday Evening Post*, "got hung up with . . . their names in the paper" (Lewis Lapham, "There Once Was a Guru from Rishikesh, Part II," 4 May 1968, 88). Ironically, one of the primary offenders was the Maharishi himself, whose penchant for photographs and sexual advance (according to Farrow's biography) led to her flight from the ashram. A cover story in *Fate* magazine observed, "There is no doubt that the Beatles and Mia helped [the Maharishi's] ascension" as a star (James Crenshaw, "The Beatles' and Mia Farrow's Guru: What Is His Power?" May 1968, 36). Mirroring her condition in *Rosemary*, Farrow again, through spiritual demands for notoriety, became a vessel for the production of classic celebrity.

Farrow's final release of 1968, *Secret Ceremony*, is an alternate version of the female gothic, reworking her persona as a fragile woman adrift in the archaic edifice, and again engaging issues of feminine perception, in this case to the extent that her character becomes almost fully delusional, in effect a young madwoman in the attic. Concurrently, Farrow's character foregrounds the perversities of the woman-child stuck in time (as *Ladies' Home Journal* had pointed out, "There is a lot of Peter Pan in Mia Farrow" [Lena Tabori, "Mia Farrow Talks," August 1968, 92]), initiating media discourse, as the decade came to a close, on insistent clinging to youth culture as a form of psychosis. In the film, Farrow plays another attachment-seeking figure, Cenci, an overgrown, orphaned child for whom liberation is the condition of being unmoored. Ensconced in a world of parental and sexual desire and violation, she latches onto a prostitute, Leonora (Elizabeth Taylor), grieving the loss of her daughter. Cenci hallucinates Leonora to be her longed-for, recently deceased mother, installing the older woman in her dark, empty London estate. Psychologically and genealogically unanchored and bereft, the shape-shifting Cenci metamorphoses, in her delusional state, from devoted daughter to nymphet to expectant mother, not only engaging in an unnaturally close relationship with Leonora, at times suggestive of lesbianism, but resuming an incestuous relationship with her mother's lover, in the wake of whose return—in an even more psychotic reconstruction of the events in *Rosemary's Baby*—she hallucinates her own pregnancy.

As part of a new order of discourse emerging just prior to *Ceremony*'s release, in which Farrow's ethereal charm—located, in part, in her persona as a figure of girlish imagination—began to decay, Cenci's madness resonated with media reconsiderations of Farrow's empirical character in the wake of the star's widely reported breakdown before the filming began. In July 1968, *Movie Mirror* reported, "Mia . . . refuses to believe [in her forthcoming divorce], but seems anxious to make-believe instead. And, as long as her fantasy had at least a tiny bit of reality to it, she could keep her pretenses" (Fred Arthur, "Sinatra Ready to Marry Again!" 50). A *Ladies' Home Journal* reporter observed, "She struck me as one of those few extra-brilliant people walking a tightrope between madness and sanity, clinging to her fantasy life with one hand and the real world with the other" (Tabori, "Mia Farrow Talks," 92). Taking their cues from celebrity discourse surrounding the new release, writers began to detect strands of psychosis throughout Farrow's screen personas; according to *Vogue*, "There has always been a hint of the demented in Mia's performances, a feeling of imploding, careening panic: she seems simultaneously to be a strange child playing at being a woman, a woman playing a little girl" (Polly Devlin, "Mia Farrow: 'Her Thin-Skinned Courage,'" May 1969, 92).

Only in her final feature of the decade, *John and Mary*, did Farrow portray a stable figure of modern feminine liberation. Appearing onscreen as a self-possessed single woman inhabiting sexually liberated cosmopolitan culture (she ventures into a romance with a man [Dustin Hoffman] she has met at a Manhattan bar and slept with the night before), Farrow is inflected with a dimension of secure autonomy. Nonetheless, Farrow remained tethered to the classicism of her well-established image, both as a young woman affixed to the older generation (her character has had an affair with a married man in his forties) and as the subject of decipherment by the mainstream media. According to the *New York Times'* Vincent Canby, "What emerges is a character composed partly of the weird waif of 'Secret Ceremony,' partly of the haunted mother of 'Rosemary's Baby'" ("Screen: 'John and Mary' at the Sutton," 15 December 1969, 68).

As the decade ended, although Farrow had become in some ways more deeply allied with youth culture (in the wake of *John and Mary*'s release, Farrow and Hoffman were seized upon by the press as spokespeople for the younger generation's perspectives on marriage and sex [see Phyllis Battelle, "Mia Farrow and Dustin Hoffman Debate: Does Marriage Have a Future?" *Ladies' Home Journal*, April 1969, 80–81, 156, 158, 160]), celebrity texts conveyed a sense of the exhaustion, even decomposition, of her star image. *Vogue* noticed that "at twenty-four, the learning shows, her eyes are scarred. She looks grieved," and commented: "Her unconventionality at times is tiresome" (Devlin, "'Her Thin-Skinned Courage,'" 80). According to *Vogue* and other magazines, Farrow was becoming an aging imitation of herself: "Her look of helplessness is false—assumed, along with shrinking vulnerability, for the audiences and the camera. . . . She becomes in turn a shattered, fragile refugee . . . Mia-the-Imp, and the Cocotte, worldly-wise. . . . When the camera stops, so does the vulnerability" (Devlin, "'Her Thin-Skinned Courage,'" 80). Reviewing *John and Mary*, Pauline Kael noted, "Everyone understood that the old fragile heroines—the Depression waifs like Loretta Young . . . needed to get well, and it's rather frightening that this little rabbit looking for a hutch is presented as a modern ideal. The waif who has done it to herself— made herself a sprite. . . . Mia Farrow is beginning to strain her 'delicious' mannerisms. Every tiny lick of the lips is just too vixenish; the childlike movements and the odd little voice are getting rather creepy" ("Gloria, the Girl Without Hope," 62).

By the close of the 1960s, Farrow had metamorphosed into a figure of haunting reproduction, an uncanny recurring version of her earlier self, again combining notoriety and the prospect of domestic containment by an older man. Farrow had alchemized from portraying an illegitimate daughter to the condition of unwed pregnancy by married conductor and film music composer Andre Previn, sixteen years her senior, whom she would wed in 1970. Once appropriated by the film industry as a figure of revitalization suturing the Establishment to the modern, Farrow and Hollywood now seemed to reject one another. Representing, along with Hoffman, according to *Time*, "the death of many myths—among them, the one of the movie star," insofar as they spurned the trappings and contractual commitments of the studio system, Farrow openly repudiated Hollywood: "The system is full of crap" (Kanfer et al., "The Moonchild and the Fifth Beatle," 50, 54). Such attitudes reportedly cost her an Oscar nomination for her role in *Rosemary's Baby*.[10]

Albeit newly scandalized and a figure of additional scandal decades later, Farrow was no longer quite the object of epistemological inquiry or modern womanhood, as she transitioned into marriage and motherhood and a quieter career in the 1970s. If, as Leo Braudy notes in *The Frenzy of Renown*, "the famous . . . are part of the audience's story about itself" (593), with the exhaustion of idealistic political and cultural efforts at metamorphosis which ultimately failed to yield radical transformations, the 1960s relinquished its passion for Farrow's celebrity. The figure of modernism as shift, the image of dynamism that was Farrow, had aged past its relevance and attraction. For the industry of Hollywood, the intensity of Farrow's stardom dissipated as the cinema of the 1970s abandoned the interrogatory magnetism of mutability for the durably resuscitative lure of the blockbuster.

NOTES

1. This number includes periodical covers on which Farrow appears individually and with other celebrities.

2. Farrow's single television film during the decade, *Johnny Belinda* (1967), contributed to her aura of foreignness insofar as she played a deaf and mute Nova Scotian girl.

3. In fact, Farrow's most prestigious awards and nominations were bestowed by the Hollywood Foreign Press Association. She received a 1965 Golden Globe as "New Star of the Year—Actress" and was nominated for Golden Globes for her performances in "Peyton Place" and *Rosemary's Baby*. In 1970, Farrow won the Golden Globes' Henrietta Award for "World Film Favorite."

4. Farrow claimed that her close-cropped hair was inspired by Julie Harris's cut in *Member of the Wedding* (1952) (Gloria Emerson, "Mia in Paris: 'I'm Kind of 20–20–20,'" *New York Times*, 15 February 1967, 22), although her coiffure closely resembled that of Jean Seberg in *Breathless* (1960). In *Rosemary's Baby*, the style recalls the simple, self-abnegating cut worn by Maria Falconetti in *La Passion de Jeanne d'Arc* (1928) through thematic as well as graphic references insofar as Rosemary's body, too, is sacrificed in conjunction with heresy.

5. Dali observed that Farrow was " 'a black moonchild, like Lilith. Her sex is not here,' he insists, pointing to his groin, 'but in the head, like a wound in the middle of the forehead'" (Kanfer et al., "The Moonchild and the Fifth Beatle," 52).

6. Farrow appears in an uncredited role in *John Paul Jones* (1959), a film directed by her father. She first appeared onscreen at the age of two in a documentary short involving Hollywood children, *Unusual Occupations: Film Tot Holiday* (1947). Farrow played her first credited role in *Age of Curiosity* (1963), a short promotional film about teenage girls produced for *Seventeen* magazine.

7. *Guns at Batasi* was released in Great Britain one month prior to the October 1964 debut of "Peyton Place." The film opened in the United States after Farrow emerged as a fledgling star.

8. This constitutes another similarity between Farrow and her "Peyton Place" character. As Moya Luckett points out, "Allison's fragility belied her desire to become a successful professional writer" (Luckett 80).

9. The film commitment was included in Farrow's television contract.

10. The *New York Times* quoted a Hollywood executive conjecturing, " 'I think one reason [Farrow was not nominated for an Oscar] is that she is young and abrasive and very independent'" (Steven Roberts, "Who (and What) Makes Oscar 'Possible'?" *New York Times*, 14 April 1969, 52). *Time* reported, "The reason: the Academicians dislike her barefoot hippie attitudes" ("Grand Illusion," 25 April 1969).

6 ★★★★★★★★★★★★
Peter Sellers
A Figure of the Impasse

CYNTHIA BARON

Peter Sellers (1925–1980) worked as a performer his entire life. As a child he appeared in variety show bits produced by the touring company his grandmother had established in England before World War I. As a teenager, he played with dance bands, sometimes touring with his father, and he worked backstage and onstage at music halls. When he was conscripted in World War II, Sellers was assigned to the "Gang Show" unit as a musician and a comedian whose expertise was impersonating officers. After the war, Sellers, Spike Mulligan, and Harry Secombe tapped into absurd and gag-centered British vaudeville traditions to create "The Goon Show" (1951–60), the legendary BBC radio program known for its silliness and sophistication and its influence on comedy groups such as Monty

---

Courtesy Photofest.

Python. Starting in the 1950s, Sellers did scores of short films, TV appearances, and comedy recordings. Between 1951 and 1980, he appeared in more than fifty features.

Sellers became a major film star of the 1960s and an actor of lasting significance through collaborations with Stanley Kubrick and Blake Edwards, who both gave the actor free rein to create his characterizations through improvisation (Howard Thompson, "Pause for Reflection with Peter Sellers," *New York Times*, 25 October 1964, X7).

Sellers's performance as Clare Quilty in Kubrick's *Lolita* (1962) enlivened the black comedy's wry look at sex in the wake of the 1948 and 1953 Kinsey reports, the publication of *Playboy* in 1953, and the arrival of "the pill" in 1960. In Kubrick's *Dr. Strangelove or: How I Learned to Stop Worrying and Love the Bomb* (1964), Sellers's characterizations of Dr. Strangelove, RAF Captain Lionel Mandrake, and President Merkin Muffley were integral to the black comedy's critique of the atomic age consensus that safety could be secured through mutually assured destruction. Working with Edwards, Sellers created other characters that captured the era's sense that modern life was absurd, for the sublimely inept Inspector Clouseau in *The Pink Panther* (1963) and *A Shot in the Dark* (1964) and the blundering, blissfully ignorant film extra Hrundi H. Bakshi in *The Party* (1968) both inhabited insane, irrational worlds even more absurd than the characters themselves.

Sellers's initial image as a radio star associated with bizarre, unconventional comedy enriched and was also enhanced by his portrayals in the Kubrick and Edwards films. His work with these directors also secured Sellers's association with characters and films that gave expression to the era's underlying sense that the world was at an impasse, in a situation in which no progress was possible, because society was marked by dissension, discord, and implacable disagreement, and because for many people living in the atomic age and then the Vietnam era, progress and reason had themselves been called into question. Sellers's roles in *Dr. Strangelove* made a joke of people's faith in progress and so resonated with audiences who saw atomic weapons as further evidence of the modern world's skewed priorities. As Clouseau, Sellers's performances make a joke of people's faith in rational thought and so expressed a sensibility shared by people who saw institutional "logic" not as a solution to but as a major cause of the decade's social crisis.

He was an improbable candidate for Hollywood stardom in 1960. One critic described him as British, middle-aged, and "likely to be taken for a book-seller on his day off" (Walter H. Waggoner, "Arrival of Sellers," *New York Times*, 27 March 1960, SM64). By the end of the decade, Sellers's com-

Sellers as Inspector Clouseau in *A Shot in the Dark*: the absurdity of modern life made visible. (Courtesy Photofest)

plex star image was colored by various associations. "The Goon Show" linked his identity to anarchical British humor. *Dr. Strangelove* connected Sellers to American Cold War black humorists like Joseph Heller. The Blake Edwards films, which gave mainstream visual tourists a glimpse of "exotic" European locales, established him as an international star and, by offering counterculture audiences a slapstick rendition of theater of the absurd, elaborated on Sellers's association with black comedy. While these associations established Sellers's image as a comedian well suited to the sixties, decisions about the way to categorize Sellers—as a British, American, or international film star—remained at an impasse throughout the decade.

Similarly, while Sellers was generally seen as a comedian, attempts to define him as an actor would continue to be deadlocked. For in the same way that his credentials as a dramatic actor were established early on by his award-winning performance in *I'm All Right, Jack* (1959), his viability as a romantic lead was established at the outset of his international career when he co-starred with Sophia Loren in *The Millionairess* (1960).[1] Sellers's image as a dramatic star with sex appeal was sustained by Hollywood publicity that presented him as an international jet-setter whose lifestyle exemplified the swinging sixties. Banking on his paradoxical image of comedian and romantic lead, the studios cast Sellers in films like *Casino Royale* (1967) and *I Love You, Alice B. Toklas* (1968).

Yet Sellers's stardom was not only shaped by Hollywood publicity and casting decisions. Corporate executives' competing visions of the industry and how it should be configured largely determined the rise and fall of Sellers's career in the 1960s. As a British actor who achieved instant stardom in the early sixties when Hollywood was investing heavily in "runaway" productions, in the late sixties Sellers would be caught in the impasse when that model became discredited and Hollywood made the transition from a film industry focused on international co-productions to a diversified American media industry designed to safeguard and maximize domestic investment.

☆☆★★★ A Star Whose Value Depended on Hollywood's Business Model

In the early 1960s, Sellers eclipsed Ealing Studios star Alec Guinness as Britain's leading film comedian. Summing up the success of Sellers's starring roles in *The Mouse That Roared* (1959), *I'm All Right, Jack*, *The Millionairess*, and *Lolita*, the American press explained that Sellers had become "one of the brightest new faces" in Hollywood by making his "talent for mimicry and impersonation into an art form as salable as any in the entertainment world today" (Richard J. H. Johnston, "Sellers, En Route to Hollywood, Talks of His 'Work' [Not 'Art']," *New York Times*, 23 April 1962, 32; Waggoner, "Arrival of Sellers," SM64). That description is telling, for it points to the reality that Sellers's rapid rise to stardom was not a simple case of talent rewarded, but instead a matter of Hollywood seeing Sellers's labor as a highly marketable commodity. In addition, with his counterculture credentials established by the anarchical humor of "The Goon Show," Sellers was prized by Hollywood because he appealed to hip American audiences that had grown tired of films designed to satisfy established "pressure groups in the United States" like the Catholic Church (Bill Becker, "Hollywood Specter: European Competition Worries Industry," *New York Times*, 26 June 1960, X7).

As inexpensive British talent, Sellers was also well suited to Hollywood's way of doing business at the time. Even in the 1950s, because foreign films were "setting new standards for sophistication" and domestic box office was still in decline as a result of TV's success, Hollywood had increased its attention to overseas markets (Monaco 3). Yet because the 1948 Paramount Decrees had taken the studios out of the exhibition business, their involvement in overseas markets went beyond a search for new audiences. Instead, with Hollywood already seeing management and distribution as its primary focus, in the 1950s the studios had started outsourcing production duties, effectively reducing costs by financing offshore productions that used inexpensive talent and technicians. James Monaco notes, "This practice, known as 'runaway production,' had become both widespread and highly controversial by the beginning of the 1960s" (11; see Becker, "Hollywood Specter," X7; Bosley Crowther, "Britain's Melting Pot: London Now Is the Bustling Center of International Film Production," *New York Times*, 12 June 1960, 115).

Despite its negative impact on American cast and crew members, in the early sixties Hollywood executives saw international co-productions as essential to the film industry's financial success. In 1960, "forty percent of all movies financed by the Hollywood majors were shot overseas" (Monaco 14).[2] While Hollywood invested in films shot in France, Spain, and Italy, its most extensive partnership was with England, a phenomenon highlighted by the Bond films released in 1962, 1963, 1964, 1965, 1967, and 1969, which Monaco aptly refers to as "ingenious hybrids of an increasingly internationalized popular culture industry where . . . British production talent blended neatly with American production and marketing skills" (194; see McDougal 150). That description would apply equally well to Sellers's films from *The Millionairess* in 1960 to *I Love You, Alice B. Toklas* in 1968 and to his collaborations with Kubrick and Edwards.

Producing films starring Sellers made especially good financial sense in the early 1960s when Hollywood productions shot overseas were subsidized by British and European governments. For example, in 1962 the studios received more than $5 million in "direct governmental subsidies" for films done in England, Italy, and France (Monaco 12). The value of such incentives, however, was soon overshadowed by developments that made investment in low-budget domestic media products safer and more lucrative. One came to fruition in 1965, when the studios became "the principal suppliers of programming for the US television networks" (Maltby 174). This was the result of many factors, including behind-the-scenes negotiations by Lew Wasserman, president of MCA (Music Corporation of America), the talent agency that represented not just musicians but also writers, directors, and actors working in theater, radio, film, and television in Hollywood, New York, and London. For it was Wasserman who recognized that international co-production might benefit Hollywood in the short run, but that it would be safer and more profitable for the studios to diversify production to include other domestic media forms, especially television and music. Wasserman's position proved correct. In 1969, Hollywood lost more than $200 million, due to increased talent costs, a drop in sales to TV, and huge box-office losses on a number of films released between 1966 and 1968, all problems exacerbated by a general recession in 1969 and high interest rates on the funds borrowed to produce those box office failures (Cook 9).

Wasserman also took the lead in another development that reduced the value of foreign subsidies and of the international stars that belonged to the system of runaway production. In a move that signaled a new vision of Hollywood as a highly diversified entertainment industry, in 1962 MCA bought Universal. That vision would carry the day after the studios' huge investments in film production led to problems in the late sixties. In 1966 Gulf & Western took over Paramount, United Artists went to Transamerica in 1967, and in 1969 financier Kirk Kerkorkian bought MGM. With the new business model in place, Hollywood executives lobbied the Nixon administration to pressure Congress to pass the Revenue Act of 1971. This legislation essentially closed the era on international co-productions. For in addition to creating federal income tax credits on corporate losses, it also established "a 7-percent investment tax credit on domestic production" and let Hollywood studios "defer taxes on profits earned from exports" if they were reinvested in domestic production (Cook 12).

In this context, as far as Hollywood was concerned, a British film star might have been a hot commodity in the early 1960s, when international productions promised to attract new audiences and secure financial gain. However, over the course of the decade, thanks to the ingenuity of talent agents, Sellers had become expensive talent. In addition, thanks to Hollywood publicity, he had also become known as an international jet-setter whose swinging lifestyle included a continually changing collection of beautiful young women, cameras, yachts, estates, and expensive cars. With

"40 percent of all Hollywood filmmakers unemployed" in 1970 (Cook 3), many of them blue-collar members of "the silent majority" that elected Richard Nixon in 1968, promoting a highly paid international star was not especially viable. With the new tax laws rewarding investment in American corporate media products, it made little sense to employ an international star like Sellers.

Thus, in the same way that Sellers's rise to fame reflected executives' vision of Hollywood as a film industry that took advantage of foreign subsidies to attract new audiences and outsource production responsibilities, his decline in the late 1960s was a sign of Hollywood's move toward an American entertainment industry, which successfully lobbied for tax laws conducive to diversified corporations able to exploit loopholes in antitrust legislation. In the late 1960s, with high-priced international stars like Sellers seen as the reason Hollywood was in a financial crisis, with rhetoric from the Blacklist period pressed into service once again, these stars were discredited for being anarchists, foreigners, and sexual deviants. That was the assessment of the executives who saw diversification as the source of Hollywood's future success and of those who had, from the early sixties forward, counted on profits from financing, distributing, and marketing film product from around the world. Material conditions like these shaped the rise and fall of Sellers's career in the sixties, yet it would be a mistake to "oversimplify the systematic component" of his stardom (de Cordova 11). To balance consideration of these factors, it should be useful to see his career in relation to the larger cultural context.

★★★★★ A Star for a Society at an Impasse

Sellers's collaborations with Kubrick and Edwards in the first half of the 1960s gave florid expression to the absurdity of mid-twentieth-century existence. Marked by their nihilism and focus on being in an absurd, impossible existential situation, the films share a great deal with the black humor of comedians Mort Sahl and Lenny Bruce and novelists Kurt Vonnegut and Philip Roth, and satires like Joseph Heller's novel *Catch 22* (1961), which "stripped the official voices of the nation of their authority" (Lytle 66).

Because Sellers's work with Kubrick and Edwards captures the absurdity of the instinct to keep going despite the perceived pointlessness of modern existence, the films also have much in common with the work of Samuel Beckett, whose writings highlight "the essential absurdity" of a world in which one "selects from a closed set, and then arranges them inside a closed field" (Kenner 94). Mapping that view in works such as the novel *Watt* (1951) and the plays *Waiting for Godot* (1953), *Endgame* (1957), *Krapp's Last Tape* (1958), and *Happy Days* (1961), Beckett spelled out the absurd "logic" of the "closed and consistent systems . . . proper to the world of IBM, of probability theory, [and] of concern with modes of short-range and long-range causality" (Kenner 96).

Bringing that sensibility and perspective into popular culture, Sellers's work with Kubrick represents what is arguably the most vivid expression of the late 1950s and early 1960s counterculture. Equally cynical but more subdued, Sellers's films with Edwards offered a droll but scathing critique of "rational" thought, for the continual success and unflappable self-confidence of utterly incompetent Inspector Clouseau hints that by comparison "competence, however great, always fails" (Kenner 75). While all these films were successful, we will never know how audiences might have responded to Sellers in other films that mounted a critique of individual and institutional "logic," for Hollywood opted to leave the un-romanticized nihilistic anarchy that Sellers embodied in the 1964 black comedies out of its product line in the second half of the 1960s. Rather than finance more films that looked at *our* support of the status quo as the problem, corporate America adroitly tapped into the despair of the late sixties "counterculture" by making films like *The Graduate* (1967), which made young love the solution to problems created by the older generation, and films like *Cool Hand Luke* (1967), *Bonnie and Clyde* (1967), *Easy Rider* (1969), and *The Wild Bunch* (1969), all compelling portraits of rebels and beautiful losers that frame social protest as an individual rather than collective action and as ineffectual and impossible by focusing on the price paid by the few who dissent.

As for Sellers, starting with *What's New, Pussycat?* (1965), Hollywood would emphasize his consumer-friendly swinging sixties image to market its "counterculture" movies. For example, he starred in films like *After the Fox* (1966), a parody of Italian neorealist films, and *Casino Royale*, a parody of the James Bond series, both of which emphasized the star's association with international co-productions. While films such as these were aimed at the cosmopolitan audience Hollywood had developed and catered to in the early 1960s, in the second half of the decade the studios found that low-budget films with American settings and characters could be "cool" commodities and less risky investments.

Americans' cosmopolitan view of cinema in the early 1960s was reflected in and shaped by the international scope of Andrew Sarris's "cultist cataloging" published in its most comprehensive form in *The American Cinema* (Taylor, *Artists* 90). By comparison, the view of cinema in the late 1960s reflected the new camp taste in underground American movies that was promoted by Jonas Mekas and created a cult following for films like *Night of the Living Dead* (1968) (see Taylor, *Artists* 98–121). One way to describe the transition is to say that corporate media began the 1960s with an interest in the world at large and a desire to lampoon the "rational" decisions of police, governments, and bureaucracy, but that by the end of the decade the Hollywood establishment saw the counterculture as a problem that could and should be managed. As a consequence, to engage hip audiences in the late 1960s Hollywood offered romanticized narratives about the price of dissent rather than black comedies about "the arbitrary nature of authority" (Lytle 65).

Yet even though Hollywood mobilized the safer, more consumer-friendly jet-setter aspect of Sellers's star image in the latter part of the decade, with Sellers so integral to the Kubrick and Edward films that highlighted the absurdity of mid-twentieth-century existence, the disruptive, nihilist challenge associated with Sellers's characterizations continued to be an aspect of his star image. It is, for example, what made him well suited to play Sir Guy Grand in *The Magic Christian* (1970). In addition, Sellers's career-defining characterizations of Dr. Strangelove and Inspector Clouseau might belong to the first half of the sixties, but his association with absurdity and anarchy could still resonate with American audiences in the late sixties; their experience of being in an absurd world, cut loose from the suspect stability of the past but without a way to craft a viable future, was perhaps even more sharply felt at the end of the decade.

The highly visible wave of social protests in America and Europe in 1968 had failed to create political change. Moreover, as if reliving the divisions of the American Civil War fought one hundred years earlier, over the course of the 1960s it seemed that many Americans had come "to regard groups of fellow countrymen as enemies with whom they were engaged in a struggle for the nation's very soul" (Isserman and Kazan 4). As the decade wore on, Americans were forced to continue debating "the meaning of their most fundamental beliefs and institutions" (Isserman and Kazan 5). Given the intensity of domestic strife in the sixties, it might be surprising that a British star would have any relevance for Americans. Yet as the actor whose performances in the Kubrick and Edwards films embodied the experience of being at an impasse, in a situation in which no progress is possible, Sellers's star image had special relevance for Americans as the sixties came to a close and Americans faced an impasse that would not break until its most polarizing figure, Richard Nixon, resigned from office in 1974.

Sellers impersonating RAF Captain Mandrake: *Dr. Strangelove* and Cold War "logic" at an impasse. (Courtesy Jerry Ohlinger's Movie Material Store)

★★★★★ From Corporate America's Comrade to Its Un-American Foe

Today, Sellers is known for his performances as Inspector Clouseau in the 1960s films *The Pink Panther* and *A Shot in the Dark* and, later, in *The Return of the Pink Panther* (1975), *The Pink Panther Strikes Again* (1976), and *The Revenge of the Pink Panther* (1978) (all five directed by Blake Edwards).[3] Current views of Sellers are also likely shaped by work such as Roger Lewis's 1997 biography *The Life and Death of Peter Sellers* and Stephen Hopkins's 2004 film of the same name. Accounts such as these set aside questions about the star "as actor (as a professional manipulator of signs), as picture personality (as personality extrapolated from films)," and as the film star portrayed in the popular press of the 1960s (de Cordova 146–47). Instead, their focus is on the "star (as someone with a private life distinct from screen image)," particularly as portrayed in accounts made public after Sellers's death (de Cordova 147; see Walker *Peter Sellers*; Sellers; Starr; Sikov). For example, based on his research into Sellers's life, Roger Lewis explores "the pervasive melancholia" in Sellers's films, and he finds that in addition to "deep personal insecurity," Sellers "was constant only in his pathetic rage at being Peter Sellers" (xxi, xxiii). Lewis proposes, for example, that the more Sellers "was paid (he was given a Rolls Royce as inducement to read a script), the more he loathed himself, and the cars, women, alpine chalets, Mediterranean yachts, etc. only served to remind him that he wasn't happy" (xxiii).

Remarkable as it may sound, this view of Sellers, as a deeply troubled individual, has no relation to the way audiences and even journalists saw Peter Sellers in the 1960s. The first intimation that Sellers's life might not square with the image created by his films, and by the press coverage of his starring roles and swinging lifestyle, did not arrive until 1969, when the BBC aired a documentary shot during the production of *The Magic Christian* entitled "Will the Real Peter Sellers Stand Up?" It is significant that Sellers attempted to keep the documentary from being aired because it depicted him as "a depressive and moody character"; it is even more significant that this unhappy image was "the last thing that the public and critics alike expected to see" (Rigelsford 173).

The "story" of Sellers's moodiness was hardly the story of the day. In 1969 the BBC also aired an interview with Sellers and Spike Mulligan on "Film Night," and while the filming of *The Magic Christian* was the occasion that prompted the interview, "when questions were opened to the audience they were predominately about The Goon Show" (Rigelsford 173). Even after the unflattering documentary aired, Sellers's troubled personal life continued to be of little interest to his fans. Instead, his radio, TV, and film performances were audiences' primary focus. For example, after Sellers, Mulligan, and Harry Secombe visited with BBC talk show host Michael Parkinson about the upcoming television broadcast of "The Last Goon Show of All," the show became "so popular with both its host and the public that it was screened" again as Parkinson's final program that season (Rigelsford 173).

Some might argue that the contrast between Sellers's star image in the 1960s, as the bright, endlessly creative, thoroughly hip, entirely cosmopolitan man with the ability to slip the noose of convention and conformity, and the more recent view of Sellers as a tragic, deeply troubled individual involves a distinction between an artificial and a more "authentic" view of Sellers. However, biographies and biopics are designed to meet audience expectations and, as a consequence, they reveal as much about the "logic" of star discourse as they do about the star that is the subject of their discussion. Richard de Cordova's observation, that early on movie audiences were led to explore "a series of questions directed toward the discovery of the reality behind the representation," points to how that logic works (112). Noting that "fascination over the players' identities [has been] a fascination with concealed truth," he reminds us that stars' private lives "emerged as the ultimate or most ulterior truth" and that star discourse consistently fixes "upon the sexual as the ultimate secret" (140).

In the case of Peter Sellers, publicity in the 1960s exploited rather than concealed the typical secret by providing a steady stream of reports about the star's involvement with women. He was increasingly identified with the swinging sixties after separating from his first wife, stage actress Anne Hayes, in 1962, for in addition to press reports about various affairs, publicity highlighted Sellers's marriages to a string of younger women: Swedish starlet Britt Ekland, British aristocrat Miranda Quarry, and TV actress Lynne Frederick. With that avenue already traveled, contemporary studies about Sellers are required to unearth another, more basic secret. So, while Sellers's sexual exploits were used by corporate Hollywood to promote its products in the 1960s, the secret used today to sell books is that the constant company of the most beautiful women in the world did not make Peter Sellers a happy man. His troubled personality becomes the linchpin in explanations for the rise and fall of his career in the 1960s. No one asks: Why were the studios initially so interested in Sellers's anarchic "Goon Show" humor, and why were they then more interested in the seemingly safer but in the end more divisive strategy of using Sellers's jet-setter image to sell films in the second part of the decade?

Rather than reckon with many film historians' view that 1965 represents the end of one period of Hollywood cinema and the beginning of another (Monaco), and cultural historians' assessment that what we have come to think of as "the sixties" emerged in about 1964 (Lytle), accounts that focus on Sellers's private life tend to divide his career into the period before and after the thirty-eight-year-old star's heart attack on 6 April 1964. This mild heart attack led to a series of far more serious attacks over the next few days. However, that is not the reason Sellers's brush with death has been seen as a significant event in the star's life. Instead, with the "ultimate secret" as the basis for determining the trajectory of a star's career, the context is what makes it salient, for Sellers's first heart attack occurred just after he had, with additional assistance from amyl nitrate, made love to his twenty-one-year-old Swedish starlet wife of two months. As one can imagine, when crafted by writers as skilled as Sellers biographer Ed Sikov, narratives peppered with moments like this make very good stories.

Others, however, propose research into different narratives, in that a focus on a star's titillating secrets obscures the fact that a star image is not a reflection of an actor's personality but instead is "an entity constructed by culture industries" (Beckett Warren, correspondence, 11 November 2008 1).[4] Examining star images as discursive formations that corporate media us to sell their products and those of other corporations—indeed, to sell consumption in general—makes marketing choices, the shaping of audience tastes, and Hollywood's methods of controlling talent and profit margin more pressing questions. Taking this approach, publicity about the star is material that can shed light on corporate strategies to secure and increase profit.

In Sellers's case, in the early 1960s the popular press was filled with lavish praise about this inexpensive talent that promised to bring in proportionally significant profit (see Waggoner, "Arrival of Sellers," SM64–66; Crowther, "Britain's Melting Pot," 115; Bosley Crowther, "Buying Sellers: New British Comic Much in Demand," *New York Times*, 1 May 1960, X1; Stephen Watts, "Before and Behind the Camera with Sellers," *New York Times*, 11 December 1960, X11; Bosley Crowther, "More Best Sellers: Britain's New Comedy Champ Scores Again," *New York Times*, 1 April 1962, 113; "Sellers' Season," *New York Times*, 1 April 1962, 223; A. H. Weiler, "Silver Screen's Gold: Fine Percentage of Quality in Films Seen Here during Last Six Months," *New York Times*, 14 June 1963, 65; Bosley Crowther, "Screen: Sellers Keeps Crime Rate Up," *New York Times*, 3 April 1963, 39; Flora Lewis, "The Ubiquitous, Multifarious Sellers," *New York Times*, 23 June 1963, 187). Material in the popular press suggests that in the early sixties, Sellers film appearances and lifestyle embodied an image of the counterculture that matched corporate America's impatience with "over-organization and creative dullness" (Frank, *Conquest* 9).

For example, a 1960 issue of *Life* magazine tells Americans that before that year, Peter Sellers had been "a household word only in households of sophisticated Britishers" (W. K. Zinsser, "Young Man Riding High," *Life*, 20 June 1960, 63). He was, in other words, a unique commodity, with a seal of approval from audiences in the know and so beloved as to be a familiar, cherished object, a "household word." With Sellers's value established by cosmopolitan "Britishers" living a world apart from middle class conventions, he could become an object of cult connoisseurship, akin to the "jazz, sex, drugs, and the slang and mores of black society" identified by Norman Mailer as vehicles for escaping mass culture (Frank, *Conquest* 12). Marshaling vivid imagery in its "pitch" for Sellers as a product that hip Americans should know about, *Life* reports:

> This year, at 34, he is the hottest name in English films. His new movie, *I'm All Right, Jack*, which opened recently in the U.S. to the unanimous delight of critics and audiences, won him Britain's academy award this spring. His LP comedy records, one of which will soon be released in the U.S., have sold more than 150,000 copies in England. He is, as his manager puts it, "being chased up hill and down dale" by major Hollywood and British movie producers.   (63)

The article goes on to detail Sellers's "rich consumer tastes" that include his "attractive blond wife—former actress Anne Hayes" and his new estate at legendary Chipperfield, where Richard III is reported to have cursed the townswomen for mocking his crooked form (63, 69). To help Americans understand why Sellers could and should appeal to "sophisticated" counter-culture taste, it explains that the performer had been involved in "The Goon Show," a radio program with "a devout weekly audience of nine million" that featured humor described as "'avant-garde,' 'surrealist,' 'abstract,' and 'four-dimensional'" (64). While it might seem strange that *Life* would intertwine comments about Sellers's "rich consumer tastes" and his avant-garde humor, this document of corporate American media offers good evidence about the surprising but essential connection between corporate and counterculture America in the early 1960s.

Thomas Frank has shown that in the late 1950s and early 1960s American business saw "the counterculture not as an enemy to be undermined . . . but as a hopeful sign" (9). Noting that many in the "corporate world deplored conformity, distrusted routine, and encouraged resistance to established power," Frank explains that American executives "welcomed the youth-led cultural revolution . . . because they perceived in it a comrade in their own struggle to revitalize American business and the consumer order generally" (9). Thus, Sellers's humor did not make him an opponent of corporate media but instead someone to be promoted by business, and *Life* magazine knew that it need not soft-pedal Sellers's anarchical "brand" of humor but instead could cheerfully explain:

> The Goons' irreverent charades seldom failed to draw protests from the old guard, thereby proving that Goonery was not mere pointless joking. To Sellers and Mulligan, comedy is very serious business. Farce is their weapon, and with it they demolish more enemy installations than they ever could with anger. The enemy is pompousness, and its ranks include snobs and stuffed shirts, fools and phonies.   (Zinsser, "Young Man Riding High," 64)

While this article goes to great lengths to establish Sellers's counterculture credentials, a 1969 *New York Times* piece that sought to shed light on the recent murders of actress Sharon Tate and others at the residence of director Roman Polanski skewers Sellers and other international jet-setters for their anarchical and un-American behavior (Steven V. Roberts, "Polanskis Were at Center of a Rootless Way of Life," 31 August 1969, 43). Published after Nixon had been elected by "the silent majority," at a time when the cosmopolitan image of the Kennedy administration seemed like something from the distant past, the article makes it clear that corporate Hollywood no longer found common cause with members of a counterculture that made fun of the old guard. With the country in a recession and the film business in a financial crisis, corporate media did not see anarchic and "foreign" affiliations as valuable assets but instead as the two aspects of the counterculture most incompatible with their ideas on how to "revitalize American business and the consumer order in general" (Frank, *Conquest* 9).

The *Times* article reveals that as far as "the Hollywood Establishment" was concerned, international stars like Sellers had become economic liabilities (Roberts, "Polanskis Were at Center," 43). Instead of being cheap labor able to generate sizable profit for corporate Hollywood, by the late 1960s Sellers's "team of personal managers" had made him an expensive part of any Hollywood film package (Walker, *Peter Sellers* 175). As a consequence, it was in Hollywood's best interest to cut ties with Sellers when he did not deliver the kind of profit expected from their investment in the high-salaried star. *Dr. Strangelove* "had been Columbia's biggest hit of 1964, pulling in the then-sizable sum of $5 million in the United States alone" (Sikov 236). When production delays on *Casino Royale* increased costs, however, and the film "opened to universally scathing reviews," Sellers was "unofficially blacklisted" by Columbia, even though the film "did surprisingly well at the box office" (Starr 136).

Rather than applaud Sellers for using humor to demolish "snobs and stuffed shirts," in 1969 Hollywood reactivated Blacklist rhetoric about the threat of anarchists, foreigners, and perverts to discredit the high-priced international, counterculture talent that was supposed to have saved Hollywood. The *Times* article provides a good picture of the contempt Hollywood executives had developed for Sellers and others who had failed to increase their profits. The degree to which the international jet-setters are savaged is striking. According to the article, the murders at the Polanski residence brought into focus "disparate yet connected" lives that "displayed some of the glamour and intrigue" one would associate with formulaic movies (Roberts, "Polanskis Were at Center," *New York Times*, 43). Characterizing the murder victims as people "whose twisted paths crossed on the night of Aug. 8," and referring to their circle of friends as being aptly "described with all the current clichés: mod, hip, swinging, trendy," the article castigates the "rootless vagabonds" for being "at home in a dozen places, and yet belonging nowhere" (43).

Quoting movie critic Charles Champlin, the article explains: "The impermanence [of the group] makes for an edginess, an urgency, an unreality—or more precisely, for an almost involuntary detachment from the

ongoing concerns which move and occupy most mortals" (Roberts, "Polanskis Were at Center," 43). Peter Sellers is not only named as a member of
the group, but his comments are used as evidence of its "rootless way of
life," for he is quoted as saying, "If Roman had a premiere in Paris, why
we'd all fly over there for it. Or we would have lunch in London and dinner in Copenhagen" (43). Detailing the swingers' expenses on stylish
clothes, fast cars, vacations in the Alps, and their preference for marijuana
and other drugs (that can't be taxed) over Scotch (a staple of corporate
taste), the *New York Times* comes back to the things that are most objectionable about the group: "They were more European than American in many
ways, especially in regard to sex, which was always plentiful and, actually,
rather unimportant" (43).

This assessment reveals that Hollywood's decision to cast Sellers in films
such as *What's New, Pussycat?*, *Casino Royale*, and *I Love You, Alice B. Toklas* and
to promote the swinging sixties aspect of his star image was a complicated
move. For, if Hollywood's use of the star's jet-setter image had proved
hugely profitable, the studios could have used their embrace of that image
as proof of their "cool." However, since it was only moderately successful,
in the late 1960s Hollywood used Sellers's freewheeling lifestyle as a basis
for renegotiating its arrangements with the star, so that he would be, once
again, inexpensive talent.

Hollywood's continued use of Sellers's associations with co-productions
shot in swinging London and exotic European locales also left the studios
room to move. If the plan had proved to be exceptionally profitable, the
jet-setter would have continued to get good press. However, with *Casino
Royale* lumped into the group of films that should have been more profitable, Sellers was of little interest or use to the studios. From the perspective of corporate Hollywood, in the late 1960s Sellers and the other
international jet-setters represented a kind of labor (expensive) and commodity (international, foreign, even un-American) that had not facilitated profit. However, rather than raise the question of labor and profit
margins, corporate media could mobilize the "logic" of star discourse to
discredit their expensive "foreign" talent. As the 1969 article reveals, it
could suggest that whatever happened in their careers, including murder, could be traced to their "ultimate secret," in this case their "European" and thus unnatural and un-American sexual habits. It could even
hint that the stars' "European" and anarchical sexuality was the reason
for Hollywood's reduced corporate profits. Faced with losses of $200 mil-
lion, that must have seemed like a good story to share with American
audiences.

★★★★★ A Talent Well Suited to Runaway Production and the Atomic Age

Sellers's transition from hot new star in the early 1960s to someone essentially blacklisted at the end of the decade is a reminder that the career of anyone working in Hollywood is symptomatic of developments in the entertainment business. Yet each instance is at least slightly different. In the case of Peter Sellers, his rise to fame is not only emblematic of developments in the culture industries in the early 1960s. Because *Dr. Strangelove* was probably the most visible critique of mutually assured destruction, assessments of Sellers as a star of the sixties necessarily turn to questions about the degree to which or ways in which Kubrick's film articulated or even instigated resistance to the idea that people just have to accept life with the bomb. In addition, because Sellers's characterization of Inspector Clouseau was recognized at the time and continues to be seen as a cogent expression of the absurdity of modern life, reflections on Sellers's lasting significance should explore questions about the importance of silliness in critiques of official culture.

The early part of Sellers's Hollywood career belongs to the time when the Bond films first captured American audiences' attention with their international casts, exotic locales, and comic self-consciousness; it also belongs to the first wave of the "British invasion" that led to the phenomenal success of the Beatles in 1964. By 1960, London had become the center of the film-making world. Noting the role of tax advantages and government subsidies, *New York Times'* critic Bosley Crowther tells American readers that London is now "where international artists meet, make deals with international operators and turn out internationally flavored films" (Crowther, "Britain's Melting Pot," 115). Describing the scene, Crowther lists the co-productions being shot in London at the time; he mentions *The Millionairess* and in passing notes, "Obviously, Peter Sellers is the hottest actor in Britain" (115).

His take on London and Sellers is echoed by another critic writing about the film business in 1960. "Never has Europe affected Hollywood so much," explains Bill Becker, because in Hollywood's view, "foreign filmmakers are not only making more pictures but they are making better pictures." As Becker reports, according to Columbia Pictures' executive Mike Frankovich, who would later blacklist Sellers, in contrast to the lively, entertaining films being produced at the time by England and European countries, Hollywood goes along in the same old static rut, with the same material and the same faces, the same old people playing young parts." Becker amplifies that point with an observation by Hollywood producer Mark

As Sophia Loren's co-star, England's brightest comic becomes Hollywood's up-and-coming star. (Publicity still, *The Millionairess*, collection of the author)

Robson, who illustrates the integral connection between corporate and counterculture America at the beginning of the 1960s: "Hollywood products often lack a point of view, and the films that attract the most interest abroad . . . are those that have been opposed by various pressure groups in the United States." Sellers, of course, figures into these calculations; describing the films shown in New York and Los Angeles in recent months, Becker writes, "Every other theatre, it seemed, was playing Ingmar Bergman or Peter Sellers" (Bill Becker, "Hollywood Specter," X7).

Americans' view of Sellers's instant stardom in 1960 is an odd perception given the longevity of "The Goon Show" and Sellers's work as a music hall entertainer from the time he was a child. Their newfound awareness of Sellers does, however, suggest that in 1960, Hollywood's interest in international films was indicative of and an additional cause of a change in mainstream Americans' way of thinking about film and popular culture. It appears that prior to 1960, middle-class America saw international stars and international films as largely foreign and alien. For in 1960, Crowther announces a "radical" change in his year-end assessment of movies. He explains that because the foreign films released in America that year were higher in quality than the English-language films, he had, for the first time assembled two "top ten" lists, to recognize the accomplishments of the foreign films, "while maintaining the distinction imposed by the foreign language barrier" (Bosley Crowther, "The Year's Best Films: Critic Selects Two 'Top Ten' Lists, in English and Foreign Languages," *New York Times*, 25 December 1960, X3). This new openness to popular culture outside the United States would increase rapidly in the early 1960s: in Crowther's 1963 top-ten film list, he explains that he had put "the foreign-language films with the English-language films [because] all films now qualified for equal consideration on the 'top 10' list"; Crowther's list featured three foreign films, three British pictures, two American films shot overseas, and two "Hollywood pictures" (Bosley Crowther, "Top Films of 1963: No Apologies for This Year's 10 Best," *New York Times*, 29 December 1963, 47).

Thus, Sellers's instant stardom makes sense in light of this cultural moment, when a cosmopolitan perspective was attractive to Americans looking for a break from routine—especially if it gave them the feeling they were breaking with conformity at the same time that it satisfied their desire for sophisticated consumer objects. As it quickly coalesced in 1960, Sellers's star image carried that combination of connotations. Americans were first introduced to Sellers's anarchical humor and association with hip sophistication in *The Mouse That Roared*, a runaway production financed by Columbia and shot in England. Because of his clever portrayals of the "monocled Count 'Bobo' Mountjoy, wimpy Tully Bascombe, and senile Duchess Gloriana," Americans came to see him as the "funniest actor England [had] sent to America since Alec Guinness" (Starr 33–34, 36). Next, his credentials as a bona fide British actor established an association with another type of sophistication, one that also suggested nonconformity because of its distance from mainstream America. In 1960, the British Society of Film and Television Arts named Sellers Best British Actor for his work in *I'm All Right, Jack*, notably the same year Laurence Olivier was nominated for *The Devil's Disciple* (1959) and Richard Burton for *Look Back in Anger* (1959). Completing Sellers's associations with nonconformity and sophistication, his "ill-matched but oddly touching liaison" with Sophia Loren in *The Millionairess* "conferred a sex appeal on Sellers's image" not yet suggested by the two other films (Walker, *Peter Sellers* 116).

That multivalent image proved to be a valuable commodity in the early 1960s American consumer market, to the point that by 1963 Sellers had become a "household word" with American audiences. He is referred to as the "ubiquitous Peter Sellers" and as "our old friend Peter Sellers" (Weiler, Silver Screen's Gold," 65; Lewis, "Ubiquitous, Multifarious Sellers," 187; Crowther, "Sellers Keeps Crime Rate Up," 39). In terms of Sellers's status with American audiences, it is clear that *Dr. Strangelove* and the two Edwards films in 1964 were well timed. An article that publicizes *Dr. Strangelove* as Sellers's upcoming film surveys his career and describes his work in the early 1960s as "a blessing in infinite disguises" (Lewis, "Ubiquitous, Multifarious Sellers," 187).

It is also clear that the films were well suited for their time. In an article from the year the three films were released, *Times* critic A. H. Weiler opens with the observation: "Our anxious atomic age and a riotous Harlem are not conducive to peace of mind. But for reasons known only to necromancers . . . our filmmakers have made this past half-year a festive, diverting time. . . . A dispassionate viewer, who cannot pinpoint precise reasons for this comic outpouring, must assume that it helped calm the nerves of tense citizens seeking diversion in times of stress" (A. H. Weiler, "Funny Film Year: Comedy Output Thus Far Has Been Both Abundant and Entertaining," *New York Times*, 26 July 1964, X1). From there Weiler discusses a collection of films, recalling that early in the year, Kubrick had "shocked, astounded, surprised and, above all, amused movie-ticket buyers with his serio-comic spoof of potential nuclear disaster"; he also tells readers that even if they had not been "entirely satisfied with 'The Pink Panther,'" they should see *A Shot in the Dark* because it was "a howlingly comic, fast-moving, artistic enterprise" (X1).

Weiler's comments about the calming influence of diversion are significant, for they reveal that the controversy surrounding *Dr. Strangelove* when it opened in January had largely died down by July. Even though Weiler suggests that Kubrick "may be criticized for his treatment of the subject," he acknowledges that exhibitors and audiences "have not been bored with the return on their investments." Similarly, early on Crowther had criticized the film for discrediting the military and the president, but at year's end it was in his top ten list because it was "an extraordinary cinematic creation" ("The 10 Best Films of 1964," *New York Times*, 27 December 1964; see also Bosley Crowther, "Is Nothing Sacred?: Two New Films Make Mockeries of Some Very Serious Things," *New York Times*, 2 February 1964, X1, and Bosley Crowther, "Hysterical Laughter: Further Thoughts on 'Dr. Strangelove' and Its Jokes about the Bomb," *New York Times*, 16 February 1964, X1). Discussing critics' conflicting views when the film opened, Margot Henriksen explains that "*Dr. Strangelove* was hailed as a cultural breakthrough and it was condemned as a sick, traitorous, and defeatist joke" (327). That is accurate, and yet because the film served primarily to enhance corporate profits and was soon embraced as a great film by one of its most visible critics, it is perhaps unlikely that it was a cultural breakthrough or a traitorous joke. For example, Pauline Kael's review identifies why the film sustained the status quo. Putting Weiler's assessment in different terms, Kael describes it as a diversion, one that intimated that the only possible response to the threat of annihilation was laughter and accommodation: "What may have been laughed to death was not [the Cold War mindset that engendered nuclear] war, but some action about it" (79). Considered in this light, *Dr. Strangelove* was a harbinger of the late sixties "counterculture" films about beautiful losers.

At the same time, the film did show "cold war reality for what it was: immoral, insane, deadly—and ridiculous" (Henriksen 318). In doing that, *Dr. Strangelove* echoed the "sardonic rejection of [official culture's] optimistic rationalism" expressed by writers such as Joseph Heller and Kurt Vonnegut (Lytle 44). The film's popularity also enhanced the visibility of work like Gar Alperovitz's *Atomic Diplomacy*, published soon after *Dr. Strangelove* was released. Alperovitz's book suggested that America knew that Japan was on the verge of defeat even before the bombing of Hiroshima and Nagasaki. Lytle notes that before the publication of *Atomic Diplomacy*, "few Americans had doubted the wisdom or justice of dropping the bomb [for it had not occurred to them] that alternatives existed" (70).

Lytle proposes that Alperovitz's book, in conjunction with *Dr. Strangelove* and the other black comedies of the period, raised questions that "shook the foundations of some of the unexamined truths" young people had accepted. In another time, these questions might have been overlooked, but in 1964 they "had special resonance because they arose as the escalating war in Vietnam raised similar questions" (Lytle 70). Thus, *Dr. Strangelove*, the first film from the 1960s to be named to the National Film Preservation Board, might have been one of many factors that led to the collective action against the Vietnam War, a more narrowly defined and thus less formidable problem than mutually assured destruction in the atomic age.

In that same vein, Sellers's collaborations with Edwards also led to the creation of a character that tacitly called into question "the basic assumptions of civilization," and in doing so was entirely "in synch with the absurdity of late twentieth-century life" (Sikov 207, 208). When *The Pink Panther* and *A Shot in the Dark* were released, Inspector Clouseau was recognized as a character that had "all the solemnity of the conventional detective of fiction" but one that created an entirely different picture of the world because he was "also absurd" (Stephen Watts, "No 'Shot in the Dark': Play Is Carefully and Gaily Revised by Peter Sellers, Blake Edwards," *New York Times*, 19 January 1964, X9). The films were seen as black comedies, with old-fashioned slapstick and classic vaudeville gags used in a way that suggested Sellers and Edwards had "a conscious policy in what they were doing, even a philosophy" (Watts, "No 'Shot in the Dark'"). In the popular press of the time, Edwards explained that the value of working with Sellers rested on his "almost surrealist approach to the insanity of things" and the interest he shared with Edwards in the "mad" tradition of "disaster-prone comedy" known to American audiences through the films of Mack Sennett and Laurel and Hardy (Watts, "No 'Shot in the Dark,'" X9).

As Clouseau, Sellers presented audiences with "a self-absorbed, diffident, yet powerful presence, around whom the action and the rest of the cast whirred and whirled" (Lewis x). Given Sellers's design and portrayal of Clouseau, the character was not only stoic in the face of disaster but also "able to continue functioning in the face of an unending series of calamities" (Sikov 208). That "ability" made the character uniquely suited to an absurd world that destroyed competent individuals; for example, Chief Inspector Dreyfus repeatedly lost his mind "under the threat to rationality that Clouseau's brainless anarchy represents" (Sikov 209). Stupid, funny, sympathetic, and frustrating, the characterization of Clouseau that Sellers created through improvisation captured the kind of bumbling that William Whyte had identified in *The Organization Man* (1956), the critique of corporate culture that in the early 1960s had become a bestseller (Lytle 51–53). In *The Pink Panther*, Clouseau wins the day, for while he is framed by his wife and arrested for the crime he sought to avert, the inept, cuckolded detective becomes the envy of ordinary policemen, who mistake him for the suave jewel thief who is also his wife's lover. In *A Shot in the Dark*, Clouseau is one of the few characters alive and sane by the end of the story, not because of his powers of ratiocination but instead because he inhabits an irrational world that rewards blundering.

Clouseau is like a character in Samuel Beckett's contributions to the literature and theater of the absurd, for he belongs to a world in which "simple objects proliferate" and "the more trivial the matter the more space is devoted to its analysis" (Kenner 87, 82). In addition, as envisioned by Sellers and Edwards, disaster-prone comedy is, like Beckett's work, "an exercise in symmetry and ritual" (Kenner 81). Like other "stoic comedians," Sellers and Edwards "imprison themselves" in the tradition of slapstick comedy to work out "its elaborate games," and their methodical process "requires no more than a closed set of elements and a set of rules for dealing with them" (Kenner 96).

Sellers's characterization of Clouseau has been associated with Buster Keaton's silent-era stoic comedians and more recently Rowan Atkinson's

disaster-prone Mr. Bean. Sellers's characterization of his signature character has also been compared to Jacques Tati's portrayal of Monsieur Hulot,
the absentminded source of seemingly endless disasters depicted by
writer-director-actor Jacques Tati in four feature films between 1953 and
1971. The link between Clouseau and Hulot is especially pertinent, for as
Sellers told the American press at the beginning of his Hollywood career,
he wanted to "key his comedy to the keenly observed technique of
Jacques Tati" (Watts, "Before and Behind the Camera with Sellers," X11;
see Waggoner, "Arrival of Sellers," SM64). Thus, insofar as Sellers crafted
a character at the center of films that took the limitations of reason as
their subject, one might borrow the epithet Hugh Kenner used to describe
Samuel Beckett and characterize Peter Sellers as another "comedian of the
impasse" (70).

Yet the context in which Sellers employed his craft was quite different
from Beckett's, for Sellers was a movie star whose image was formed by
corporate Hollywood's publicity and casting decisions. In addition, he was
essentially "plunged into international prominence" in the early 1960s
(Johnston, "Sellers, En Route to Hollywood," 32). For example, in 1962 he
was among the select celebrities invited to entertain President Kennedy and
other guests at the annual White House Press Dinner. With his image as
British comic transformed by being cast with Loren in *The Millionairess*, in
October 1962 Sellers became the second celebrity invited to do an official
Playboy interview. With his star image colored by associations with anarchic
comedy and the sixties sexual revolution, in April 1964 Sellers was the first
man featured on the cover of *Playboy*; the issue's photo-essay with Sellers is
a parody of famous screen lovers. A personal friend of Princess Margaret
and Lord Snowden, in 1966 Sellers was awarded the title of CBE (Com-
mander of the Most Excellent Order of the British Empire). With Sellers
involved in producing films as well, his last project of the decade, *The Magic
Christian*, released in February 1970, resulted from his longtime interest in
the novel by satirist, New Journalist, and screenwriter Terry Southern.
Given the casting of Beatle drummer Ringo Starr as Youngman Grand and
its flamboyant send-up of greed and class privilege, the film would become
"something of an underground classic" (Starr 157). It seems fitting that the
decade would end with Sellers returning to his roots in "Goon Show"
humor.

An assessment of Sellers as a star of the sixties depends on how one
frames the context and trajectory of his career. Given Hollywood's transition from an international film industry to an American entertainment
industry, it is surprising that Sellers's image still resonated with late sixties'

American audiences. Yet it also makes perfect sense, for his association with absurd comedy could have special appeal for American audiences caught in the impasse of conflicted views on civil rights, the Cold War, and the Vietnam War. Given his recognized gifts as an improvisational actor, one can see how Sellers's work with Kubrick could have led to one of the sixties' most memorable films and how his collaboration with Edwards could have given rise to a fictional character that can still make the absurdity of modern life visible and tolerable by turn.

NOTES

1. Press coverage of Sellers's work does reveal an uncertainty about whether or not his "external" approach to characterization (finding the character's voice and other means of physical expression) was "true" acting. That quandary had, of course, been created by Lee Strasberg's polemical publicity for the Actors Studio in the 1950s, which popularized the idea that the "external" British approach produced inauthentic performances while his scientific discovery of "the Method" made "true" acting possible (Baron).

2. Overseas productions were also good business for Hollywood's highest-paid agents, actors, and directors. Beginning in the 1950s, Jules Stein, the founder of MCA, and MCA president Lew Wasserman "stepped up the number of movie deals that [the highest-paid and thus most] severely taxed MCA clients were 'forced' to film" in Europe as a way to take advantage of a new law that allowed "actors and directors who spent seventeen out of eighteen months in Europe [to pay] no taxes during their time overseas" (McDougal 151, 150).

3. Fueled in part by the work of writer-director Blake Edwards, the Pink Panther franchise includes TV shows, video games, commercials with the animated Pink Panther figure, and films such as *Inspector Clouseau* (1968) with Alan Arkin, *Trail of the Pink Panther* (1982) with archival footage of Sellers, *Curse of the Pink Panther* (1983) with Roger Moore, *Son of the Pink Panther* (1993) with Roberto Benigni, and *The Pink Panther* (2006) and *The Pink Panther 2* (2009), both with Steve Martin. While the franchise as a whole has proved to be highly profitable for corporate media, some of the most financially successful products are the 1970s films with Peter Sellers. The box office for *The Return of the Pink Panther* was second only to *Jaws* (1975) and *The Revenge of the Pink Panther* was the tenth highest grossing film of 1978 (Sikov 341, 355). Their commercial success, along with the critical acclaim of Sellers's performance in *Being There* (1980), led to Sellers making the cover of *Time* magazine on 3 March 1980, shortly before he died on 24 July.

4. I want to thank Beckett Warren for sharing his insights on stardom, for talking about cult taste, and for reading and commenting on the chapter (correspondence, 11 November 2008).

7 ☆☆☆☆☆☆☆☆☆☆☆

Julie Andrews
Practically *Too* Perfect in Every Way

DENNIS BINGHAM

As a phenomenon of movies and culture, Julie Andrews's career in the 1960s has gone mostly unexamined. She was a rarity to start with: a postwar Broadway musical comedy star without the stagy eccentricities that kept divas such as Mary Martin, Gwen Verdon, Ethel Merman, and Carol Channing from ever becoming film stars. Overcoming what Peter Bart at the time called "the long-standing dicta that Andrews was neither photogenic nor sexy enough to be a movie star," she finally won over the film industry in 1963–64 ("The Hollywoodization of Julie Andrews," *New York Times*, 6 September 1964). Andrews was blessed with a warm, immaculate singing tone—a voice frequently described as "freakish"—as well as a face that could express devotion, exasperation, strength, but most of all the shining attribute of the classical, pre-1970s Hollywood star: sincerity.

Andrews made her leap from Broadway to Hollywood in the decade when American movies became internationalized and British talent seemed to be taking over the screen. From Richard Burton, Richard Harris, Peter O'Toole, and Albert Finney to Vanessa and Lynn Redgrave, Peter Sellers, Julie Christie, and Maggie Smith, British actors were everywhere one looked in the 1960s. Unlike the other British stars, except for the film and stage veteran Burton, who co-starred with her on Broadway in *Camelot* in 1960–61, Andrews did not suddenly burst onto the international scene during the decade. Moreover, she probably would have become a household name in *Mary Poppins* (1964) and *The Sound of Music* (1965) if none of the surrounding Anglophilia had existed. Andrews was tied to an older musical comedy tradition and to the values on which it rested. In her world, institutions were sound and secure, trained voices and cultured talents were prized, and film musicals were made frequently. Before Andrews made her first film (at the behest of America's uncle, Walt Disney) she had become part of American culture, at a time when Broadway songs still featured on radio playlists and millions of original cast albums were sold.

In a hat trick that, coincidentally, Barbra Streisand would repeat at the end of the 1960s, Andrews was signed to her first three films, representing an enormous investment. In Andrews's case, principal photography on all three movies was finished before a single one of them was seen by the public.[1] Andrews's first and third movies, *Mary Poppins* and *The Sound of Music*, were phenomenal, persona-defining successes that she, in fact, would never match and by which she would be mercilessly typecast, by the public if not by moviemakers. This was in spite of her second film, *The Americanization of Emily* (1964), a romantic comedy that drew good reviews and showed her versatility, but was a relative failure at the box office.

A paradox haunts Andrews's stardom. She was born in 1935 and thus was only two years older than the famous "class of 1937," the birth year of New Hollywood stars Jane Fonda, Jack Nicholson, Robert Redford, Warren Beatty, and Dustin Hoffman. However, her association with the dying genre, the musical, her "peaches-and-cream" persona, and her typecasting as nannies and governesses stitched her star to Old Hollywood and the Establishment. Like a vast cohort of movie stars many years her senior, Andrews was cast aside in the vast generational and cultural turnover at the end of the decade.

Andrews thought her problem was typecasting. Even at her height, she declined roles that portrayed her as being in charge of children, even if the projects were light years in tone away from *The Sound of Music*, like *The Prime of Miss Jean Brodie* (1969), for which Maggie Smith would win an

Oscar. Andrews had other, less obvious problems. The New Hollywood Cinema was emphatically a new *American* cinema, partly because the run-away international productions of the 1960s also led to big budgets. A dras-tic move by Hollywood at the end of the decade away from big budgets meant smaller-scale subject matter, closer to home. Accordingly, the British stars who soared to stardom in the 1960s fell to earth in the 1970s. Six of Andrews's eight 1960s films, furthermore, were produced by one of the major studios. Despite the widespread assumption that independent pro-duction was standard procedure since the 1950s, with the studios acting as distributors and sometimes financiers, the studios were very much holding on when Andrews came into movies, with some of the old lions such as Walt Disney, Jack L. Warner, and Darryl F. Zanuck still maintaining control of their companies. Hence, although Andrews and all her directors, except Disney's Robert Stevenson, were freelancers working for the studios on the basis of one film or perhaps two, she represented the conventional genres and styles favored by an Old Hollywood nearing its absolute and final end. Their failure was her failure.

In addition to these symptoms and liabilities, there is one more, which I'll introduce in a personal anecdote. As a smart-aleck college student in the mid-1970s, I engaged my mother in one of my favorite things: teasing her about her love of *The Sound of Music*, a movie that represented the glossy Hollywood version of everything I was then rejecting in life, includ-ing conforming and being Catholic, well-behaved, and obedient. One day she hit back with a riposte for which I had no answer: "Ohhh, you just don't like *The Sound of Music* because it's about a woman." This changed the terms of the arguments against the film from the usual raps against raindrops on roses and movie Nazis menacing cute kids to something I wasn't prepared to deal with and haven't stopped thinking about since. There is no denying that the backlash that hit Andrews full-force at the end of the 1960s was part of the cultural tsunami that swept away nearly all signifiers of the "old" culture and values. It is difficult to ignore, how-ever, the reality that the female star as institution was discarded along with the Old Hollywood and that Andrews was the last female star in the lumi-nous old manner. As the entertainment industry embraced demographics at the end of the 1960s and the direction of Hollywood movies tilted heav-ily toward young males, a certain variety of female spectatorship was snubbed. One feels the contempt in the critical revulsion toward Andrews and *The Sound of Music* once its phenomenal popularity took hold. Andrews had won an Academy Award for her debut film, starred in the highest grossing film of all time to date, and was named the top box-office draw for 1966 and 1967. Thirty-two years would pass before another woman (Julia Roberts) achieved that honor. More was coming to an end here than the popularity of one movie star.

In a sense, Andrews's star image predicts its own fleetingness. The Julie Andrews character in films is a stranger who never seems fully at home. In most of her 1960s films she plays a visitor, a newcomer, if not an alien. Mary Poppins flies into the lives of the Banks family from nowhere in particular and departs when the wind changes; Maria in *The Sound of Music* has been a novice in a convent when she comes to work for the Von Trapps. In *Darling Lili* Lily Smith/Lili Schmidt is of mixed British-German heritage and equally divided loyalties. *Torn Curtain* (1966), *Hawaii* (1966), and *Thoroughly Modern Millie* (1967) never explain her accent, and thus naturalize her foreignness. *The Americanization of Emily* is one of the few films in which her character is in her element and on her own territory, rather than a newcomer or a striver in someone else's land. *Star!* (1968), the film besides *The Sound of Music* in which she plays an actual person, casts her as Gertrude Lawrence, a stage star who, like Andrews, left her native England for bigger stardom in America. Moreover, her characters are usually trapped in the past;only in *Torn Curtain* does Andrews play in a contemporary setting. Her image is somehow out of time and space, and out of synch with the American sixties.

The public's brief, flame-like love affair with Julie Andrews and the abruptness with which the flame was extinguished points up a bit of what was lost amid the cultural turnover of the late 1960s. She reigned as a superstar in the years 1964–67 but was dethroned between 1968 and 1970. As Mary Poppins was "practically perfect in every way," Julie Andrews was rejected as too perfect, too polished, for an era that came to distrust the slick, the composed, the obviously professional. Her movies, persona, and performances in the eight films she made in the 1960s provide a guided tour through the cinematic and cultural transitions that marked this lightening rod of an era. In what follows, I trace these shifts through a brief discussion of her 1960s films.

☆☆☆☆★ *Mary Poppins*

One might think that Julie Andrews, or any actress, would be lost in the whimsy and spectacle of Walt Disney's live action and animation combination. However, Andrews's performance in *Mary Poppins* emits for posterity the charge of newness and discovery that comes from a great star debut.

Mary Poppins in the afternoon? Disney meets Deren? Not exactly, although Poppins's anticlimactic gaze as the reunited Banks family leaves her behind holds its own brand of ambiguity to which no one else has the key. (Digital frame enlargement, *Mary Poppins*)

Commentators over the years have assumed that Andrews's Academy Award for *Mary Poppins* was "at least partly a consolation prize from Hollywood sentimentalists who thought Julie should have got the film role in [*My*] *Fair Lady*" ("Now and Future Queen," *Time*, 23 December 1966). (For that film, the film's producer, Warner, famously opted to cast the more marquee-friendly Audrey Hepburn as Eliza Doolittle, a role Andrews had created and played for three and a half years on Broadway and in London.) In line with this view, Andrews's performance in *Poppins* is the kind of understated, subtle acting that traditionally *fails* to win Oscars. It offers little dramatic emoting, physical transformation, or psychological complexity. Not that the performance is not complex; P. L. Travers said, after meeting Julie Andrews, "I hadn't spoken to her for five minutes before I realized she had the inner integrity for the part" (Stirling 119). Andrews's ability to convey private confidence, which is comic, poignant, and even heroic in its effects, gives the performance its power. It is also the opposite of what one expects from stage actors, who presumably have to be brought down from projecting-to-the-balcony acting habits. So seamlessly does she make the transition from the boards, while keeping the tone away from either cutesy knowingness or heavy-handed irony, that Julie Andrews the Queen of Broadway was now forgotten.

The conceit of *Mary Poppins*, from a child's eye, is that the heroine comports herself as an adult but possesses the heart of a child. She is a contradiction, a withholding mother who releases pleasure and magic, denying her own powers and keeping as firm a handle on emotion as she does her flying umbrella. She represents both order and disorder. In the musical genre, moreover, people express themselves in song and dance. Thus we are to believe that Mary Poppins is most herself when she sings "Just a Spoonful of Sugar," a song in the Disney "Whistle While You Work" vein, or a ballad in waltz time like "Feed the Birds." Believe not what this Mary Poppins says, but what she sings.

☆☆★★★ *The Americanization of Emily*

Emily Barham is one of only two good nonmusical parts Julie Andrews had in the 1960s and her first "straight" role since a London play she did while a teenager. Andrews plays the standard female conscience of the Hollywood social problem film. "Most English families haven't seen that many eggs or oranges in years," says Emily, war widow and driver for an American admiral's aide (James Garner) in London in the run-up to D-Day. "But it's just one big Shriners' convention to you Yanks, isn't it?"

A mild satire of courage under fire as celebrated in movies like *The Longest Day* (1962), *Emily*, which takes place in the days before, during, and after D-Day, awkwardly combines the war film and the romantic comedy. As interesting as it is to see a Hollywood film taking up weighty issues, much of *Emily* plays like a college debate tournament. Yet it provides Andrews with as good a "straight" role as she was likely to find in mid-1960s Hollywood. The character is indignant and righteous, but also caring and loving. Andrews thought that *Emily* would inoculate her against any typecasting incurred by *Mary Poppins* and *The Sound of Music*. It might have, had audiences gone to it in anything like the numbers in which they attended the two blockbuster musicals.

☆☆★★★ *The Sound of Music*

The pre-credits opening of *The Sound of Music*, with the aerial views of the Alps, delivers the spectacular effects that mid-1960s audiences expected in a Todd-AO/stereophonic sound roadshow attraction, while echoing the opening of Wise's previous Oscar-winning musical, *West Side Story* (1961). Mere mention of the movie's title, and perhaps of the actress's name, most often evokes that image of Julie Andrews in a mountain clearing, arms stretched out, inviting the spectator to share her rapture. "You had me at 'The hills are alive . . . ,' " the ordinary spectator might have said as the film broke every box office record in its initial roadshow run.

The Sound of Music is as maudlin as its many critics allege. Screenwriter Ernest Lehman tones down some of the saccharine elements of Howard Lindsay and Russell Crouse's Broadway script. Nonetheless, anyone who doesn't wince at a line like "Why does the flag with the black spider on it make father so cross?" either isn't paying attention or has been mesmerized into submission in the way that Pauline Kael's infamous review alleged. But Andrews gives herself so wholeheartedly to the sentimental material that she literally brings it out the other side, making realism out of the most anti-realistic stuff. Hers is one of those "performances of a lifetime," when character and actor merge at just the right time in the actor's development and the result is an indelible person created on film. Why does Andrews seem so dominant in The Sound of Music? Christopher Plummer says that her performance "was real. There was nothing 'musical comedy' about it, just the actual naked Julie Andrews on the screen, her own heart. . . . If you can do that on the screen, you're going to be a star" (DVD comm.). The actress's musical comedy gifts are often called upon, however. While emerging from a bus on her first visit to the Von Trapp manse, for example, she lets her guitar case get wedged as a barrier, requiring her to struggle in order to get out the door, all while lip-synching on location to playback of "I Have Confidence."

The shot through the gate upon Maria's arrival at the Von Trapp estate marks the first time in the film that we are positioned in Maria's point of view. Nonetheless, Maria seems a figure of identification in most of the film, rather than an objectified figure. At times, she seems the only human character in the film, stumbling over her skirts as she runs to the Von Trapp front door, not just as a comic pratfall but as an expression of over-eagerness and nerves. William Reynolds, accepting his Academy Award for editing The Sound of Music, explained his découpage principle: "When in doubt, cut to Julie Andrews" (Denkert 210).

Because Andrews is so much at the center of the film, she bore the brunt of the backlash against it. Kael, who would in coming years help set the tone for the New American Cinema, found most offensive "Julie Andrews, with the clean, scrubbed look and the unyieldingly high spirits, the good sport who makes the best of everything; the girl who's so unquestionably good that she carries this one dimension like a shield. . . . What is she? Merely the ideal heroine for the best of all possible worlds. And that's what The Sound of Music pretends we live in" (177). For those caught up in the cultural and aesthetic changes of the 1960s, The Sound of

Is there an iconic star performance that is as scorned, and as loved, as Julie Andrews's in *The Sound of Music*? She may have asked Robert Wise at the beginning, "How are you going to get the sugar out of this thing?" but Andrews radiated sincerity and conviction in an incurably calculated Broadway property. (Digital frame enlargement.)

Music and Julie Andrews were the enemy, an unthinking, unquestioning force for the status quo. Kael knew what to call this force: "the sentimental American tone that makes honest work almost impossible." Richard Nixon a few years later knew what to call it, too: the Silent Majority.

Clearly, the movies had created a new Julie Andrews in the public mind. "I can't knock *The Sound of Music* and *Mary Poppins*," Andrews told Charles Higham in 1977, even before she could know how enduring the two films would be in the home video age, "because they gave such an awful lot of pleasure to such an awful lot of people. But that kind of exposure does put one into the greatest danger. . . . Now I can see that I was too quickly bracketed in one category, and I couldn't escape from it" ("The Rise and Fall—and Rise—of Julie Andrews," *New York Times*, 21 August 1977).

Andrews's "middle period" films emerged in the shadow of *The Sound of Music*, which in eighteen months overtook *Gone with the Wind*'s twenty-six-year record as the highest grossing film ever, and which could be seen in most cities for up to *four years* after its initial release. All of her middle-period films were commercial hits in their own right. In quick succession Andrews starred in a Hitchcock thriller, one of the "literate" epics of the era, and another original musical.

★★★★★ Torn Curtain

Made after *Hawaii* but released first, *Torn Curtain* marks the only instance in Andrews's star period where she seemed abandoned by her director. Andrews, who dyed her hair strawberry blonde to play Maria and grayed it and pulled it back severely for Jerusha Hale in *Hawaii*, would surely have become a Hitchcock blonde had the director wished it. However, he seemed to have little concept of her character. The plain, dreary, dun-colored set that is meant to pass for an East German hotel room draws attention from the star's equally dull costuming and hairstyling. Perhaps Andrews didn't know how to play contemporary roles, since this is indeed the only one of her eight sixties films set in present day. More likely, she received little help from Brian Moore's screenplay or from Hitchcock's direction. Andrews plays Sarah Sherman, the fiancée of a famous scientist (Paul Newman) who appears to defect to East Germany. Bewildered and betrayed, she follows her lover there, where she has little to do but tag along and become a part, but not an integral one, of intrigues that are not very intriguing.

Andrews's reputation—as if it needed more impugning among cineastes amid *The Sound of Music* backlash—was done no good by remarks made by Alfred Hitchcock in his famous interview with François Truffaut, implying that Andrews and Paul Newman were cast in *Torn Curtain* because they were "hot," not because they were right for their roles or even particularly talented. The many who took his comments seriously must have forgotten that the director's most recent idea of a "Hitchcock heroine" had been "Tippi" Hedren, the utter failure of whose *Marnie* (1964), Hitchcock's previous film, seemed to have dampened not only the director's trademark exactitude but his legendary flair with actresses. Newman retorted, "I think he owed it to us not to say we were miscast after he approved us. . . . We were stars, and we brought in fans at the box office" (qtd. in Stirling 191).

★★★★★ *Hawaii*

In the Vietnam era, *Hawaii* was a film that explored the history of American adventurism and arrogance abroad in the form of religious certainty. Based on James Michener's 937-page book, *Hawaii* is an example of how serious and ambitious the big roadshow films of 1960s Hollywood could be. *Hawaii* opens in 1819, when an awkward and gauche young Calvinist missionary, Abner Hale (Max Von Sydow), is introduced to Jerusha Bromley (Andrews) in the hopes that he can journey to Hawaii as a married minister, who thus won't be tempted by the native women. Jerusha makes her entrance at the top of the stairs of her parents' New Hampshire home. Hale meets his putative fiancée by sneezing in her face, ruling out the romance conventionally signaled by this kind of scene.

Jerusha looks wonderingly at Hale as the film lap dissolves out on Andrews's blue eyes. Later, when Jerusha accepts Abner's clumsy proposal of marriage, Andrews glows with the charisma of a movie star.

It follows that Abner would mate with a woman like Andrews's Jerusha. She is a model of the clergyman's wife, alluring without being threatening. Who but Andrews, asked George Roy Hill, "can play a convincing young lady of breeding in the 1820s in New England. What other names spring to mind? People of the 1820s—particularly in New England—were closer to the lands of their birth than to the Americans of today" (Windeler 124–25). Is Jerusha shaped to the radiant persona of Julie Andrews, or does Andrews use her gifts to create the character? One would assume now, as Glenn Erickson does, that "*Hawaii*'s only nod to commercial concerns is the casting of the magic name Julie Andrews. After *Mary Poppins* and *The Sound of Music* a producer could get funding for almost any project with her name attached, freeing [producer Walter] Mirisch and his writers to tell [James] Michener's story without the compromise of happy endings" (DVDTalk.com). However, before *The Sound of Music* phenomenon broke, director George Roy Hill reportedly "had fought to cast" her (Windeler 124); by the time the film opened, Andrews had top billing, despite her secondary, "wifely" role.

It's unknown, without archival research, exactly who cut *Hawaii* from its 189-minute running time at its premiere engagements to 161 minutes for its national and international roadshow release, and none of Andrews's biographers pick up on the fact that the film was recut at all. One's view of her performance, however, depends very much upon which version of *Hawaii* one sees.[2] Andrews was badly slighted in the *Hawaii* that most of the world saw in the 1960s. Given that she was the world's most popular movie star, it's unclear why the distributor would excise some of her best scenes, to the extent where her character doesn't make sense. A review of the longer version praised Andrews for bringing "both sensuality and sensibility to a role that might easily have wallowed in sweetness and light," words the actress must have found suitable for framing but which would have been impossible to apply to the remnants of the Jerusha character left in the recut film ("Shouts and Muumuus," *Time*, 21 October 1966).

In the shorter version, the young woman in love with a seafaring whaler, Rafer Hoxworth (Richard Harris), whom she thinks has spurned her (in truth his letters have been kept from her), marries Abner Hale because she believes he could be her last chance at marriage. In the fuller version, she accepts his clumsy proposal because at least life with him will not be without purpose and adventure, and indeed, as a niece of the president of the seminary at Yale, she has been somewhat prepared for such life. We also get more of a sense of what she is leaving behind; a scene on her wedding day with her younger sister and a shot of her parents as she sails to the Pacific with her new husband are also cut. However, most of Hoxworth's scenes, filled with action and conflict, remain, showing the male-oriented assumptions about what footage the film company can afford to lose and still have an exciting movie. They also make the spectator wonder what sort of husband he would have been, a whaler thousands of miles away for months at a time, keeping his wife in comfort while despoiling native girls on his journeys.

In the premiere version, Jerusha stands up to Abner during the lull after the ship clears the stormy seas at the Cape of Good Hope. "Mrs. Hale," Abner gasps, as his wife, seasick for weeks, makes her first appearance above deck, heaving overboard the large bunch of bananas from which he had forced her to eat. "My name is Jerusha," she storms. "You bullied me, Abner. You bullied me through the sin of your pride. Never again will I submit to your bullying. I am as good a judge of God's will as you. And God never intended that a woman as sick as I should be so hatefully . . ." She breaks off as a sailor, whose Bible Abner took from him after the sailor got drunk but before the same man skillfully saved the ship in the storm, asks for his book back. When Abner refuses, Jerusha again crosses him, in a Christian if not a biblical sense, giving the man her own Bible. "God has no meaning to me," she tells him in another trimmed sequence, "if He doesn't reveal himself, even to an evil man, with love."

These excised scenes show not just the strength of Jerusha's character and of Andrews's performance, but her dramatic function as a merciful counterweight to Hale/Von Sydow's judgmental intolerance. *Hawaii* depicts a woman in the traditional role as nurturer, but it shows the value of the character and the female star as a well-rounded person, and not just an appendage of the male protagonist. Hill and the screenwriters, Daniel Taradash and Dalton Trumbo, spare the spectator her wedding vows with a man she may not love. Thus they never seem like a romantic couple, requiring the spectator to project any growing sense that Jerusha and Abner belong together and indeed to decide whether or not they do. Jerusha, in both versions, shockingly dies offscreen. Hill relieves the spectator of the masochistic experience of watching the star die, while showing that, in retrospect, her death was inevitable, even if we learn the news when Hoxworth appears, demanding to see Jerusha. "I killed her," Abner declares, passively motioning to her grave marker, which we see in an insert. Hill, whose later blockbuster hit *Butch Cassidy and the Sundance Kid* (1969) would help usher in a male-dominated period in American cinema, makes the film's climax a banal exchange between men. *Hawaii*, fittingly, is also about the end of matriarchy and about the relationship of two women, Jerusha and the local queen, Malama, played by Joycelyne La Garde, who had not acted before and received the film's only Academy Award nomination for acting. Both Malama and Jerusha are dead by the film's end. The women's demise is as fitting a metaphor for the waning importance of women in the impending New Hollywood as is the producers' relegation of Andrews's most assertive moments to the cutting room floor.

☆☆☆☆★ *Thoroughly Modern Millie*

Thoroughly Modern Millie is the closest any Andrews film came to displaying the bubbly comedienne of Broadway and of her 1962 TV special with Carol Burnett. It is close in tone to *The Boyfriend*, the 1920s pastiche in which Andrews made her Broadway debut at the age of nineteen. The actress viewed the spirited, adventuresome young woman in the Big City in 1922, fervent in her desire to be "a modern," as "the last chance I'd have to do the ingénue" (Windeler 130). Andrews's Millie Dillmount is joyous, perfectly timed, comic, and energetic. As a musical comedy performance piece by Julie Andrews, *Thoroughly Modern Millie* nearly achieves the audience intimacy of a one-woman show.

Millie signals Andrews's desire not only to get loose of the "nanny" type, but also to swear off characters defined by their moral superiority. Her first films, even the misfire *Torn Curtain*, all set her morally above the ordinary person. In *Millie* she fairly revels in the character's ordinariness, and the film showcases Andrews's talents in a way that signifies looseness and "fun." "Julie as you love her," cheered the posters, "singing, dancing, delighting." "Here was the clincher, for all audiences," said a Universal executive, "Julie Andrews, back again after *Hawaii*, in a happy picture with music, doing what the public liked" (Howard Thompson, "Studios Again Mining Gold with Lavish Film Musicals," *New York Times*, 26 October 1968). While one naysaying critic claimed, "Julie Andrews' star's bright charm and prodigious energies cannot make a hit all by themselves" ("Thoroughly Maudlin," *Time*, 7 April 1967), Universal learned otherwise, as the film grossed a total of $40 million worldwide (Harris 284).

The film attempts to spoof or "send up" the popular culture of an entire era. Ben Brantley, reviewing the Broadway recreation, called the movie "failed camp," which "never seemed to grasp the style it was sending up" ("All Right, Everyone: Smile!" *New York Times*, 19 April 2002). By Susan Sontag's definition, "one must distinguish between naïve camp and delib-

Millie is so spontaneous she might even dart out of the light. Jimmy (James Fox) pulls her back in. *Thoroughly Modern Millie* is the closest Andrews got on film to the bubbly performer of Broadway and her TV specials. (Digital frame enlargement)

erate camp. . . . Camp which knows itself to be Camp ('camping') is usually less satisfying" (282). In this reading, Millie is another Andrews visitor, Alice in a campy twenties wonderland as conjured up on soundstages four decades later. Certainly, the film reads as camp, whether knowingly produced by the film's gay producer and Andrews, the lesbian icon. Muzzy, played by the gay male icon Carol Channing in a rare film performance, is a wealthy socialite who "takes instruction" individually from what looks like each member of the Village People—wrestlers, German flying aces, trapeze artists—"always gathering the nuts of life," as ever-naïve Millie says admiringly of Muzzy in the film's final line. Millie is the naïf, innocent of whatever frolics may be going on around her. Is the naïve Millie, the classic "femme," as Stacy Wolf defines Andrews, enthralled by a queer world, even as she misrecognizes it and herself? Andrews's sincere innocence never lets on that Millie knows she's anything other than a young woman consumed with the prospect of being a flapper.

The film is not nearly distanced enough for ridicule. Its title character is made instantly sympathetic; we are never out of her cinematic point of view. This is established indelibly in the title sequence, a series of eyeline matches and reaction shots that interpellate for Millie what this twentieth-century Big City stuff is all about. Andrews displays a talent for understated irony that she had earlier brought to many of Alan Jay Lerner's wry lyrics for *Camelot*, in which she reportedly played Guinevere as something of a comic femme fatale. In the brilliant credit sequence—the combination of a great song and

Andrews's wonderful way with it, Hill's Kuleshovian montage, Andrews's gifts as a mime and deft costuming and production design—Millie/Andrews transforms visually from the nineteenth century, with high-button shoes and shoulder-length curls, to the twentieth, in which you "raise your skirts and bob your hair" in the time it takes to sing the title song. (The sequence could be from an early musical, such as *Love Me Tonight* [1932], shot silent, with the prerecorded song being the only sound.) At the same time that the editing puts us in Millie's reality, Millie looks at the camera, while title cards and rinky-tink piano music make extra-diegetic asides that take us out of an objective diegesis and into a larger 1920s movie world. The film keeps us in Millie's point of view while also making fun of her naïveté.

Millie "spoofs" musicals: Millie, in the midst of a number, "Jimmy," whose lyrics really do include "Jimmy, oh Jimmy, silly boy, gee what a real swell guy," retires to her closet to change into her "p.j.s," whirls around, sees "us" there, turns back around and closes the door with herself inside. She whistles—an Andrews specialty dating back to "What Do the Simple Folk Do?" in *Camelot* and her bird duet to "A Spoonful of Sugar" in *Mary Poppins*—and then tap-dances unseen! Furthermore, while most of Andrews's films cover her freckles with makeup, this one accentuates them, to emphasize the character's youth and innocence. Andrews, even in Jean Louis's vampiest costume, does not lose Millie's essential innocence. The film even makes fun of Disney, with Mrs. Meers, the farcical villainess played by the seventy-two-year-old Beatrice Lillie, offering the faux-innocent Miss Dorothy (Mary Tyler Moore) a poison apple. Millie tartly reminds her friend that a little "dope" "didn't hurt Sleeping Beauty or Snow White." Of course, reference to the *original stories* would not be anachronistic for a movie set in 1922, but, with the line spoken by Mary Poppins herself, it's hard to imagine a 1967 audience thinking of anything but the Disney versions from 1959 and 1937, respectively, or conversely to imagine the audience thinking of the 1967 connotations of "dope."

The myriad spoofs of the sixties were in retrospect not only camp but postmodern pastiche, irony and queer undercurrents in movies and television, in their infancy. While pastiches of the 1980s and 1990s restate the constructedness of culture, a 1960s pastiche like *Millie* plays for nostalgia but is too cool to directly indulge it. When 1960s culture "spoofs" an entire period, it neither makes the era alive for the spectator nor analogizes the past to present themes and concerns. What "spoofs" of the past like *Thoroughly Modern Millie* do is hold back time, presuming the superiority of the present, while preventing progress by hindering a true understanding of the past. While "modernity" is elaborately illuminated in the film as the term applied to women at the time of suffrage and to the United States after the Great War, this 1967 film dashes even a forty-five-year-old concept of the term, as Tea, the ancient Chinese on the Van Hossmere estate, turns up incongruously to signal his approval, pronouncing Millie "a good old-fashioned girl." *Millie* flunks standards set by *How Men Propose*, a 1913 one-reel comedy directed by Lois Weber in which three ardent suitors come upon a modern female journalist conducting research and mistake her for an "old-fashioned girl" waiting demurely in the parlor for a proposal of marriage. Millie is not thoroughly modern enough for the "first-wave feminist" era. Thus, Andrews star image is, once again, placed in a recent past that is made to seem out of touch with modernity.

Millie adds to the number of films, including *Mary Poppins* and *The Great Race* (1965, by Andrews's future husband-director, Blake Edwards), which toy with first-wave feminism. By confining a women's independence movement securely to the past, these Hollywood films render it the stuff of nostalgia. Andrews, then, can be perceived as part of a project of patriarchal conservatism, even if decades later she can be seen as a pleasurable identification figure for female spectatorship. Millie's line upon finding that "Jimmy" is really the Rockefellerian Van Hossmere, "I don't want to be your equal. I want to be a woman," might have come from a film made in 1947, when postwar wives were being hustled from the factory floor to the kitchen. Andrews was identifying herself with ideologies that, while proto-feminist, would be jaw-droppingly outdated in only a few years. Her next film, *Star!*, on the other hand, flouted conventions in ways apparently indecipherable in the gender nowhereland of the late 1960s. Either way, Andrews couldn't win.

☆☆☆☆☆ Grande Dame, Not-So-Grand Finale

At the beginning of 1968, a magazine proclaimed that Julie Andrews "has, in fact, become perhaps the most important star in the history of show business. . . . At the age of thirty-two, she is young, healthy, and beautiful. Her career is at a peak it should hold for many years to come" ("Has Success Spoiled Julie Andrews?" *Coronet*, January 1968). Hyperbole like this shows how overblown media rhetoric can be, especially in the late 1960s, when nobody knew what was coming around the next week's *Variety* box office report. Nineteen months passed between the release of *Millie* in March 1967 and that of *Star!* in October 1968. The world convulsed during that period of war, tumult, social unrest, and tragedy, out of which came profound and lasting cultural shifts.

Julie Andrews fell out of favor during that year and a half, and nobody told her or those around her. This may have happened for these reasons: (1) the colossal failure of *Star!*; (2) her divorce from Tony Walton in May 1968, while living with Blake Edwards, whom she would marry in November 1969; (3) the highly publicized troubles of *Darling Lili*, writer-director Edwards's $25 million romance-war/spy film-musical/Andrews vehicle, in production during most of 1968; (4) the final death throes of Old Hollywood, as expensive musicals put into production in the euphoria over *The Sound of Music* opened and lost millions for their studios; and/or (5) in a nutshell, the zeitgeist.

★★★★★ *Star!*

By 1968 there were two irreconcilable sides to Julie Andrews. In *Star!* they collided disastrously. One was the *Mary Poppins / The Sound of Music* nanny stereotype that had hardened in the minds of the public, in the press, and among many in a fast-changing industry. The other was the Julie Andrews known to the actress herself and those who had worked with her: the consummate trouper, a multi-talented singer, actress, and comedienne. People like Robert Wise, Saul Chaplin, and George Roy Hill did not think of Andrews as a particular type but as a hard-working, collegial talent with "a greater range," as Wise said, "than had been called on for any film so far" ("Silver *Star!*"). Andrews was fated, or at least slated, to make the musical biopic of Gertrude Lawrence (1898–1952), the great star of West End and Broadway theater, since early in her movie career. Wise, Chaplin, and Andrews agreed to make "The Gertrude Lawrence Story," so said Twentieth Century-Fox's "publicity manual" for *Star!*, on 4 September 1964, at a luncheon ten days after filming wrapped on *The Sound of Music*.

Wise took "a realistic approach to theatre . . . and not just . . . the glamorous side of Gertrude Lawrence's life" ("Silver *Star!*"). Musical biopics in the studio era were essentially dramatized revues, such as *Yankee Doodle Dandy* (1942) or *The Jolson Story* (1946), which illustrated a famous musician's impact on society. This format lent itself with surprising success in the 1950s to the melodrama and realism of the new warts-and-all mode. *Love Me or Leave Me* (1955), *I'll Cry Tomorrow* (1955), and *The Joker Is Wild* (1957) for example, provided acting and singing showcases for their stars, Doris Day, Susan Hayward, and Frank Sinatra, respectively. They told showbiz-set stories involving gangsters, contentious marriages, alcoholism, and other various human foibles. Wise directed some of the most powerful (nonmusical) warts-and-all entries (*Somebody Up There Likes Me* [1956], *I Want to*

Live! [1958]). Put these together with his blockbuster musicals of the 1960s and *Star!* is the result.

The screenwriter William Fairchild, Wise, and Chaplin laid out a three-part concept: a 1940 black-and-white Academy ratio John Grierson–style documentary presents Gertie Lawrence's life as it's known then to the public; the spectacular 1968 roadshow film with Julie Andrews shows what actually happened in Lawrence's life. Meanwhile, seventeen songs by Noel Coward, George and Ira Gershwin, Cole Porter, and many others punctuate, illustrate, and comment upon the progress of Lawrence's life and career. The numbers, a bit more obviously than in an integrated or organic musical, are performed for our benefit and are showcases for the film's star. Moreover, the glamorous Gertie, who dressed regally, spending herself into bankruptcy on both sides of the Atlantic, required 125 costume changes, said to be a record for the time, as well as jewelry rented from Cartier's and insured for three million dollars. For all this, the film never looks overproduced, unlike some of the musicals in the late-1960s cycle (including *Darling Lili*). The Gertie of Fairchild's treatment was "generous, impulsive, extravagant, and maddening. . . . Seemingly always contradictory. She was supremely elegant and of the earth, earthy. She could behave with perfect dignity and decorum at one moment and call her dinner companion a bitch at the next" (William Fairchild, *The Gertrude Lawrence Story* Notes on Revised Treatment, 10 December 1965, Robert Wise Collection, USC).

For Wise and his team, *Star!* was a showcase. The director told a writer, "I really didn't want to make the Gertrude Lawrence story. What I really wanted after *The Sound of Music* was a star vehicle for Julie" (Dunne 68). Perhaps there was a bit of arrogance here, that superior talent will out. While someone with Gertrude Lawrence's indifferent singing talent could never play Julie Andrews, Andrews, practically a perfect singer in every way, might even "improve" on Lawrence in the sense of translating star magnetism from one medium to another, as Cagney had done with George M. Cohan in *Yankee Doodle Dandy*. A great irony is that, since Gertrude Lawrence had bought the rights to *Anna and the King of Siam*, Rodgers and Hammerstein had to write *The King and I* for her (qtd. in Morley, *Private* 500).

Now Lawrence would be played by the actress who was Lady Rodgers and Hammerstein for the 1960s public. More fundamentally, Lawrence and Andrews had both come up through hardscrabble early family lives and tours of the British music halls. The younger actress had been exposed growing up to much of the established star's music. A male impersonator, Ella Edwards, was on the bill of a 1948 Royal Command Performance at the London Palladium with Andrews, singing "Burlington Bertie from Bow," which Andrews sings as Lawrence in the film (Windeler19). Andrews also must have been used to being compared to the performer who, like her, was an Englishwoman who found great success on American shores, ended an early marriage to an Englishman and entered into a lasting second marriage with an American, and finally made the United States her permanent home. Sandy Wilson wrote, "I wondered if we might be about to assist at the birth of a new star, someone as remarkable in her way as Gertrude Lawrence" (Windeler 32). Late in 1964, amid the news media's love affair with the new star, the *Los Angeles Times* ran a story headlined, "Julie Andrews Just Right for Gertie—This Biography May Click." "How perfect," burbled the article, "Miss Andrews has that same lovely quality, that same delightful British voice, so gay, so titilizing" (qtd. in Stirling 158).

In the four years from the film's inception to its release, however, quiet misgivings were forming. Noel Coward, whose willingness to allow himself to be portrayed enabled the project to go forward, nevertheless told Fairchild in 1966, "I've always been against a film on Gertie's life. . . . There's no story—poor girl who became a success, then just success, success, success" (memo from Fairchild to Chaplin, 9 June 1966, Robert Wise Collection, USC). In his private diary Coward was more direct. The casting of Andrews as Lawrence, he wrote, was "about as suitable as casting the late Princess Royal as Du Barry. However, she's a clever girl and will at least sing well" (Stirling 158).

When the film opened in New York, the reviews were biting. *Time* dubbed it "The Character Assassination of Gertrude Lawrence as Performed by the Inmates of Madame Tussaud's" ("Lawrence/Tussaud," 8 November 1968). Over and over, reviewers interpreted the warts-and-all treatment as sheer nastiness. Renata Adler noted "some sort of clash between [Andrews's] special niceness and the attitude the film has toward Lawrence" (*"Star!* Arrives" *New York Times,* 23 October 1968). The differences between Lawrence and Andrews as singers were also too much for the reviewers. Lawrence, wrote *Time*'s critic, "could wander off-key in every bar, yet the song's content remained pure and intense. Andrews is ten times the musician Lawrence was; her voice never varies a hemisemidemiquaver from the written notes." While "Lawrence always suggested a melancholy sensuality, Andrews continually gives the feeling that beneath the lyrics, everything is supercalifragilisticexpialidocious" ("Lawrence/Tussaud").

☆☆☆☆★ *Darling Lili*

Of all of Andrews's films, *Darling Lili* is the one that would be the most offensive to a 1960s sensibility. *Darling Lili* says, "Don't worry, it' only a movie; there's no relation to political or social life here." While American screens in the late 1960s were as overrun by what Vincent Canby called "wretched World War II rehashes" ("Is Hollywood in Hot Water?" *New York Times*, 9 November 1969) as they were by big musicals, World War I by the sixties was a meaningless, remote war that only occasionally made a fit setting for antiwar statements (*Paths of Glory* [1957] or *Oh What a Lovely War* [1969]) or war-is-hell melodramas full of dastardly antiheroes and told from the German point of view (*The Blue Max* [1966]). *Darling Lili* makes Lili Smith/Schmidt a German spy in World War I for no reason except to have some pretext for Julie Andrews to play a woman in the thick of the frontlines. Lili's backstory provides her with an English father and a German mother and thus wavering allegiances. She has no qualms or convictions about betraying the Allies and leaking secrets to the Germans. There are no consequences for her treason and no disgrace. At the end of the film (in its 137-minute original version), after the armistice is indicated by a lightning-quick end-of-the-war montage, Lili reprises the stage number "Whistling in the Dark," which had opened the film. She performs for an English audience, with her beau and his comrades-in-arms all happily reuniting with her backstage.

Darling Lili, therefore, was a museum piece by the time its first cut was put together. Just as *Star!* could have been a hit in 1958, and maybe even in 1965, but not 1968, *Darling Lili* plays stubbornly, as if the sixties and the Vietnam War had never occurred. The Great War of *Darling Lili* is just slightly more real than the Snoopy and the Red Baron subplot popular in *Peanuts*; the movie's World War I is a series of tropes, props, and costumes designed to deny war. Even the casting of Rock Hudson as the romantic lead reveals a sensibility from 1959, not 1969: Mata Hari Does *Pillow Talk*.

Lili was in editing for a year and a half before Paramount released it nationally in America on 25 June 1970, a month before its Radio City Music Hall opening. Thus the studio let the $25 million movie play off across the country before the New York critics were turned loose on it. When they were, the reviews were mixed, but the box office returns were not: just three million dollars in rentals. During the interim, Vincent Canby reported that MGM had "scrapped" two planned Julie Andrews musicals. One of these was *She Loves Me*, a 1963 Harnick-Bock show based upon the 1940 MGM film *The Shop around the Corner*. The studio reportedly bought Andrews out of her contract, paying her one million dollars not to make a film. The other was *Say It with Music*, a songbook musical tribute to Irving Berlin, originally planned as the last hurrah of producer Arthur Freed, later passed to Andrews and Edwards. Three days after Canby's report appeared, Andrews and Edwards were married, on 12 November 1969.

★★★★★ A Star Tripped

In the 1970s Andrews's career was subjected to plenty of postmortems. Had she been overexposed? (Chris Chase, "Julie Andrews Fights Back," *McCall's*, May 1973). Perhaps, but eight films in six years really is not excessive for a major star of any era, and may be rather typical. Julie Andrews protested, "I just tried to pick nice roles" (Windeler 172). In his 2009 book on Blake Edwards, Sam Wasson writes, "Audiences obviously were not ready to see [Andrews] spending time in the shower [or] going to bed with leading men. . . . Nor were they even ready to think of her re-married. Both on screen and off, her changing image was at odds with the chaste maternal icon the world desperately wanted intact. 'I guess everybody felt Mary Poppins was getting soiled or something,' [Edwards] remembers."

Later in the same paragraph, however, Wasson declares, "Well aware that Andrews' wholesome-nanny image was incompatible with the new America, the studios promptly erased her from production" (157). So, which is it? Does "the world desperately want" the "chaste maternal icon intact," or is that icon "incompatible with the new America"? The former derives from the concept of the star persona, which can be varied only in the right role, and only when the public has been carefully prepared, while the latter is specific to the new reality of the late 1960s. A harbinger of the changing realities that would affect movies along with most other aspects of culture appeared to Andrews when location shooting of *Darling Lili* was forced to move from Paris to Brussels after the production became caught up in the general strike of France. This brush with "May 1968," the immense implications of which dwarfed the production problems of a fanciful Hollywood movie, might have been symbolic of the changed world that would soon confront Andrews and the rest of Old Hollywood. A third viewpoint sees the radiant performer Julie Andrews whose talent and ebullience have escaped the sixties, as subsequent generations have grown up seeing *Mary Poppins* and *The Sound of Music* on television and home video, and even *Thoroughly Modern Millie* was well enough recalled to inspire a hit 2002 Broadway version with a mostly new score. Andrews, ironically, is as well or better remembered than many actors with far more successful careers.

NOTES

1. Streisand's first three films, unlike Andrews's, were all musicals. Also, unlike Andrews she got to re-create the Broadway role that established her in the first place. That role, in *Funny Girl* (1968), made her, like Andrews, an Academy Award winner with her debut film (see Bingham chap. 13, "Barbra and Julie at the Dawning of the Age of Aquarius").

2. In 1990, the film was restored to its 189-minute length for an MGM/UA laser disc; I saw a 35 millimeter print of this version at the Ohio Theater Summer Movie Series in Columbus in 2001, and it also was issued in 1996 on VHS. However, when the company in 2005 released a DVD that turned out to be the 161-minute cut, fans of the film were dismayed, given the lengths to which the restoration team had gone to reassemble a film thought to have been lost (Erickson). Ironically, MGM/UA has done film scholars a favor, however, for at least we can compare the two versions.

8 ★★★★★★★★★★★

Sidney Poitier
It Is No Great Joy to Be a Symbol

ARTHUR KNIGHT

By the end of the 1960s, Sidney Poitier—the second African American to be nominated for a major acting Academy Award (1959); the first African American to win a Best Actor Oscar (1964); the first African American to be ranked the top U.S. box office draw (1967); in short, the first black movie star—had become an icon. But he was an icon given deeply divergent meaning, depending on the perspective of the beholder. In one view, he was an icon of American individual possibility and the possibility of a more equal and just, integrated United States. In another view, though, he was an icon of restriction and constraint, not just the first black movie star but still, as the decade closed, the *only* black movie star, "SuperSidney," a "showcase nigger" (Bogle 183; Clifford Mason, "Why Does

Courtesy Photofest.

White America Love Sidney Poitier So?" *New York Times,* 10 September 1967, 1D, 21D).[1]

The first perspective remains the popular and official one into our present. Poitier's post-sixties activities bolstered this view; for example, in the 1970s he directed and performed in a series of comedies in which his straight man burnished the stardom of Bill Cosby, and in the 1990s he portrayed civil rights giants Thurgood Marshall and Nelson Mandela in television miniseries. And this perspective has been certified by a host of awards, including an honorary Academy Award (2002), by hagiographic appearances on "Oprah," and by Poitier's three volumes of autobiographical writing. In the wake of Barack Obama's election to the U.S. presidency, *New York Times* film critics Manohla Dargis and A. O. Scott listed Poitier as first among the "[cinematic] role models who helped expand the possibilities for fictional blacks, and real ones" ("How the Movies Made a President," *New York Times,* 18 January 2009, 9AR).

The second perspective stands as the dominant critical and scholarly one. In 1973, Donald Bogle labeled Poitier "an old [uncle] tom dressed up with modern intelligence and reason" (176), a judgment reiterated through many editions of his seminal book, *Toms, Coons, Mulattoes, Mammies, and Bucks: An Interpretive History of Blacks in American Films.* This estimation distilled several years of criticism of the star, which had built to a notorious peak with Mason's above-cited 1967 article and Larry Neal's "Beware of the Tar Baby" (*New York Times.* 3 August 1969, D13). And this estimation—that the characters and narratives that form the foundation of Poitier's star image were severely limited and have served to restrict African American images in American film—continues to ramify (see Levine, Slane, and Sexton).

The dichotomous readings of Poitier emerge out of the split that developed across the sixties between, broadly speaking, the established, integrationist civil rights movement and the emerging Black Power movement. In the decades since, this split has healed somewhat, but it still informs the history and criticism of representations of race in American film and culture. Because the two readings of Poitier have roots in such an important and fraught episode in U.S. political, social, and cultural history, the epochal but also incomplete civil rights era, they each have aspects that remain convincing. More opportunities for black performers did open up in Hollywood after Poitier. Things changed. *And* the roles Poitier played and the narratives that contained them were limited in ways that continue to the present. Maybe things haven't changed that much.

This essay necessarily rehearses key aspects of the dichotomous readings of Poitier. But it also seeks a way of reframing Poitier's stardom that might enrich or complicate, even as it doesn't unify, the two positions on Poitier, and that is a close attention to Poitier as an actor, the nuances of his performance style and technique and, particularly, his performance of pleasure. It's true that Poitier's characters are generally limited and the stories that contain them are usually sentimental, apolitical, and compromised. It's true that Poitier was shaped by and helped express a historical moment that created significant progress in the United States. But it's also true that one of the things that distinguishes a Hollywood star is a sense, conveyed through the details of performance, and often aided by a persona created outside the confines of his films, of presence beyond character or story, a "presence" that may wriggle slightly, if inevitably only temporarily, free of the history that contains ordinary viewers.

The inspiration for my focus, Poitier's search for joy, and approach, a close attention to the details of performance, comes from two sources. The first is Poitier's critics. Even his most ardent critics praise Poitier as a performer, but neither critics nor champions have examined Poitier's acting in detail. Calvin Hernton, one of Poitier's most articulate early critics, called Poitier a "great" actor (60). Bogle lauds his "talent" (176). Even harsh critics, like Clifford Mason, called Poitier an "excellent" actor (21D). James Baldwin in a careful consideration of Poitier's stardom in the late sixties wrote of him as "beautiful, vivid, and truthful" in even some of his most limiting roles, "somehow escap[ing] the film's framework" ("Sidney Poitier" 51, 58). All these critics also focus their assessments of Poitier around the issue of pleasure. Hernton, for instance, emphasizes how important it was that Poitier "is not an entertainer, not a singer or a comedian or musician. Rather, he is strictly an *actor*" (56). Hernton thus emphasizes that Poitier forgoes many of the conventional and, in the case of blacks given work in Hollywood, stereotypical means for representing pleasure. But Hernton notes (as do many others) that Poitier is not permitted to portray romantic, physical, (hetero)sexual passion, which is an expected pleasure in most Hollywood movies.

My second inspiration is Poitier himself. He clearly took himself seriously as an actor, both in terms of acting as a craft and in terms of acting as a struggle for agency in American filmmaking. He insisted, for instance, on the label *actor* in his first interview with *Ebony* in 1959 (Lerone Bennett Jr., "Hollywood's First Negro Movie Star," *Ebony*, May 1959, 100; see also Funke and Booth). He was also aware from early in his career of the power and the limits of his stardom, and he expressly linked this awareness to pleasure. Here, late in 1962 just as he was about to start filming for the role that would win him an Oscar, he testifies at congressional hearings on "Employment Practices in the Performing Arts": "It is no great joy for me to be the only Negro out there. I am too often used as a symbol and as a reference of how they are making efforts to rectify the disgraceful situation of discriminatory practices in hiring for the film industry" (U.S. Congress 12). Poitier describes himself as doubly bound by his representative status: within the stories of his films, he stands for American racial-social progress. His very presence in Hollywood is supposed to be a manifestation of this. But his isolation—in his movies' stories, in the general Hollywood labor pool, and, emphatically, in the realm of Hollywood stardom—is in profound tension with this understanding of progress. Poitier is "out there" all alone, and for Poitier this dilutes one of the significant values stardom carries for a star and creates for the audience: Joy.

This essay, then, explores in detail how Poitier performed pleasure, or, as often, how he performed a refusal of pleasures that could be construed as stereotypical or demeaning and how he portrayed the *quest* for pleasure, under and through the conundrum of being at once exceptional and representative: The First Black Star.

★★★★★ The Abnormal Normal: An Overview of Poitier's Sixties Films

During the sixties, Poitier appeared in sixteen movies. His roles ranged from an infantry sergeant in the Korean War film *All the Young Men* (1960) at the start of the decade to a black "revolutionary" on the lam in *The Lost Man* (1969) at its end. In between he played a frustrated working-class everyman in the adaptation of Lorraine Hansberry's play *A Raisin in the Sun* (1961); an expatriate jazz musician who falls in love and decides to return to the United States in *Paris Blues* (1961); a prison psychiatrist recalling his failed efforts to treat a pathological racist in *Pressure Point* (1962); an itinerant handy man pressed into building a chapel for a group of nuns in *Lilies of the Field* (1963); a villainous Moorish king in a period action movie, *The Long Ships* (1964); a reporter assigned to a U.S. Navy sub chaser at the apex of Cold War tension in *The Bedford Incident* (1965); Simone of Cyrene, who helps Christ carry the cross on his way to Calvary, in the star-studded *The Greatest Story Ever Told* (1965); a newspaperman who befriends a blind and, importantly, white girl in *A Patch of Blue* (1965); a graduate student manning a suicide prevention hotline in *The Slender Thread* (1965); a horse dealer, gambler, and quick draw in the western *Duel at Diablo* (1966); an unemployed engineer who takes a teaching job in a London school for troubled youth in *To Sir, with Love* (1967); a Philadelphia homicide detective pressed into helping solve a murder when he gets trapped in a small southern town in *In the Heat of the Night* (1967); an impressively accomplished doctor and the suitor to the daughter of an eminent, and white, liberal family in *Guess Who's Coming to Dinner* (1967); and a hustling trucking company owner cornered into dating a black maid, whom he then falls for, in *For Love of Ivy* (1968).

It's important to see Poitier's catalogue of roles in this distilled form for several reasons. First, the sheer number of roles Poitier played was unprecedented for an African American actor. The black performers who preceded or were contemporary with him as potential movie stars—performers like Lena Horne, Dorothy Dandridge (the first African American to be nominated for a major acting Oscar in 1954), or Harry Belafonte in the forties and fifties or Brock Peters or Sammy Davis Jr. in the sixties—all did considerably less work. Only monumental character actors of the thirties and forties like Louise Beavers or Hattie McDaniel (the first African American to win an Academy Award, for best supporting actress in 1939 for *Gone with the Wind*) worked more regularly than Poitier. And none of these performers were movie stars, performers who had lead roles in films the Hollywood studios were confident would draw large audiences; who, thus, were offered consistent, headlining work; who had roles crafted with them in mind; who won critical attention and professional recognition; and who developed an image that exceeded their individual films and became a subject of national, even international, fascination. Second, while such regular movie work was unusual for black actors, it was ordinary for white actors. Male stars in Poitier's generational cohort like Marlon Brando, Paul Newman, Peter O'Toole, and Jack Lemmon did similar amounts of work during the decade. Finally, in contrast to his African American predecessors and peers but again more like his white peers, Poitier played a variety of roles, including several, most pointedly in *The Bedford Incident*, *A Slender Thread*, and *Duel at Diablo*, in which race went unmentioned and unnoticed in the worlds represented in the films. And most often Poitier's characters inhabit worlds presented as ordinarily (though not unproblematically) multiracial, rather than as all-black, which had been the commonplace Hollywood framework for previous potential black stars.

All these features of Poitier's sixties career support the progressive, integrationist reading of his stardom. At the same time, many of these same features of the Poitier catalogue supply evidence for the critical view of the star. While no one complained of the frequency with which he was employed, for many Poitier critics the "range" of his roles was more putative than actual. Restricting this range are the facts that Poitier is so often

ne helper of whites and that he is so often isolated from other African
Americans. As troubling for his critics was that Poitier is so often placed in
relationships with white women that either hold no possibility for heterosexual romance (the nuns in *Lilies of the Field*) or where the possibility is
titillatingly dallied with but then restricted or qualified. For example, in *A
Patch of Blue* Poitier's character sends the white girl to a school for the blind,
despite their attraction to one another. In *To Sir, with Love* his character
fends off a flirtatious student but, less explicably, also the overtures of a
fellow teacher. Perhaps most famously, in *Guess Who's Coming to Dinner*, a
passionate courtship is signified through one brief kiss. Perhaps most
bizarrely, in *The Long Ships*, Poitier's character vows celibacy until he has
achieved an extremely difficult goal, thus chilling all the scenes with his
wife and the other women he encounters, all of whom would have signified as white to audiences in 1964, and leaving the rather steamy, and
campy, romantic field to his Norse enemy. And most finally, in *The Lost Man*
the relationship he develops with a white social worker trying to help him
escape ends in a hail of police bullets. In only three films—*A Raisin in the
Sun*, *Paris Blues*, and *For Love of Ivy*—is Poitier allowed a relationship with a
black woman. In the first, the dramatic events of the story mitigate against
the expression of romantic and sexual attachments; in the second, the relationship is almost as chaste as in *Guess Who's Coming to Dinner* and in stark
contrast to the depiction of a parallel relationship between white characters;
only in *For Love of Ivy* does Poitier share some extended love scenes with his
partner, which are still, by the standards of the era, quite restrained.

Emblematic images from *All the Young Men* and *The Lost Man* might best
encapsulate the problems critics see. In the first, Poitier provides a direct
blood transfusion to one of his wounded men, winning the loyalty of his
troops. In the last, Poitier dies holding hands with the white social worker
who has become his lover, again symbolically mingling white and black
blood. Poitier seems virtually always tied to, even defined by, certainly val-
orized by, whites, almost never African Americans.

 **"Masquerading as an African American":
Poitier before Stardom**

In the case of Poitier, however, the phrase African American
requires some careful consideration and compels attention to his pre-stardom
biography. If "African American" is taken to mean a person of some black
African descent born and raised in the United States, then Poitier's status
in relation to this identity is not simple. He was born in Miami in 1927, but

by accident.[2] His parents were farmers from a remote island of the Bahamas who were marketing their produce when baby Sidney arrived prematurely. Consequently, Poitier spent the first fifteen years of his life in the Bahamas—eleven years on Cat Island, with no electricity, cars, or running water, and the next several in a shantytown in the Bahamian capital, Nassau, where he first experienced modern technologies and also had his only year and a half of formal education. In his new urban environment, he also developed a tendency to get in trouble. Concerned for his future, his parents sent him, the only one of their seven children who could emigrate legally to the United States, to live with a relative in Florida.

As he recounts it even in his earliest interviews and profiles, Poitier quickly ran into what he called the "barbed wire" of U.S. racism, which confounded him (see, for example, "Talk with the Star," *Newsweek*, 13 May 1957, 115). The Bahamas were not a utopia of interracial harmony, but Cat Island had been virtually all-black and Nassau, also predominantly black, had offered both all-black neighborhoods and a well-established black middle and professional class. Compared with the legalized Jim Crow racism of the U.S. South, the daily racial order of the Bahamas could be experienced as fairly benign, especially if a young man stayed out of trouble with the law. Not so in Miami, where Poitier was threatened for unwittingly violating racial codes (for example, making a delivery to the front door of a white home) and was traumatized by police for being in the wrong part of town.

He quickly fled to New York, where he arrived at sixteen, virtually penniless and with no connections. For several years he scraped together a living at menial jobs and then, in a desperate attempt to find work more interesting than washing dishes, he answered an audition call for actors at a Harlem "little theatre," the American Negro Theatre. He had never set foot in a theater and was laughed out of the room for his thick accent and his near illiteracy.

What happened next is the linchpin of the Poitier star story. Here is an account, chosen for its complete ordinariness in the Poitier star text, from a profile in the middlebrow magazine *Coronet*: "Mortified but determined, Poitier invested fourteen dollars in a radio and bought stacks of newspapers and magazines. He taught himself to speak clearly and read well in six months, and successfully passed his second audition" ("Self-made Powerhouse," *Coronet*, July 1959, 14). By this account, which remains consistent from Poitier's first star profiles to his autobiographies, Poitier essentially remade himself. He transformed his Bahamian accent into a U.S. American one. And while he did not become formally educated, he proved himself educable and committed to the idea of being educated. At the same time, he proved himself highly motivated and self-reliant, qualities with an American lineage running back through the autobiographies of Frederick Douglass and the slave narratives to Benjamin Franklin's autobiography and tutelary works. Through its ritual repetition in Poitier's star profile, this episode would become central to Poitier's persona and attraction as a star.

These qualities, however, didn't just get revealed in interviews and profiles. They also informed many of the characters Poitier played, from Walter Lee Younger in *A Raisin the in the Sun*, a man desperately looking to escape a life of menial labor, to John Prentice in *Guess Who's Coming to Dinner*, a man from humble origins who has become a doctor of world renown; from Homer Smith in *Lilies of the Field*, an itinerant carpenter striving to leave his mark on the world, to Jack Parks in *For Love of Ivy*, a scrappy hustler committed to going straight and making good. Even in roles where self-reliance and educability are not a manifest part of Poitier's character, we can see, or rather *hear*, them in his unique way of speaking, which might be best described as accentedly unaccented. When Poitier's Gordon Ralphe first meets Selina D'Arcy, the blind protagonist of *A Patch of Blue*, she says, "You sound like the radio." This reflexive comment is at once accurate and insufficient: Gordon speaks more standard and normatively accented American English than Selina, but Poitier's voice is not a standard radio voice. It is a distinctive combination of painstaking enunciation and rhythms that swerve from stately and formal to lilting, all shaded lightly by traces of Poitier's Bahamian accent. In short, Poitier sounds more American—in a continental and cosmopolitan sense—than most "Americans." He also does not sound typically, in Hollywood terms of his era, African American.

These sketches of Poitier's sixties work shouldn't be taken to suggest that his episode of self-education immediately catapulted him to stardom. With several lucky breaks Poitier did move in a couple of years from the school of the American Negro Theatre to touring with an all-black professional theater. But when that initial surge ended, work came in fits and starts. Another break came when he was cast in an important role in a Hollywood social problem film, *No Way Out* (1950), where he won favorable notice playing a young doctor treating a racist sociopath. But at this moment in the early fifties, there was no "natural" next step for a black actor who didn't sing or dance and couldn't or wouldn't be stereotypically comic. While white performers of similar age—a Marlon Brando, Paul Newman, or Rod Steiger—could find many opportunities to work on stage, in TV dramas, and film, and could sometimes gain notice, like Brando or Newman, very quickly, Poitier struggled to patch together modest movie roles, with occasional day labor thrown in, through the early and middle fifties.

These struggles had two important effects on Poitier. They kept him in New York City, where he grew increasingly familiar with the many black artists and activists who were playing important roles in organizing the developing civil rights movement. And his struggles to work, along with the connections he made, encouraged Poitier be activist himself, leading him, for example, to push the actors' union to agitate for more roles for African Americans.

As Poitier rose to stardom at the end of the decade, however, his struggles to find work and especially the effects they had on his political formation were glossed over in star profiles in favor of the story of self-transformation and rapid rise. In part this elision was necessary for political reasons: many black artists were avowed leftists and suffered terribly from the anticommunist Blacklist of the forties and fifties. An African American performer who proudly and publicly claimed his connection with, for example, the pro- (or at least not anti-) Soviet artist-activist Paul Robeson simply could not become a star, or even a minor mainstream presence, in the United States. Consequently, Poitier did not advertise such connections, even though he had them. And, importantly, he did not disavow them.

But this elision was also necessary for maintaining the myth of the star as, first and foremost, an individual whose unique qualities account wholly for his success, a myth that's vital to supporting the idea that the United States is fundamentally a meritocracy. Poitier's obscured grounding in the community of African American activists and artists and his construction as, and struggles with being, exceptionally representative are crucial for understanding the divergent views of his stardom's meanings in the 1960s and beyond. However, Poitier's complex dis/connection from this artistic community shouldn't only be analyzed in terms of the politics of the forties, fifties, and sixties. Poitier's personal formation—his rural upbringing, his Bahamian-ness, his self-education—also played a role, keeping him aslant, in ways both voluntary and involuntary, black *U.S.* America. Caribbean transplants had a long history in New York, but they were also viewed with some suspicion by U.S. African Americans. Critic Nelson George (who supplies the title for this section), recalling his adoration of Poitier during his 1960s Brooklyn boyhood, captures this vividly: "I'd never known Sidney was . . . West Indian when I'd first seen his work and, very likely, it would have negatively affected my view of him. . . . I'd always viewed [the Caribbean's] transplanted natives as snobby, snotty, and uppity, based on my own experiences. . . . There was real tension between us and them, skin color be damned" (George 17). For his part, Poitier saw his work in relation to the developing struggle for civil rights. In his first national profile piece in the late fifties, he made this clear: "I am a Negro. For this reason, I try to do and say nothing that might be a step backward. I believe in integration, though I'd rather call it equality of opportunity" ("Talk with the Star," *Newsweek*, 13 May 1957, 115). At the same time, perhaps based on spending his first decade as a subsistence farmer, Poitier—while never ignorant of his great luck and the help he had received—also clearly saw his work as, importantly and finally, *his*, and he insisted that it be framed by considerations of his individuality.

By the late fifties, Poitier was working regularly enough to make a middle-class living as a movie actor, but he was a journeyman. His presence and availability was both supported by and shaped the roles Hollywood producers could imagine for him. Consistently, and following an American tradition that goes back at least to *Moby Dick*'s Ishmael and Queequeg and *The Adventures of Huckleberry Finn*'s Huck and Jim, they imagined roles for him that paired Poitier with white men. In *No Way Out*, the black/white pairing had centered on white racial hatred so deep it could only be stopped, and it's not clear for how long, through the near-mortal wounding of the white antagonist. But as the civil rights movement rose into national consciousness with the Supreme Court's 1954 *Brown v. Board of Education* decision, the 1955–56 Montgomery, Alabama, bus boycott, and the federal government's 1957 intervention in desegregating the schools of Little Rock, Arkansas, Hollywood began to reimagine the black/white pairing allowing a narrative of struggle toward dramatic reconciliation. The apotheosis of this reimagining was the film that finally secured Poitier's stardom in 1958, *The Defiant Ones*.

Poitier and Tony Curtis (in 1958, the established star of the movie) play convicts who escape when a prison transport bus crashes. Curtis is a racist and Poitier has little trust in or patience for whites. However, the pair are shackled together, so although they have escaped prison they cannot escape one another. Forced to cooperate, they begin to bond through a series of misadventures until they finally find a haven with a white woman and are able to remove their shackle. Exhausted by their journey, Curtis falls into a fevered sleep, and the woman convinces Poitier to leave. When he awakens, Curtis discovers the woman has sent Poitier into a trap. Enraged by her villainy, Curtis chases after Poitier and finds him jumping a freight train, with a posse in hot pursuit. Poitier calls Curtis to join him and Curtis tries, reaching up to grasp Poitier's outstretched hand. But in his weakened state, Curtis can't hold on and falls, tumbling down an embankment. Poitier pauses a moment, and then leaps from the train to join his injured friend, whom he cradles in his arms and sings to as the posse closes in and the movie ends.

Poitier's work in *The Defiant Ones* earned him an Oscar nomination for Best Actor. He did not win, but the film's success made it clear that Poitier's name above the title could sell. He could draw white as well as black patrons. He could be a star. But already the complexity of his nascent stardom was manifest to African American audiences. James Baldwin saw *The Defiant Ones* twice. In downtown New York, the predominantly white audience members "were much relieved and joyful" by the film's end. In Harlem, the audience yelled at Poitier, "Get back on the train, you fool!" "That didn't mean," Baldwin insists, "that they hated Sidney: They just weren't going for the okey-doke. And if I point out that they were right, it doesn't mean that Sidney was wrong. That film was made to say something to white people. There was nothing it *could* say to black people—except for the authority of Sidney's performance" (Baldwin, "Sidney Poitier" 58).

★★★★★ Serious Sidney: Performing No Joy

In the first of many features that would appear in *Ebony* on Poitier and his films, Lerone Bennett Jr. worked to sum up Poitier's acting skills:

> With the flick of an eye, he can convey contempt, anguish, glee, or hatred. His round, handsome face can be naïve and trusting, sullen and savage. His voice, a magnificent instrument that has been compared with the organ-like perfection of Paul Robeson's *Othello*, can mumble and gurgle, caress and coo, sparkle or spit fire.
>
> ("Hollywood's First Negro Movie Star," *Ebony*, May 1959, 100)

Besides noting that Poitier was "good to look at, tall, regal and self-possessed," as would be expected of a "matinee idol," though one who "wears [his hair] *au naturel* in the African style" (100), Bennett also called on outside experts. Stanley Kramer, who had directed Poitier in *The Defiant Ones* and would go on to work with him in *Pressure Point* and *Guess Who's Coming to Dinner*, compared Poitier's range to Brando's: "He can be a pathetic and pitiful character, and he can go instantly to moments of overwhelming, savage emotional power" (100). Actress Ruby Dee, who appeared with Poitier in four films in the fifties and was, when Bennett was writing, with him on stage in *A Raisin in the Sun*, likened her colleague to a "panther": "He has a discipline that looks like a lack of discipline. A controlled freedom . . . something like tamed passion. He has a calm kind of violence" (102).

All these distillations of Poitier's acting tend toward the severe. Bennett's first sentence seems to set the ratio: three parts contempt, anguish, and hatred to one part glee. On the one hand, this simply reiterates the conventions associated with serious acting. As Stanley Kramer suggests, Brando might have been described in similar terms. On the other hand, this tendency toward severity reveals the constraints Poitier worked under in his bid for stardom as an actor rather than an entertainer. Brando could play Sky Masterson in *Guys and Dolls* (1955) without dimming his reputation for intensity. For Poitier comedy, lightheartedness, and pleasure were fraught territory, liable to call to mind "the standard [Hollywood] procedure for handling black personalities, the Negro Entertainment Syndrome" (Bogle 188). In fact, even as Bennett was asserting that "[Poitier] does not dance or sing," Poitier was onscreen singing (badly) in *The Defiant Ones* and (dubbed) in the all-black cast musical *Porgy and Bess* (1959). In short, Poitier couldn't just *be* serious as a black star, and then choose to be funny or light. He had to make and claim space for an African American to perform seriousness in Hollywood.

Amongst Poitier's sixties films, *All the Young Men, Paris Blues, Pressure Point, The Long Ships, The Bedford Incident, The Slender Thread,* and *The Lost Man* have Poitier performing undiluted seriousness. Collectively they show both the attractions of this mode of characterization as well as its limits. In these films, Poitier's performance is predominantly reserved and impassive, conveying the authority and dignity of his character. For example, in *Pressure Point* and *The Bedford Incident,* he is a professional observer (a journalist, a psychiatrist) whose work requires objectivity, and Poitier portrays this by crafting a steady, unsmiling demeanor. This demeanor at once contrasts with the unstable subject he is observing; grounds his characters' dignity, as he avoids clashing with his intentionally provocative foils; and, finally, makes the moments when he does "emotionally explode" or "shout back" (Bogle 179), which he does at the climax of each story, both abrupt but also controlled and never physically violent, further emphasizing Poitier's characters' dignity. In most of these films, there is a distinct sense that Poitier's characters are being tested, both as individual men and in racial terms. These characters are apprentices (a sergeant thrust into a leadership position; a psychiatric intern) who must display authority to earn (further) authority, but Poitier's race makes the apprenticeship novel. Under these circumstances, Poitier's comparative impassivity becomes a drama all its own: What, the spectator is encouraged to wonder, must he be suppressing? Even as his features remain still, did I see the hint of anger (and more than a hint would seem justified) in his hooded gaze, the trace of tension in his brow?

None of Poitier's performances in these films were esteemed at the time or are now recalled as his best, perhaps because the pattern they imposed was too restrictive and Poitier couldn't finally act his way out of, or through, it. In *Paris Blues*, where he plays a jazz musician and arranger against Paul Newman's driven musician-composer, Poitier's "shout back" comes early and the stakes are low; Newman's character is absurdly demanding, but he's not questioning Poitier's musicianship or being a racist. After this, Poitier's performance settles into a stable sobriety, admirable for combating stereotypes of black jazz musicians as dissolute but less interesting when it undermines the potential pleasures of the romance Poitier has with Diahann Carroll's character. *The Long Ships* and *The Lost Man* are still more problematic. In *The Long Ships*, Poitier is a tyrannical king, but his seriousness, which is given form in several physical outbursts, seems simply fretful. Since Richard Widmark, the story's hero, chose a performance style that winks at the absurdities of a silly period adventure story, Poitier ends up looking stuck. And in an important way, he was. For Poitier, and for *Ebony*, which hailed him, pictured in costume as Sheik Ali Manush, as "actor of the year" on its cover, this role was a "break-through" for allowing a "Negro to be given a [major] villainous part" ("Top Actor of the Year," *Ebony*, March 1964, 4). In Poitier's estimation, this opportunity had to be taken in earnest. In *The Lost Man*, Poitier plays a black activist who has decided to forgo non-violence in favor of robbing factory payrolls to support vaguely outlined revolutionary activity. The film opens with a long passage of crosscutting between a smiling young boy and a sternly stone-faced Poitier, who proves utterly immune to the child's attempts to charm him. Even as the robbery he plans goes awry and each of his potential escape routes is blocked, Poitier remains unwaveringly cool and interior, giving a sense that he is nearly as hemmed in by his own self-policing affect as he is by the cops.

Poitier's ongoing struggle to perform seriousness would appear plainly misguided, if it weren't for *In the Heat of the Night*, the one undisputed success he had in pursuing this mode. The movie was one of the three hits that contributed to Poitier's becoming the nation's leading box office attraction in 1967–68,[3] and while Poitier received no awards for the film, *In the Heat of the Night* was nominated for seven Academy Awards and won five, including Best Actor for Poitier's co-star, Rod Steiger, and Best Picture, helping to make it the most canonical of Poitier's films. Poitier would reprise his character from *In the Heat of the Night* in two early seventies films—the first attempt to create a cinematic "franchise" featuring a black star.

Much of the power of Poitier's performance in *In the Heat of the Night* is distilled in his delivery of one crucial line: "They call me *Mister* Tibbs." In the film's story, Poitier plays a Philadelphia homicide detective, Virgil Tibbs, detained on suspicion of murder when he is found in the middle of the night at the train station in Sparta, Mississippi. It's quickly established that the sheriff, Bill Gillespie (Rod Steiger), and his men are both unsophisticated at police work and racist, but a background check on Tibbs confirms his profession and his story that he was changing trains while making his way back north from visiting his mother. Having missed his train, Tibbs agrees reluctantly to examine the victim's body, and his forensic skills immediately exonerate a white suspect who was arrested after Tibbs. Through this opening section of the film, Poitier portrays Tibbs as coolly wary; attuned to the dangerous situation he has found himself in, he carefully controls both his voice and his body. Once his credentials are established, he allows some heat into his vocal performance, but he remains a paragon of confident restraint, assuming cooperation—from morgue workers, from the white suspect—with the unspoken force of a demand. However, Tibbs's quick dismantling of Gillespie's next suspect prompts the sheriff to attempt to remind Tibbs where he is and who's in charge. Gillespie drawls, with his voice rising and accelerating in anger, "Well, you're pretty sure of yourself, ain't you, Virgil? 'Virgil.' That's a pretty funny name for a nigger boy that comes from Philadelphia! What d'they call you up there?" Poitier's Tibbs, who was initially almost conciliatory in his presentation of the counter-evidence, pauses, narrows his eyes slightly, and delivers his famous line with heightened volume (though it matches rather than tops Steiger's), even tone, hyper-clear enunciation, and the slightest catch between "me" and "mister" to emphasize the latter word. Gillespie immediately tops Tibbs in volume and speed, demanding his deputy deliver Tibbs to the station, and Tibbs as quickly returns to his cool demeanor from earlier in the film, though now with a hint of hauteur—almost a smile—and says he will send the evidence he has gathered to the FBI. This drives Gillespie to a higher pitch, still, and he lunges for the box Tibbs holds. Tibbs barely flinches, gripping the box firmly, and repeats, nearly in a whisper, his resolve to send the evidence to the FBI. Gillespie has Tibbs locked up for withholding evidence, putting him literally under his charge, but now there is no doubt in the viewer's mind who should be, and in a just world would be, in control.

In many ways the increasingly tangled story of *In the Heat of the Night* is absurd, but it did give Poitier a framework for modulating his performance of essential seriousness that none of his other films had. Three moments in the film are vital for this process. The first comes when Tibbs and Gillespie are visiting Endicott, a wealthy and powerful planter Tibbs suspects may be connected to the murder. Tibbs engages Endicott in conversation about his hobby of growing orchids, using an interested tone of voice and even some encouraging half-smiles as he also probes the materials of the greenhouse

In successive shots from *In the Heat of the Night* (1967), his most successful performance of seriousness, Poitier's Virgil Tibbs first angrily demands respect from and then displays contempt for the southern sheriff who is trying to intimidate him. (Digital frame enlargements)

for evidence. Finally, Endicott asks why they've come, and Tibbs explains carefully, even hesitatingly, in deference to Endicott's position in the community as well as his unreconstructed racism, that they wanted to question him. Shocked by the presumption, Endicott slaps Tibbs. Tibbs *immediately* slaps him back. The choreography of this exchange of blows, covered in one shot, makes it clear that Tibbs doesn't hesitate, not even a full second, in his action. Tibbs's demeanor, which returns as immediately to his resolute cool erasing any trace of his earlier strategic warmth and deference, also conveys that this action was intended, not reflex. Later, Gillespie has Tibbs to his apartment. Gillespie talks of his loneliness, and Tibbs commiserates, offering up his first full-fledged smile in the movie, but when Tibbs goes too far, comparing himself to Gillespie, Gillespie taunts him—"Now don't get smart, black boy"—and Tibbs restores his mask of cool seriousness, returning, it seems, to his self-presentation from the start of the film. This operation is reversed at the very end of the film, when, after Tibbs has found the killer, Gillespie deposits him at his train. Initially their parting is prompt and taciturn: a handshake and a "bye-bye," and the two men go their separate ways. But then Gillespie turns back and calls out, "Virgil." Tibbs is almost through the door of the train, but hearing the call, he reverses course by a step, coming back into view. Gillespie says quietly, and with a small smile on the last words, "You take care. Ya hear?" Tibbs equally quietly says, "Yeah," and then smiles fully and launches himself with vigor onto the train, leaving Gillespie to wander down the platform. At last, the pleasure of full communication is reached, and then sundered.

Analyzing this scene, James Baldwin saw it as "a fade-out kiss" that "gave me the impression, according to my notes the day I saw it, of 'something strangling, alive, struggling to get out.'" Baldwin argues that what is conveyed here is that "it is a terrible thing, simply, to be trapped in one's history, and attempt, at the same time . . . to accept, deny, reject, and redeem it—and, also, and on whatever level, to profit from it." He applauds the struggle presented by the "choked," "moving," yet "rigid" performances of Steiger and Poitier, but also believes that, in the end, "white Americans have been encouraged to continue dreaming, and black Americans have been alerted to the necessity of waking up" (*Devil* 67–69). Even at its very best and carefully modulated, the resolute performance of seriousness could only go so far.

★★★★★ "With the Flick of an Eye, He Can Convey...Glee": Poitier Performs Pleasure

Poitier may remain best remembered for the seriousness that in some ways trapped him as a star in the sixties, but it was not his only mode. Seriousness—dignity, certainly—was a component in every role he performed, but in a number of his roles throughout the decade he used his sobriety as a foundation from which to launch performances of pleasure and even joy. Poitier's carefully patterned performance in *In the Heat of the Night* has some commonalities with these other performances. As in that film, he usually extends from his seriousness to give a sense that the pleasure he displays is *earned*, but in *A Raisin in the Sun, Lilies of the Field, To Sir,*

With Love, *Guess Who's Coming to Dinner*, and *For Love of Ivy*, he plays with the ratio of pleasure to seriousness, often reframing the Poitier persona to suggest something like serious lightheartedness.

The inclusion of *A Raisin in the Sun* on this list may seem surprising. It takes up the painful topics of a black family's struggle to hold itself together in the face of economic hardship, racism, and the individual family members' overlapping senses of being isolated from and entrapped by one another. The story has two main conflicts. The first is over what to do with a $10,000 inheritance the family receives; the second is over what to do once most of the money has been swindled. Poitier's character, Walter Lee Younger, is pivotal to both conflicts, and they allow him to enact a trajectory that runs from anger and bitterness to elation, abjection to an earned and complex joy. The film was an adaptation by African American playwright Lorraine Hansberry of her successful, and at the time unprecedented, Broadway play. Poitier had originated the role of Walter Lee on the stage in 1959–60, certifying his developing film stardom with a demonstration of his stage skills, and the film allowed him to reprise this most actorly role. It also gave him his only role in the sixties fully conceived by an African American writer.

Through the first two-thirds of the film, Poitier's Walter Lee is sullen and irritable, even mean, and finally despondent. He feels trapped in his dead-end job, and he wants his mother to allow him to use the insurance payment from his father's death to partner with some friends in a liquor store. She refuses and instead spends $3,500 on the down payment for a house in a white neighborhood. At the start of the story, Poitier portrays Walter's emotions viscerally, with abrupt flashes of anger sweeping his face, a raised, clipped voice, and rapid, expansive gestures that claim considerable space in the two-room flat the family shares. But as his mother remains obdurate, Walter becomes increasingly affectless until, when Mama announces the purchase of the house, he seems to implode, reclining full-length in a chair and, when he rises, shuffling out, headed to the tavern. Seeing her son so defeated, Mama reverses herself and puts Walter Lee in charge of the remaining funds, and over the course of three successive scenes, Poitier lights Walter up. First, he reflects intently on his new situation, nearly blank-faced, looking inward; then, when the family visits the house they're buying, he gains confidence, smiling, and returning to his expansive gestures but now with fluid ebullience rather than barely contained jagged rage; and finally, as the family packs, he arrives home bursting with happy energy, leaping over crates, dancing with his wife, good-naturedly teasing his sister, and making all of these actions flow into one another.

In short order, however, the second conflict looms, leading to the destruction and revision of Poitier's performance of pleasure. A white man, Mr. Lindner, from the family's new neighborhood association, arrives and attempts—in the name of neighborliness and race relations—to buy them out. Poitier slowly, reluctantly dims Walter's smile as he comes to understand the offer, and then after Walter dismisses the offer, he slowly, somewhat hesitantly restores it. But then Walter discovers that the family money he has invested has been stolen by one of his partners. He descends into a panicked self-loathing and decides to call Lindner back and "put on a show" for him, which he rehearses, getting down on his knees and weeping, before his horrified mother, wife, and sister. When Lindner returns, Walter finds he can't perform his abjection and instead holds firm. Poitier keeps his voice level, accelerating only when Lindner tries to interrupt and drawing out his words at other times to give himself time to think; he begins the scene rocking back and forth and avoiding eye contact, but to create the sense of Walter's mounting courage, Poitier gets gradually stiller. When he is done, Poitier stands perfectly still and straight for several moments, letting the other performers swirl around him, a reversal of the dominant pattern in the rest of the film. Then he reenergizes Walter for his final moments onscreen, but with a calmer, quieter force that seems more secure than the quicksilver happiness we witnessed earlier. Mama describes Walter's revised anti-show as "kind of like a rainbow after the rain," and Poitier's multifaceted performance in the last third of the film warrants this description.

None of the rest of Poitier's sixties performances of joy have quite the same range as his Walter Lee, perhaps because none of his other roles asked him to risk Walter Lee's anger and meanness as an addition to, or detour from, his performances of seriousness and struggling toward joy. Still, *Lilies of the Field, To Sir, with Love, Guess Who's Coming to Dinner*, and *For Love of Ivy* were four of Poitier's most successful films: He won his Academy Award for *Lilies, To Sir* and *Guess Who* joined *In the Heat of the Night* to make his big box-office trio, and *Ivy*, his last commercial success of the decade, was also the first in which he took a direct creative hand, writing the story on which it is based. And within the narrower affective range they develop, all rely on Poitier's insistence on grasping for pleasure.

Lilies is the most overtly comic of the films, but it relies on Poitier's ability to portray a character who changes from an apparently carefree drifter ("People gotta have some joy in livin'") to a man with a mission imposed upon him to a man who accepts the mission as his own (and then must accept the help of others) and, finally, to a man who can be free, not drifting. Homer Smith, who stops in the desert for water for his car, is pressed into service building a chapel for a small order of East German refugee nuns. The commanding mother superior keeps Homer on the hook by not paying him ("Slavery time is over," he insists) and instead giving him the possibility of building something of his own. In many ways, Poitier's performance here is a variation on the final third of *A Raisin in the Sun*: he enters the film happy but not genuinely under his own control, and here he comes as close as he ever would to Bogle's "Negro Entertainer Syndrome"; he gives the nuns goofy English lessons, moving from standard English to a marked "black" English—"Ah stands up, y'all"—and later he sings the film's theme song, "Amen." At the mid-point of the film, though, Poitier's Homer has had enough and gives a flash of Virgil Tibbs: "Get yourself another boy," he seethes. In the second half of the film, Poitier rebuilds Homer's joy, but as in *Raisin*, he alters his performance signs: his smile is moderated, his gestures calmer, and his voice and speaking style calm and carefully enunciated (no more "black" English), to give a sense of depth to this joy.

Poitier's performances of joy in the other three films—the pleasure of reaching his students and finding a vocation in *To Sir*; the pleasure of gaining his and his fiancée's parents' approval, as well as discovering his resolve even if they don't approve, in *Guess Who*; the pleasure of finding love in *Ivy*—are more straightforward, more conventional, and less compellingly patterned than in *Raisin* and *Lilies*. But all share an important quality that makes Poitier's performances in these films particularly winning, and particularly "star-like": They allow Poitier to play with a version of his "self" or, more accurately, a piece of the star persona that was well known by the late sixties. In *Guess Who's Coming to Dinner*, Poitier essentially gets to play the Poitier of the present, an unquestionable American movie star who has earned his place onscreen with Hollywood institutions Katharine Hepburn and Spencer Tracy. It's true that Poitier's character, John Prentice, is a medical doctor rather than an actor, but he is a medical doctor of such world renown that his jet-setting life suggests celebrity. Because the outcome of the story cannot be seriously in doubt (would Hepburn and Tracy deny love or countermand the U.S. Supreme Court, which had declared state laws banning interracial marriage unconstitutional while the film was being shot?), Poitier modulates his performance in smaller units than in many of his other films, moving frequently from happiness to sobriety and back within a scene. Often Poitier shows Prentice attempting to suppress or check his pleasure out of respect for what others feel is the seriousness of the situation, and failing. His smile and his confidence break through despite—though, of course, really *because of*—himself. The best example of

In *Guess Who's Coming to Dinner?* (1967), Poitier's Dr. John Prentice is lighthearted in the face of questions from his prospective father-in-law (Spencer Tracy) about how he expects his and his fiancée's biracial children to fare in the world. (Digital frame enlargement)

this comes during John's first conversation with Mr. Drayton, Tracy's character. Drayton asks if John and his daughter "have given any thought to the problems your children will have?" John assures him, soberly, that they have, but as he continues to recount his fiancée's thoughts he begins smiling broadly, "She feels that every single one of our children will be President of the United States, and they'll all have colorful administrations." Seeing that Drayton doesn't seem inclined to laugh with him, John again turns briefly sober, but in response to Drayton's next question, he again brightens: "Frankly, I think your daughter's a bit optimistic—[here Poitier almost giggles] I'd settle for secretary of state." Once more Drayton does not rise with him, and John coughs lightly to allow himself to cover his face and control his demeanor. But Poitier has done his work, making plain with his playfulness that while the film's topic is serious, the outcome—and his pleasure *and* the general pleasure of these two families (and the analogy is meant to extend to the audience)—is secure.

The part of himself that Poitier plays in *To Sir* and *Ivy* is both less abstract and, in its way, less immediate that in *Guess Who*. In these two films, Poitier lets his "masquerade as African American," in Nelson George's words, slip and owns his West Indian heritage. The narrative of Poitier's Mark Thackeray winning over and shaping his undisciplined students unfolds as a series of skirmishes. Thackeray carries them all, and the finale (to return to Lerone Bennett's word) a "gleeful" dance that the students hold, celebrating their achievements and their teacher. Thackeray dances with his students—very badly. Poitier smiles beautifully throughout this sequence, perhaps with the pleasure of knowing he can perform a disavowed activity *poorly*, that he has escaped the stereotype of the black entertainer and can be his character, as well as himself, which is to say: Not a dancer, but someone who can have fun dancing. One moment early on in this trajectory is especially important. The students, testing whether they can really ask Thackeray about anything, as he's promised, ask him about his background. The story he tells is much like Poitier's own: he was poor, emigrated to the United States, worked washing dishes and the like. Surprised, they ask how he learned to speak so "posh" and he cracks them up, and himself, with a burst of thick patois. Maintaining the sparkle in his eye and animated countenance, but now overlaid with seriousness, he delivers the lesson: "The point is, if you're prepared to work hard, you can do almost anything. You can get any job you want . . . you can even change your speech, if you want to. "Poitier has his Mark Thackeray consistently return to his sober, teacherly persona throughout the film. In fact, the final images of the movie are Thackeray, who has received an engineering job offer, sitting alone at his desk after an encounter with some new students who clearly need his discipline, tearing up the job letter before getting up and striding purposefully from the room with his serious "game face" on. But his burst of patois and his dancing suggest that joyous *play*—the intentional, pleasurable altering of the representation of the self; even losing "control" of the self, as in some moments in *Guess Who*—can be crucial to an effectively "serious" self.

For Love of Ivy takes up this idea. Poitier's Jack Parks is being blackmailed by the children of a white family who don't want their maid, Ivy, to leave their employ and think a boyfriend might make her happy (the bumbling kids know that in addition to his legitimate trucking business Parks runs a gambling operation, too). Understandably, Parks resents this as does Ivy (Abby Lincoln) when she finds out, and much complication ensues before, in the manner of romantic comedy, all works out. Wha foreordains this ending is that Ivy upon first meeting Parks immediately knows he is from the West Indies, and on being called out, Poitier ha Parks drop his reserved wariness: he tilts his head back slightly, smile broadly, perhaps even a bit rakishly, and laughs from deep in his ches Through all the complications that ensue, this first connection remains Poitier shows Parks finally winning Ivy by dropping his cool and acknow! edging his pleasure, even in just thoughts of her: "I found myself grinnir [here Poitier inserts a suppressed, mildly astonished laugh] a lot, at not!

ing in particular. "The last line of the film, which meshes Parks and Ivy's smiles, is Poitier's: "What have you got against West Indians?" Here Poitier most reflexively plays with his star identity—and under the sign of Hollywood's normative pleasure in heterosexual romance, grabbed now for blacks, who have previously been denied this pleasure in the movies. The line and the moment that contain it are densely significant. One implicit answer to the question, the answer Ivy and the star's fans share, is, "Nothing. We love you. "The question is also a rhetorical rebuke to Poitier's critics, saying, in effect, "You don't know—and you certainly don't own—me. I am not—at least not simply—African American. "And, finally, since the line is delivered in Poitier's painstakingly cultivated "American" voice, the line asserts that Poitier is capacious, multifold, many: A superstar *and* a black star.

★★★★★ Conclusion

Recall James Baldwin's analysis of the ending of *The Defiant Ones*: all that Poitier's leap from the train to succor his white partner left African American audiences was "the authority of Sidney's performance." But the question lingers: How separable was Poitier's authority as a performer from his leap? Throughout the sixties Poitier worked to express what he, and many, felt was the essential seriousness of the times and the seriousness of the opportunity, the responsibility, to at once revise the history of and expand the possibilities of black representations in Hollywood films. At the same time, Poitier looked for ways to present the pleasure that attracted audiences to the movies—that had attracted *him* to the movies when he first saw them in Nassau—and that, in complex ways, attended his quintessentially American success. The task proved at once possible and impossible. He was lauded, his stardom soared, many of his films succeeded, and he secured a place in Hollywood that would allow him not only to perform but also to produce and direct and open further paths for African Americans in the next decade. But he also couldn't change the world, he couldn't create more black stars, and he couldn't figure out how not to be trapped in seriousness or to draw the complexities of the civil rights era into consistent narratives of pleasure. Very likely Sidney Poitier's stardom will always be read in conflicting and contradictory terms. Close attention to his performances shows those very conflicts and contradictions playing, ceaselessly and "in the flick of an eye" or a smile or hand, over the represented body of the first black star as he struggles to find and display joy.

NOTES

1. There was yet another view, which waned as the other two rose but which shouldn't be forgotten: for white supremacists even one black star was one too many, and Poitier was an icon of the decay of the properly white nation (see, for example, "Star Studded Film Glamorizes Interracial Marriages," *Film Comment*, Winter 1969, 30–32, reprinted from *Thunderbolt: The White Man's Viewpoint*, December 1967).

2. My capsule biography of Poitier draws from a range of sources. Two, Aram Goudsouzian's *Sidney Poitier: Man, Actor, Icon* (2004) and Poitier's *This Life* (1980), have been especially helpful and should be consulted by anyone wishing full accounts of the star's life.

3. Top box-office star power is determined by a poll of exhibitors done annually by the Quigley Publishing Company since 1932. Poitier appeared on the list three years in a row, 1967 (number 7), 1968 (1), and 1969 (6). While Poitier's concentrated rise and decline on the Quigley list was not unprecedented, it was, and remains, uncommon for a star to reach the number-one position and then move so quickly off the list never to return.

9 ★★★★★★★★★★★

Brigitte Bardot
From International Star to Fashion Icon

KELLEY CONWAY

Beginning in the mid-1950s, Brigitte Bardot exerted an enormous impact on film, fashion, and celebrity culture, introducing a youthful, sexy image of French femininity to both domestic and international audiences. Among film historians, she is primarily remembered today for two films, *Et Dieu . . . créa la femme* [*And God Created Woman*] (1956), in which her persona of the insolent "sex kitten" first emerged, and Jean-Luc Godard's *Le Mépris* [*Contempt*] (1963), which offers, among other things, a complex and self-conscious treatment of Bardot's appearance and star persona. In between and beyond these two highlights of her career, Bardot appeared in a wide range of mainstream French comedies and melodramas, many of which are unjustifiably neglected by film historians. In melodramas such as

---

Courtesy Photofest.

En cas de malheur [*Love Is My Profession*] (Claude Autant-Lara, 1958) and *La Vérité* [*The Truth*] (Henri-Georges Clouzot, 1960) and in comedies such as *Cettes acrée gamine* [*Naughty Girl*] (Michel Boisrond, 1956), Bardot shows surprising range and appeal. But her importance extends far beyond the actual films in which she appeared—indeed, while films launched her career, she quickly became what would now be called a "multi-platform" celebrity. She is thus a compelling figure of transition in several contexts: she served as a bridge both from one model of femininity to another and as a link from popular to art house culture, and from cinema stardom to fashion icon and public celebrity. Bardot had one foot in 1950s femininity and the other in the sexual revolution: she was the blond, big-busted pin-up girl who ostensibly existed for the pleasure of the male viewer, but she was also the barefoot, sullen "teenager" dressed in blue jeans who connoted adolescent rebellion and attracted female imitators worldwide (Vincendeau *Stars*). Bardot was both a creature of mass-media stardom who gained initial visibility on the covers of French fashion magazines and from the paparazzi photographs taken on the beaches of Cannes, and an object of fascination for intellectuals such as Simone de Beauvoir, Françoise Sagan, François Truffaut, Jean-Luc Godard, and Edgar Morin (Schwartz). She appeared primarily in mainstream commercial films, but she is also considered a generative factor in the rise of the French New Wave, inspiring a new, looser acting style and symbolizing rebellion against an older generation (de Baecque). Although Bardot's importance in the French context has already been well documented, less is known about her international trajectory, specifically her reception in the United States.

A paradox lies at the heart of Bardot's American stardom: she became a hugely important film star in America without ever actually making a film there. She is a French star who influenced profoundly the ways in which Hollywood did business, yet she expended very little energy on public relations there. Long before Bardot became a media sensation in the United States, French actors Maurice Chevalier and Charles Boyer, among others built enduring careers in Hollywood (Danan; Phillips). And, of course, foreign actresses such as Greta Garbo, Marlene Dietrich, and Ingrid Bergman were (and remain) powerful symbols of the Hollywood cinema as a whole But these performers differ from Bardot in that they actually moved to the United States, built and nurtured their public personas, and appeared in English-language films. Bardot did not even visit America until 1965, when she promoted *Viva Maria*. She passed through again in 1966, but only to get married quickly and quietly in Las Vegas to a German "playboy." So, what is the nature of this unlikely "international" stardom? How did it emerge and evolve? How did Bardot acquire such extraordinary visibility in the United States and around the world without taking part in Hollywood's star system?

Bardot's impact on American film culture has already begun to be explored. The success of Bardot's breakthrough film *And God Created Woman* prompted both independent distributors and studios to fund foreign art films by directors such as Jean-Luc Godard, Ingmar Bergman, and Tony Richardson (Balio). Bardot's success also helped spark an expansion in the promotion of popular French film in the United States, resulting in a significant recasting of the relationship between Hollywood and French cinema as one of cooperation rather than competition alone (Schwartz). That Bardot would have the power to incite shifts in the ways in which Hollywood collaborated with foreign production companies and promotion entities reminds us of the importance of actors as causal forces in film history. Bardot's impact on the American film industry is especially startling when one examines more closely her fluctuating reception in the U.S. press.

★★★★★ The Uneven Formation of an Image

Bardot was the object of attention in the American press well before the November 1957 release of *And God Created Woman*. From 1952 to 1957, some twenty articles were published on Bardot between the *Los Angeles Times* and the *New York Times* alone. Typically, the articles are reviews of the early, relatively unremarkable films in which Bardot appeared. Bardot was not a readymade "bombshell" or the "French Marilyn Monroe," as one might have expected from her subsequent image. Instead, the *Los Angeles Times* described her in 1952 as a ballet dancer and thus the likely successor to Leslie Caron (26 October 1952, J20). The reviews for *Doctor at Sea* (Ralph Thomas, 1955), a British comedy, celebrate Bardot's comic abilities and call her "the new Simone Simon" (*New York Times*, 2 March 1956, 17). Instead of the luxurious and intentionally messy blond mane with which Bardot is now associated, she wore her hair short and dark for *Doctor at Sea*. It would take five years and the release of *And God Created Woman* before Bardot's image fully coalesced into the one we recognize today. Once *And God Created Woman* was released in the United States, the press references to ballet and to Bardot's comic abilities fell away in favor of commentary on her extraordinary physical attractiveness and a critique of her acting skills.

In September 1957, two months before *And God Created Woman* was released in America, *Esquire* published an article about Bardot that exemplifies the abrupt change in the language with which Bardot would be

described for the next few years. Bardot is "France's newest love goddess
. . . a pouting, sulking, sensual child-woman, [who] fascinates European
men, including Pablo Picasso" (3 September 1957, 55). The film is "badly
written" and "badly directed" and "badly acted by Bardot," but "after it
opens with a ten-times-life-sized CinemaScope shot . . . of Bardot completely
nude and bottoms up, nobody seems to mind its artistic deficiencies." This
discourse, that Bardot is gorgeous but without talent, will dominate the
subsequent discussion of her film performances.

Bardot so struck Bosley Crowther of the *New York Times* that his writings about her deserve special attention. He disliked *And God Created Woman*,
yet wrote no fewer than three articles about Bardot in the year following
the American release of the film. Bardot, he claimed, a "round and voluptuous little French miss," is "undeniably a creation of superlative crafts-
manship" (22 October 1957, 41). The film, he goes on to assert, is "clumsily
put together," but "she is a thing of mobile contours—a phenomenon you
have to see to believe." Crowther's rhetoric positions Bardot as a kind of
extraordinary, French-made, artisanal product. But she is not the equivalent of an exquisite Hermès bag or a shiny Citroën; she is an extremely sex-
ualized and therefore problematic French export. For Crowther, Bardot
quickly comes to symbolize everything that is wrong with European cinema of the time. In an article published several weeks later concerning a
crop of foreign films in U.S. theaters, Crowther complains that recent foreign films are "obsessed" with sex (*New York Times*, 3 November 1957, 137).
He takes as his primary example *And God Created Woman*, which he calls a
"witless drama that is concerned with nothing but the stimuli of sex." Foreign imports, which include Fellini's 1957 *Le notti di Cabiria* [*Nights of Cabiria*]
and Sacha Guitry's 1953 *La vie d'un honnête homme* [*The Virtuous Scoundrel*],
indicate a "sag in culture" and a "slump in the energies of artists." Crowther
spends a disproportionate amount of time on *And God Created Woman* in the
article and, moreover, his style shifts when he writes of Bardot, falling into
excessive alliteration: "Its story is a tedious little tattle about a vastly voluptuous little dame who lives in a village on the Riviera and makes panting,
pawing monkeys out of them. That's all. "Nine months later, Crowther
again puts Bardot front and center when he criticizes the practice of dubbing foreign films. The bulk of the article consists of a comparison between
the subtitled and the dubbed versions of a comedy in which Bardot starred
called *Une Parisienne* [*La Parisienne*] (Michel Boisrond, 1957). According to
Crowther, in the French-language version of *La Parisienne*, Bardot is "a
symbol of saucy sexiness, breath-taking, at times, in her exposure of purpose as well as just plain flesh, but nonetheless amusing as a purely Galli

grotesque," while in the dubbed, English-language version of the film, "her whole person takes on an aspect of open vulgarity [and] she appears just another little teaser, trying hard to make like Marilyn Monroe" ("Changing Voices: Foreign Films with English Dialogue," *New York Times*, 7 September 1958, X1). Thus, an article whose subject is ostensibly the problems created by the practice of dubbing becomes a backhanded appreciation of Bardot's "Gallic" qualities. Crowther cannot leave Bardot alone, whether to condemn her or to grant her some value as an exemplar of French authenticity.

From the release of *And God Created Woman* in 1956 into the early 1960s, commentary on Bardot's physique dominates her American reception. But there are other, subsidiary, themes in the American press coverage of Bardot, which indicate that journalists were experimenting with different interpretive frameworks for characterizing the actress. One such theme is "the foreign star." In the fall of 1957, Bardot is linked in the *New York Times* with other "queens" of the "foreign Hollywoods," including Italy's Gina Lollabrigida, Germany's Romy Schneider, Spain's Carmen Sevilla, England's Diana Dors, India's Nargis, Greece's Melina Mercouri, and Japan's Fujiko Yamamoto. The article consists primarily of photographs with small captions devoted to each star, but the framing idea is rather interesting: that foreign film industries have their own stars, many of whom are little known in the United States but who are important nonetheless:

> Americans see a few of the movies of these other Hollywoods and know a few of their queens, like Gina Lollobrigida. But most foreign films are shown only within their nation's borders or in lands that speak the same language. For all that, the glamour and power of, say Mexico's Maria Felix among her own people and those of South America should not be underestimated. Such a star is idolized, imitated—and probably is indestructive, for foreign audiences seem more loyal than those in the United States. Sometimes one of these queens, a Sophia Loren or Maria Schell, is lured to Hollywood. But most of them find careers in their own lands fully satisfying—and income taxes lower.   ("Queens of the Foreign Hollywoods," 10 November 1957, 253)

Leaving aside the question of relative rates of income taxation, the article's assertion that other nations' film industries possess their own star systems that thrive outside of Hollywood's orbit is a rare articulation in the American press of the viability of foreign film industries. However, this theme did not dominate the coverage on Bardot in the United States; it was usually assumed that she was coming to Hollywood shortly to develop further her career.

★★★★★ France's Fabulous Young Five

Bardot's foreignness is emphasized again in 1958, but this time she is linked not to other foreign female film stars but instead to other young, financially successful, and influential cultural figures in France: novelist Françoise Sagan, twenty-two; painter Bernard Buffet, twenty-nine; fashion designer Yves St. Laurent, twenty-two; and Roger Vadim, twenty-nine, Bardot's ex-husband and the director of *And God Created Woman* (P. E. Schneider, "France's Fabulous Young Five," *New York Times*, 30 March 1958, SM12). Bardot's youth had already been emphasized in the press preceding the release of *And God Created Woman*. But in this article, published six months after the initial fanfare around the film, Bardot is not simply beautiful and young, but a symbol of a new and very particular kind of celebrity associated with the rise of youth culture in the late 1950s and 1960s. The new breed of celebrity lacks political convictions, rejects traditional mores, and enjoys extraordinary financial success. The article goes so far as to estimate the annual income for each of the "Fabulous Young Five," as well as the number of books sold by Sagan, the number of paintings sold by Buffet, and the U.S. box office position of *And God Created Woman*. Bardot is also linked to this group of celebrities because of her apparent emotional vulnerability: "Like Françoise Sagan, she carries within her opulent bosom an incurable wound caused by a basic loneliness and insecurity, and seeks alleviation in the same opiates as do the youth characters in Sagan's novels." Here, then, Bardot is not just a particularly young and attractive foreign film actress, but a member of a select group of cultural arbiters. She is young, famous, rich, and emotionally wounded, just like France's most intriguing artists and writers. This article thus simultaneously elevates Bardot to the milieu of high art (she is as important as a novelist and a painter) and provides an obvious link to American figures such as James Dean, who similarly connoted youth, fame, and vulnerability.

Given the positive American reception of Brigitte Bardot, which is reflected in the truly voluminous discourse about her in the press ranging from breathless descriptions of her appearance to hyperbolic estimations of her cultural cachet, one might have expected Bardot to capitalize quickly on her success in the United States by making films there. Indeed, that is exactly what the American press expected to happen: "She'll Be in Hollywood Before She's 21" (*Los Angeles Times*, 15 August 1954, I12). Long before and after the American release of *And God Created Woman*, it was taken for granted in the American press that Bardot would come to the United States and act in Hollywood films. In 1956, the *Los Angeles Times* reported that Ott

Preminger was considering Bardot for the lead in *Bonjour Tristesse* and that Preston Sturges and William Wellman were also planning films featuring the actress (20 July 1956, 25; 29 August 1956, A11). The following year, it was announced that the Distributors Corporation of America was seeking a film project for Bardot and that it would soon bring Bardot to the United States for a tour (*Los Angeles Times*, 5 February 1957, 25). In 1958, Bardot and Frank Sinatra were provisionally paired for a film called *Paris by Night* to be produced by Raoul Lévy and written by Vadim (*New York Times*, 2 February 1958, X7). According to Hedda Hopper, Bardot was offered a role in *Ripe Fruit*, a film to be directed by Anthony Mann (*Los Angeles Times,* 19 March 1958, C10). In 1959, it was announced that Bardot, Marlon Brando, and Danny Kaye were the top choices of producer Dave Siegal for starring roles in Nelson Glueck's *Rivers of the Desert*, a biblical drama (*Los Angeles Times*, 20 February 1959, A9). The *New York Times* reported that Bardot would act in a film called *Fool's Paradise*, to be shot in Paris, in both French and English, and distributed in the United States by Twentieth-Century Fox (28 January 1960, 26). Also in 1960 there was talk of a film to be directed by Billy Wilder featuring Bardot and Maria Schell (*New York Times*, 16 July 1960, 9). Yet another article published in 1960 spoke with confidence about a co-production agreement signed by MGM and the Cipra Company of Paris "to make a series of major feature films in both English and French versions," including an adaptation of Noel Coward's *Private Lives* featuring Bardot (*New York Times*, 4 December 1960, X7). In fact, not one of these films came to fruition. Bardot never traveled to the United States to appear in a film and, although she did have a cameo appearance opposite James Stewart in the 1964 American film *Dear Brigitte*, her portion of the film was shot in Paris.

Why did Bardot's American film projects fail to materialize? There are several possible explanations. According to some sources, contractual obligations prevented her from taking on new projects. Hedda Hopper, for example, who interviewed Bardot in Paris in June 1958, reported, "She won't be making any American films for two years as she's signed up here" (*Los Angeles Times*, 18 June 1958, B6). Others suggested that Bardot resisted making films in the United States because she didn't want to become a cog in the "machine" of Hollywood. Charles Boyer, who appeared with Bardot in the film *La Parisienne*, said in 1958, "She is scared that if she comes over here [to the United States] she will be 'just another' sex type" (*Los Angeles Times*, 5 August 1958, 21). There is considerable evidence that Bardot simply did not want to travel to the United States. In the first volume of her memoirs, Bardot mentions frequently her fear of flying and her horror of encountering new places and new people (Bardot). Hedda Hopper's comment in 1964

confirms this: "She's always wanted to make an American film if she didn
have to come here" (*Los Angeles Times*, 7 May 1964, C10).
We may never know the precise reasons why Bardot did not pursu
film acting in Hollywood. What seems striking is that she managed to sta
in the American public eye as long as she did without the benefit of fre
quent publicity tours, roles in Hollywood films, or even roles in commer
cially successful French films exported to America. (None of her subsequen
films was as successful as *And God Created Woman*.) In fact, Bardot did nc
remain in the limelight, as least as a film actress, for as long as we migh
assume. As early as the fall of 1958, the American discourse on Brigitte Bar
dot began to shift. Journalists' fascination with her appearance and th
audacious expression of her sexuality coexisted now with the notion tha
she had tainted the cinema. The *Los Angeles Times* expressed concern abou
art cinema's embrace of "sex appeal" and predicted, "The consequence c
this . . . is that it will remove the difference between American pictures an
foreign pictures and all product will seem the same. All Europe will b
trying to make Brigitte Bardot pictures" (Philip K. Scheuer, *Los Angele
Times*, 26 October 1958, E1). In a review of a film called *Faibles Femme
[Women Are Weak]* (Michel Boisrond, 1959), Bosley Crowther once agai
blames "Bardotism" for a new crudeness he sees in French cinema. Bardo
does not even appear in the film—it stars Alain Delon as a Don Juan fig
ure—but never mind, she is to blame for the film's crudeness. The French
Crowther claims, used to be able to make films that were "witty and amus
ing about sex" such as *La Kermesse héroïque [Carnival in Flanders]*, *La Ronde
Le Plaisir*, or *Fanfan la tulipe*: "But something's been happening lately, an
we have an uneasy fear it reflects a commercial reaction to the movemen
Brigitte Bardot. Suddenly, it seems, the French pictures on the delicate topi
of sex are becoming deliberately erotic and laced with uncouth suggestive
ness" ("French Fall-Out: Gallic Film Makers Go Low for Bardotism," *Nev
York Times*, 14 June 1959, X1). Crowther was not alone in his reaction t
European cinema. By 1965, Pauline Kael would complain casually in
review of a book of Ingmar Bergman's screenplays that "art or foreig
movies had come to mean Brigitte Bardot in and out of towel and sheet an
Italian Amazons in and out of slips and beds" (*New York Times*, 21 Februar
1965, BR43). Thus, despite Bardot's solid portrayal of willful and sexuall
liberated women in *Love Is My Profession*, *The Truth*, and *Viva Maria*, an
despite her strong performance in Godard's *Contempt* as the enigmatic, dis
dainful wife of a screenwriter, this notion that Bardot had tainted the cin
ema, both French cinema and art cinema more generally, appears to have
hardened into standard opinion by the mid-1960s.

☆☆★★★★ "Decline"

Even in 1960, the American press began to hint that Bardot's box office power was in decline. In an article about *La Femme et le Pantin* [*The Female*] (Julien Duvivier, 1959), a reviewer emphasized the decline in Bardot's status:

> Less than three years ago, when Brigitte Bardot was undulating across local screens in "And God Created Woman," foreign film importers were calling the actress the hottest box-office attraction on the art-theatre circuit. . . . Yesterday, a collaboration between the star and [Julien Duvivier] arrived in New York, dubbed into English and bearing the blunt title, "The Female." The Lopert Films release received exactly the kind of opening it deserved— as a second feature at low-priced neighborhood theaters.
>
> (Eugene Archer, *New York Times*, 28 April 1960, 29)

Even more striking, a 1961 article about the increased visibility of European film actresses in the United States scarcely mentions Bardot. The article notes that foreign actresses "are becoming as well known in Peoria as in Paris," and is lavishly illustrated by photographs of Jeanne Moreau, Monica Vitti, Marie Laforêt, Annie Girardot, Anita Ekberg, Melina Mercouri, and Ingrid Thulin (Seymour Peck, *New York Times*, 24 September 1961, SM54). Crucially, Bardot is not pictured. She is mentioned, but only briefly: "Main Street talks about BB almost as much as about MM [Marilyn Monroe]." The absence of Bardot in this article is especially notable because it argues that European actresses are permitted to be more sexually frank than their American counterparts, which was exactly the kind of remark made about Bardot previously.

But the turning point in the perceived importance of Brigitte Bardot as a film actress is really 1962. True, some aspects of her American reception remained the same. Bosley Crowther still loathes her, but he can't stop writing about her: "She slops through [*A Private Affair*] in slacks and scanties, with her hair looking like a sheep dog's head. . . . The unspoken irony of the picture is that an actress who is so poor at her job should be the representation of the bitterness of fame in such a film" (*New York Times*, 29 September 1962, 14). Columnists such as Hedda Hopper are still reporting on potential American films roles for Bardot, this time announcing a Bardot role opposite Marlon Brando (*Los Angeles Times*, 17 January 1963, C8). But much had changed. An article about the ubiquity of the interview format on television begins by mentioning Bardot, but it makes her sound like a has-been: "The interview is as much a staple of television as Popeye, cooking hints and old Brigitte Bardot movies" (Cecil Smith, *Los Angeles Times*, 13

September 1962, A10). By 1962 Bardot had even become fodder for a Las Vegas comedy act in which Carol Channing impersonated Bardot playing Lady Macbeth (John L. Scott, *Los Angeles Times*, 3 July 1962, C7). A sharp decline in the number of articles about Bardot's film projects in the American press can be seen from 1962 onward.

Two interesting exceptions to this discourse of "decline" occurred in 1964, the year in which *Contempt* was released. Bardot's acting skills were finally recognized in the American press, at least by *Variety*, which gave considerable space to Bardot's performance: "Miss Bardot, who[m] old-timers like H. G. Clouzot, Claude Autant-Lara, Julien Duvivier and Christian Jaque tried to force to act in the more general mold, here is given her head as a young married woman who is physically amorous but begins to doubt her respect for her husband. She handles her lines well and displays a feel for a scene, and a timing and presence scarcely seen in her more undraped pix" (*Variety*, 1 January 1964).

By far the most serious assessment of Bardot's performance skills and image published in the United States was found in *Playboy*, which printed a lengthy and thoughtful article on Bardot in July 1964. Written by French novelist and biographer André Maurois, the article initially seems to be little more than a typical recap of Bardot's rise to fame and an attempt to explain the ways in which Bardot represents a "brand-new style in sex." Like so many other commentators, Maurois attributes Bardot's initial success to Roger Vadim: "It was to take an extremely intelligent director, Roger Vadim, to perceive the immense force inherent in this creature at once graceful and untamed" (André Maurois, "BB: The Sex Kitten Grows Up," *Playboy*, July 1964, 84–93, 134). However, Maurois goes on to acknowledge Bardot's agency in the creation and nourishment of her career, asserting that she is engaged in managing thoughtfully her career, that she has talent and knows how to work hard. This "young bourgeoise calculates her moves with great care" (134). These assertions, combined with his serious attempt to understand her larger cultural significance and his assumption that she has a long future in front of her as an actress, constitute an exception in the American press of this period.

✮✮✮✮✮ The Most Influential Fashion Leader in the World

So, if the American press generally positioned Bardot as a has-been actress by the early 1960s, why is it that "Main Street talks about BB almost as much as about MM"? Bardot, I would suggest, sustained her visibility in the American press throughout the 1960s not as a film actress, but rather as an international fashion icon. In 1965, when Bardot finally visited the United States for the first time in order to promote Louis Malle's film *Viva Maria*, the *New York Times* published a lengthy article on Bardot in its fashion section, paying more attention to her shoes than to her film role: "'Yes, I am a fashion influence,' acknowledged Miss Bardot, curling up on a lemon-colored sofa like the sexy kitten she plays on and off the screen and kicking off her yellow kid, square-toed, chunky-heeled pumps with brass Pilgrim buckles" (Marylin Bender, "Miss Bardot: Just an Old-Fashioned Girl," *New York Times*, 18 December 1965, 32). Underscoring her link to the fashion world is the accompanying photograph featuring Bardot arm in arm with Hélène Vager, her close friend and one of the creators of Réal, a couture house whose success Bardot helped bring about.

Assertions of the impact of Bardot's clothing, makeup, and hair on both the general public and the fashion industry dominate her coverage in the U.S. press. A typical account of her impact in this realm appeared in a 1959 *New York Times* article:

> Young women in Greenwich Village are letting their hair down in the hopes they will look like Brigitte Bardot. Seen at the Feast of St. Anthony on Sullivan Street were a number of blondes whose pale, tangled hair cascaded below their shoulders. Brunettes imitating the same wanton coiffure were just as frequent. Black-rimmed eyes and little lipstick were the order of the day. Some young women wore dark glasses, and all were dressed in tight pants and pullover tops. Feet were left as bare as possible in the flimsiest of sandals.
> (13 June 1959, 18)

Bardot's influence was seen to extend from the street all the way up to haute couture. The very first line of a *Los Angeles Times* review of the summer 1959 haute couture collections in Paris trumpets Bardot's impact: "Balenciaga may be the master of French haute couture, but Brigitte Bardot sets the fashion pace of Paris" (Fay Hammond, *Los Angeles Times*, 14 July 1959, A1). The most influential look of the season, it is reported, is not to be found on the runway but on the young women imitating Bardot's "naughty *jeune fille*" look of gingham skirts cinched tight with a wide belt and "tops that all lend themselves to falling provocatively off one shoulder." In 1959, according to the *New York Times*, Bardot is the "most influential fashion leader in the world" (10 August 1959, 22). In 1960, the *New York Times* again asserts Bardot's global impact on fashion: "The Bardot look, composed of a bird's-nest hairdo, high-heeled shoes, flounced skirts and frills on everything, is the most familiar sight on the streets not only of Paris but of cities all over the world" (9 March 1960, 28).

Bardot wearing her iconic gingham and eyelet embroidery. With Serge Gainsbourg on the set of *Voulez-vous danser avec moi?* (Courtesy Photofest)

Commentary on Bardot's impact on fashion could focus on something as narrow as a particular fabric she favored to her influence on large-scale changes in the fashion industry. For example, Bardot's influence on the popularity of gingham was the subject of many articles. In 1960, *Life* magazine reported Bardot was even influencing children's fashion:

> Style-conscious 4-year-olds are discovering the old-fashioned charms of pastel gingham, assisted by an unexpected fashion source—Brigitte Bardot. BB's widely publicized wedding garb of lace-trimmed pink checked gingham touched off a fad in France last summer which swept stores' shelves clean of the honorable but unpretentious cloth dating from 17th Century Brittany. This year U.S. manufacturers have tooled up to produce quantities of gingham for grownups and have plenty left over for little girls' play outfits, pinafores, and party dresses.   (4 April 1960)

Earlier that year, *Life* mentions Bardot also in connection with the popularity of bulky sweaters, even though she had nothing to do with this trend: "Having tried their best last summer to look like Brigitte Bardot in tiny-waisted ginghams, the pretty girls of Paris have now come up with a new twist for cold weather. Their current craze is *le gros pull*" (25 January 1960). Throughout the decade, Bardot would be credited with initiating or strengthening a number of other trends, including short shorts, the bikini, large scarves worn around the hair, "ballerina" flats, and slim "cigarette" pants (Simon, *La Mode* 68). She was also credited with popularizing two quite disparate styles of dress for women: the mod, space-age, mini-dresses created by Courrèges in the mid-1960s, as well as the long, floral dresses and embroidered vests of the late 1960s and 1970s.

But Bardot's influence went well beyond popularizing a type of fabric or a style. Haute couture had previously been associated with mature women, Paris, and established fashion houses. Now, however, thanks in part to Bardot, it was associated with young women, young designers, and even a specific town, Saint-Tropez. This picturesque town on the Côte d'Azur was first popularized by novelist Françoise Sagan and singer Juliette Greco, but thanks to Bardot's presence during the filming of *And God Created Woman* and her purchase of a home there, Saint-Tropez became even more fashionable (Simon, *La Mode* 78). In 1960, *Life* linked Bardot with the new youthful styles, young designers, and St. Tropez:

> Until recently no European woman could qualify as a fashion leader without being over 30 years of age—generally well over—and dressed to the nines by a *haute couture* designer. But this season France's newest style setters are younger girls—debutantes, aspiring actresses, Parisian working girls and *habitués* of the Riviera bohemia, St. Tropez. They are dressed by new designers, still on the

Bardot wearing a bandeau, probably on the set of *Contempt*. (Courtesy Photofest)

edge of the big time, who are more interested in having their clients look young and feminine than elegant. Among these designers are Louis Feraud and Jacques Esterel, who at one time were in business together. Both have made clothes for Brigitte Bardot, the *grande dame* of St. Tropez and France's leading exponent of the frilly look. U.S. buyers, too, have bought heavily of the bright, bouncy clothes which have caught on as far afield as Tokyo.

("Some Romance from France," *Life*, 13 June 1960, 121)

Even more important than Bardot's ability to launch individual young designers or to shift the focus momentarily from Paris to St. Tropez was her impact on the fashion industry's increasing reliance on ready-to-wear clothing. In an article lamenting the decline of the "little dressmaker" in Paris in favor of mass-produced, ready-to-wear fashion, it is suggested that Bardot spurred the movement in fashion toward "standardization" (P. E. Schneider, "Adieu to Paris' Little Dressmakers," *New York Times*, 20 September 1959, SM16). By the summer of 1960, Bardot's impact on fashion was even seen as equivalent to that of Coco Chanel: "Chanel and Brigitte Bardot have both given impetus to the development of the ready-to-wear— Chanel because she is so relatively easy to copy, Mlle. Bardot because she started a vogue for such inexpensive materials as gingham and *broderie-anglaise* (eyelet embroidery)" (Gill Goldsmith, "Paris Women Now Boast of Chic Little Bargain," *New York Times*, 5 August 1960, 11).

Bardot was seen to have influenced not only what women wore, but also where they shopped. She was specifically associated with the rise of the boutique, as opposed to the department store. In the 1960s boutiques were perceived in Europe and in the United States as new sources of relatively inexpensive yet still individualized clothing. Marylin Bender, the fashion critic for the *New York Times*, wrote of the rise of the boutique in her 1967 book, *The Beautiful People*: "Shopping in boutiques was like altering the birthdate on a passport. It certified that a woman was a swinger. Press agents who had trained their clients to drop the names of Paris haute couture or the Seventh Avenue galaxy had to re-educate them to murmur Biba (the London boutique, owned by Barbara Julanicki, where Brigitte Bardot, Julie Christie, Geraldine Chapin and Françoise Hardy bought the $10 dresses and $25 coats by the half dozen)" (Bender 228).

Clearly, Bardot's impact on fashion went well beyond that of film stars from the classical era such as Joan Crawford, Katharine Hepburn, and Marlene Dietrich, who popularized specific looks, or Audrey Hepburn, who helped ensure the visibility of Hubert Givenchy (Studlar). While it is true that one ultimately must attribute the changes in 1960s fashion to multiple and broad sociocultural shifts of the period, such as the rise of youth culture

Bardot shopping in a boutique in Capri while wearing her famous cigarette pants and ballet flats, 1963. (Courtesy Photofest)

(see Epstein and Steele), Bardot clearly played a significant role in creating the appetite for casually stylish and relatively inexpensive clothing that utterly transformed the way women dressed. Curiously, for those of us accustomed to the process by which today's film stars, singers, and athletes promote their "brands" and earn revenue by attaching their names to specific consumer products or even by collaborating on the design of entire lines of clothing, it does not appear that Bardot actually tried very hard to exert an impact on fashion or to earn much income from her visibility in this realm, at least in the 1960s and beyond. Certainly, the buildup to Bardot's acquisition of worldwide stardom depended heavily upon the placement of her image in fashion magazines, facilitated first by her mother, who had links to the fashion industry, and then by Roger Vadim (Vincendeau, "Hot Couture" 135). However, apart from her early work as a fashion model in the period predating *And God Created Woman* and the occasional licensing of her name to a product (for example, the "Lovable Bra" in the late 1950s), Bardot appears not to have sought an ongoing, lucrative link to fashion. That she nevertheless continued to have an enormous impact on how young women wanted to present themselves to the world attests to the powerful conjunction of her extraordinary appearance, her persona of the sexually liberated young woman, and the sweeping changes that occurred in the fashion and film industries at this time.

From the early 1960s onward, Bardot generally made only one film per year, and not one of them made a huge splash. The discourse on Bardot shifted decisively away from film and toward fashion. In addition to charting her impact on fashion, the American press increasingly focused on Bardot's personal problems, reporting obsessively on the birth of her child, her suicide attempts, and her tempestuous love life. Throughout the 1960s, Bardot was also written about in conjunction with her occasional and highly successful musical variety programs on French television and her recordings with Serge Gainsbourg. She retired definitively from show business in 1973, but, as late as 1976, was still capable of creating a frenzy around a particular item of clothing, when she appeared in a television advertisement for a pair of trousers and caused the company to hire an additional 130 workers to meet the demand (Simon, *La Mode* 68).

✩✩★★★ An Alternative Trajectory: The Case of Sophia Loren

It is worth comparing briefly the career of another international, non-American star to Bardot for an understanding of how Bardot's career trajectory might have developed differently. Sophia Loren was born, like Bardot, in 1934, and raised near Naples, Italy. Also like Bardot, Loren launched her film career with the help of a Svengali figure whom she eventually married, Carlo Ponti. Like Bardot, Loren was no overnight success. She acted in a string of unremarkable Italian films starting in 1950 and became well known in Italy only in 1954 as a result of Vittoria De Sica's *L'Oro di Napoli* [*Gold of Naples*], which established her image as an unabashedly sensual yet independent woman (Gundle).

By the late 1950s, Loren had become an international film star. Unlike Bardot, however, Loren went to Hollywood and acted in American films. In 1957 alone, she appeared in *Boy on a Dolphin* (Jean Negulesco), *The Pride and the Passion* (Stanley Kramer), with Cary Grant and Frank Sinatra, and *Legend of the Lost* (Henry Hathaway), with John Wayne. Her five-picture contract with Paramount provided a solid base for her developing visibility in the United States. She appeared with Cary Grant in the romantic comedy *Houseboat* (Melville Shavelson, 1958); in *Black Orchid* (Martin Ritt, 1958), she played a mob widow alongside Anthony Quinn; in George Cukor's *Heller in Pink Tights* (1960), she played a blond actress touring the Wild West. It was Loren's performance in an Italian film, however, that clinched her international fame and her critical acclaim. In *La ciociara* [*Two Women*] (Vittoria De Sica, 1960) she played a widow trying to protect herself and her teenaged daughter from retreating Nazis and a band of Moroccan soldiers in the French army. For this role Loren won an Academy Award for Best Actress, the first foreign actress to do so. She worked steadily throughout the 1960s and the 1970s, acting in Italian, French, and American films, including *El Cid* with Charlton Heston (1961), and De Sica's *Ieri, oggi, domani* [*Yesterday, Today, and Tomorrow*] (1963). Despite the initial parallels between Bardot and Loren—the slow start in a string of unremarkable films, the reliance on a male mentor, the "sex goddess" image—Loren's trajectory differs significantly from that of Bardot; she is a different kind of international film star, one whose image is aligned more closely with her films and which has depended upon the star's mobility over several decades.

There were, then, at least two very different ways of being an international, foreign star in the 1960s: one could develop and sustain, like Sophia Loren, an international career fueled primarily by making many films in many countries. Bardot's ongoing visibility is based on something else. While her performance and her persona in *And God Created Woman* catapulted her to international fame, her longer-lasting importance in the 1960 and beyond is not to the world of cinema. Three years after her break through film, Bardot's celebrity detached from her film work and she became much more important in the milieu of fashion. Even the release of *Contempt* in 1964 did not change this state of affairs. Working with a prestigious art house director like Jean-Luc Godard did not bring about additional roles for Bardot in European art films, nor did it enhance her currency as a star of commercial cinema. Instead, the 1960s saw Bardot's fame moved further and further away from the cinema and settle firmly in the realm of fashion. She appeared in her last film in 1973 at the age of thirty-nine. In the 1970s and beyond, Bardot's image became even more diffuse: still a fashion icon, her media coverage shifted principally to her commitment to animal rights. Bardot remains a cult figure to this day—a quick glance at the fashion spreads featuring models Claudia Schiffer and Kate Moss confirms this—but her image has undergone yet another shift since the height of her impact on fashion in the 1960s and the 1970s: she is now more likely to be written about critically for her controversial statements about immigrants in France.

One could read the trajectory of Brigitte Bardot in America in a number of ways: as a glitch on the part of the Hollywood system at a moment of transition in the industry—an inability on the part of producers and directors to find the right roles and shooting conditions for someone like Bardot. Rather than interpret Bardot's career as short-circuited, we could view it more positively as the story of an independent woman who said "no thanks" to Hollywood and, eventually, to the cinema altogether, and went her own way, for better or for worse. But Bardot's transition from film star to fashion icon is most productively thought of as part of a larger story of cultural change involving an expansion and an alteration of the very notion of stardom. It was a moment of crossover for many stars, from long-term studio contracts to quasi-independence; from film to television; and from film to other realms in which celebrity could be cultivated, notably fashion. The Bardot story exemplifies a moment when the most important engine of star making, the Hollywood studio system, had become only one of many ways to achieve lasting cultural visibility.

10 ★★★★★★★★★★★

Edie Sedgwick
Girl of the Year

CHRISTOPHER SIEVING

> Edie Sedgwick is the girl that everybody is talking about. No one is quite sure
> who the everybody is who is talking about her, but no matter. There is too
> little new that is happening and too many words to write and television
> talk shows to film to leave a phenomenon like Edie Sedgwick alone. Edie
> Sedgwick is being talked about because she is here, there, and everywhere.
>
> (Nora Ephron, "Woman in the News: Edie Sedgwick,
> Superstar," *New York Post*, 5 September 1965, 2:1)

At the time of Nora Ephron's September 1965 profile, Edie Sedgwick was
known to *New York Post* readers primarily as the party-hopping, out-
landishly clothed, oft-photographed companion of Pop artist and experimental moviemaker Andy Warhol. When their paths crossed for the first
time Warhol was already arguably the most infamous avant-gardist in
American film history, having outraged middlebrow sensibilities with his
soundless, intolerably protracted studies of mundane events and objects—
the two most notorious offenders being the six-hour *Sleep* (1963) and the
eight-hour *Empire* (1964), a fixed-camera, dusk-'til-dawn contemplation
of the Empire State Building. After *Empire* Warhol more fully committed to

a couple of tendencies that had marked much of his 1964 work: (live) sound film production and, following the lead of Jack Smith's cause célèbre *Flaming Creatures* (1963), a cinema founded upon the appeal of flamboyant onscreen personalities. Sedgwick, a vivacious, free-spirited debutante who had recently arrived in Manhattan by way of Cambridge, Massachusetts, would, under Warhol's guidance, become not just the most radiant star of the New York "underground" film scene but also an above-ground celebrity.

The Edie Sedgwick phenomenon that spanned much of 1965, originating in the spring with breathless mentions in the society columns of the New York dailies and culminating later in the year in fashion spreads for mass-market magazines and rampant gossip-page speculation about a Hollywood future, rests on what even at the time seemed like a paradox. The implicit question undergirding her *Post* feature—why are we paying attention to Edie Sedgwick?—is rooted in the assumption that stardom and, specifically, star *publicity* must have a clear referent; it must be grounded in and justified by some sort of tangible, marketable accomplishment. While Sedgwick may have seemed to be "here, there, and everywhere" during that chaotic year, there was one place from which her silver-haired countenance was typically and paradoxically absent: the movie screen. Even the best known of her Warhol-directed vehicles, most of which were shot in the spring and summer of 1965, were unseen and mostly unknown outside New York City, watched only by several hundred avant-garde aficionados within. The publicity accumulated by Sedgwick during her meteoric "career" *suggests* a star of the first magnitude. But star of what?

The fact that her celebrity was definitively meteoric and her rise to movie fame retarded, thanks to her own self-destructiveness and the neglect of those around her, has secured for Sedgwick a lasting stardom. Her uniqueness is not, contrary to the popular conception reproduced in a recent biography, that she was "famous for doing nothing at all" (Painter and Weisman 12) but that her stardom was in large part predicated on the explosion of the dichotomies upon which traditional stardom rests. She was a mainstream fashion icon who acted in underground movies. Her look of apparent nonchalance was achieved only after hours spent trying on clothes and putting on makeup, and her androgynous synthesis of feminine beauty (seen in her large, expressive eyes and dancer's legs) and boyish attributes (small breasts and hips and close-cropped hair) motivated one critic to liken her to "Peter Pan in drag" (Richard R. Lingeman, "Pop Sex: Some Sex Symbols of the Sixties, "*Mademoiselle*, November 1965, 221). She was both a blue-blooded socialite and a nearly destitute charity case who blew through an almost six-figure inheritance in her first six months in Manhattan. She effortlessly transgressed the class lines that separated New York's high society of aristocratic elites, its "café" society of the ebullient nouveau riche, and the underground subculture of artists existing on society's fringes; her ease at bridging these chasms put her at the crest of the "new chic" trends memorably chronicled by Tom Wolfe in the pages of *Harper's Bazaar* ("Pariah Styles: The New Chic," April 1965). Finally, whereas Warhol's series of observational, quasi-documentary studies of Sedgwick waking up in the morning, applying cosmetics, and entertaining friends suggest a gesture toward transforming her life into art, his subject had already obliterated the borderline. Sedgwick may have played "herself" in films like *Beauty #2* and *Afternoon* (both 1965), but "herself" was a role she had been honing at least since leaving Cambridge in early 1964.

Related to this willful obfuscation of "life" and "art," "rich" and "poor," Sedgwick's example is particularly compelling and unique, even within the arena of experimental cinema, for transgressing the barrier between "text" and "publicity." The construction of Sedgwick's stardom and its resultant publicity are the very subjects of all of her movies for Warhol: not only the various episodes in the so-called *Poor Little Rich Girl Saga* documenting Sedgwick's daily routine, but the scripted narratives as well. Fittingly, given Warhol's well-documented efforts to emulate classical Hollywood's industrial model at his midtown studio, the "Factory," largely through basing his filmmaking efforts around stars, these movies' sophisticated meditation on the process of star creation represents a significant contribution to the then-incipient critical reexamination of the classical Hollywood cinema. Much of the scholarly literature on Warhol and his retinue of stars, or "Superstars," ascribes authority to the director rather than the performer, a relationship that reproduces a long-held tradition in film historiography. In academic writing the Warhol Superstar is mainly a function of Warhol's larger auteurist objective: that is, in David E. James's account, his "inquiry into the mechanisms of the inscription of the individual into the apparatus and into the way such inscription has been historically organized" (68). The insights produced by this scholarship have shed considerable light not just on Warhol and avant-garde cinema but on the very nature of cinematic representation, yet they also implicitly assert that Sedgwick's media image was manufactured and manipulated by Warhol alone. What I propose to do is restore Edie Sedgwick's own agency—indeed, her resistance to some of Warhol's aesthetic goals—as a determining factor in the construction of her star image and as a significant cause of her own enduring myth.

☆☆★★★ Goddess of the Underground

Although I intend to explicate the singularity of Sedgwick's stardom, it must nevertheless be acknowledged that the arc of Sedgwick's life, in many ways, reproduced that of a more traditional media star. In fact, the conventionality of that arc explains the posthumous promulgation of her stardom in popular cultural forms like the literary oral history (Jean Stein's *Edie* [1982]) and the glossy biopic (George Hickenlooper's *Factory Girl* [2006]). More so than any comparable underground cinema figure, Sedgwick's star trajectory reads like that of a Hollywood ingénue: discovery by a celebrity filmmaker; eye-catching secondary roles in various productions; a series of specially tailored star vehicles, coupled with intense exposure in national periodicals and gossip columns; acrimonious departure from her "studio" over roles and money; lengthy absence from public view, attempted comeback, and tragic early death.

Sedgwick's debut on the public stage came quickly after her introduction to Warhol and his primary screenwriter, the absurdist playwright Ronald Tavel, at a party in January 1965. In March and early April she had brief, walk-on roles in *Bitch* and in Tavel's western spoof *Horse*, and she sat for the first of her nine *Screen Tests*: silent, unedited, four-minute portrait films for which the sitter was instructed to remain motionless. Sedgwick's early *Screen Tests*, in which she gazes rapturously into the camera lens with lips parted and eyelashes fluttering, probably came closer to fulfilling the traditional objective of the Hollywood screen test—to groom a potential star—than any of the hundreds Warhol filmed between 1964 and 1966, an aim further confirmed by the painstaking though subtle changes in makeup and lighting from film to film (Angell, *Andy* 181–82). By mid-spring Sedgwick had settled into the dual role she was to play for most of the year at the Factory. Her social career ignited as she assumed the part of Warhol's public escort and his meal ticket to the Park Avenue haute bourgeoisie; together the two appeared in each other's company at parties, discotheques, and museum openings almost nightly. With regard to her film career, she made a dramatic impact in a nonspeaking role in *Vinyl* (April 1965), Tavel's adaptation of Anthony Burgess's *A Clockwork Orange* (1962) starring Warhol's chief acolyte, Gerard Malanga, in the role of a supposedly reformed juvenile delinquent. Sedgwick was inserted into the film, an otherwise all-male affair complete with homoerotic torture scenes and s&m play, at the last minute by Warhol, ostensibly because she looked "like a boy" (qtd. in Stein 189).

For *Vinyl*'s sixty-six-minute duration, Sedgwick sits at the right foreground of the frame on a trunk, silently witnessing the action and displaying her soon-to-be-classic look: short silvered hair, heavily made-up eyes, gorgeous bare legs, black tank top and leotards, leopard-skin belt, enormous dangling earrings. Throughout she exudes utter placidity and self-absorption, demonstrating more interest in the contents of her purse than in Malanga's abuse at the hands of tormentors. Still, at various moments in *Vinyl*, as in her later films, Sedgwick also lets on that the pose is just that, as she frequently breaks character to crack a smile at a friend off-camera or at an actor blowing his line, and as she casually leaves the set for three minutes to use the Factory bathroom. It was likely the combination of her performance modes—one defined by a tranquil serenity, echoing her *Screen Test* sittings, and the other by an antic spontaneity—that bewitched the Factory regulars who watched the finished film. Tavel saw Sedgwick totally overshadowing Malanga's star turn:"The film became like one of those vehicles for a famous star, but it's somebody *else* who gets discovered . . . like Monroe in *Asphalt Jungle* [1950]. She had a five-minute role and everyone came running: 'Who's the blonde?'" (qtd. in Stein 189; emphasis in original). Sedgwick subsequently starred or appeared in both narrative projects (including *Kitchen, Space,* and *Prison*) and a cinéma vérité–style series of films depicting a typical day in her life: *Poor Little Rich Girl, Beauty #2, Afternoon, Restaurant, Outer and Inner Space,* and two rarely seen pictures, *Beauty #1* and *Face* (all 1965).

The industrial model that generated classical-era studio stars, a process minutely chronicled in Cathy Klaprat's case study of Warner Bros.' efforts on Bette Davis's behalf, barely applies to Sedgwick in many respects, yet during the peak of her public visibility she certainly behaved and was treated like a full-fledged star. Production at the Factory was rationalized around its most bankable screen personality, such that Sedgwick was featured "in every single sound film to come out of the Factory between late March and . . . Labor Day Weekend" of 1965 (Angell, *Andy* 181). Tavel was assigned to write scripts expressly for her; indeed, *Kitchen*'s eponymous location and narrative premise were tailored to allow Sedgwick to show off her trademark sleek, fishnet-stockinged legs and to exploit the blinding whiteness of her skin and hair (Tavel, *"Kitchen,"* http://www.ronald-tavel .com/pdf/011.pdf, accessed April 8, 2008).

In her starring vehicles, Sedgwick's nervous energy helped compensate for a lack of narrative momentum and camera technique. The nonstop tics and mannerisms and movements that characterized her screen presence likely made the Warholian tropes of the de-dramatized situation and the absolutely static camera more palatable for underground audiences. As a result, her showcase pictures were screened regularly in New York by the

The blinding radiance of star power: Edie Sedgwick with Roger Trudeau in *Kitchen* (Digital frame enlargement from *Andy Warhol: A Documentary Film*, PBS Paramount, 2006)

Film-Makers' Cinematheque throughout the summer and fall of 1965. Tellingly, by that autumn Sedgwick's name, rather than that of her mentor, was appearing above the title in Cinematheque advertisements placed in the *Village Voice* (15 July 1965, 10; 30 September 1965, 20).

Like many luminaries of the studio era, however, Sedgwick chafed at the lack of "depth" afforded by her roles, and the severity of the developing rift between her and the Factory began to affect her press publicity by September. She let slip to Ephron that she and Warhol had "gone about as far as they can go together, professionally." As her friend and co-star Ondine later recalled, people outside of the Factory circle "were telling her that she should concern herself with being a very famous star . . . putting it in her mind that she was the greatest thing since Greta Garbo or Marilyn Monroe— she owed it to herself to be that famous" (qtd. in Stein 220). Hollywood moguls came calling to express their interest, leading a piqued Warhol to tell *Women's Wear Daily* that Sedgwick had the choice of being "a plain old movie star" or someone who "could change the way movies look" (qtd. in Leo Lerman, "Success,"*Mademoiselle*, December 1965, 98). He became increasingly dismayed by her increasing amenability to the first option, especially after Bob Dylan's manager, Albert Grossman, began grooming her to star in a "legitimate" picture opposite Dylan. Her desertion of the Factory in early 1966 fueled speculation about her relationship with Dylan, who reportedly wrote the songs "Just Like a Woman" and "Leopard Skin Pillbox Hat" under her inspiration. The final straw arrived when Grossman instructed Sedgwick to stay away from Warhol, due to the extreme hype surrounding the pair, and requested that Warhol remove Sedgwick's featured reel from exhibitions of his 1966 magnum opus, *The Chelsea Girls* (Stein 229).

But the rumored project with Dylan never materialized, nor did the plum parts allegedly dangled by the studios. Sedgwick's media profile accordingly diminished rapidly in 1966, although she made front-page news in October by nearly perishing in an apartment fire she carelessly, albeit accidentally, started. (She repeated the incident at her room at the Chelsea Hotel the following spring.) The lone positive press notices she garnered in this period, prior to her return to obscurity at her family's California ranch in fall 1968, were for landing the lead role in *Ciao Manhattan* (1972), a film conceived and initiated by Sedgwick's longtime confidant, Chuck Wein. Wein originally envisioned *Ciao Manhattan* as a free-wheeling, wide-ranging exploration of New York's bohemian sixties milieu, but the project spun out of control in quick order, thanks to the filmmakers' general disorganization but also to Sedgwick's diminished capacity as a performer. Some black-and-white footage from Wein's 1967 shoot made it into the finished feature, but the majority of what was released as *Ciao Manhattan* was filmed in 1970, after a long period of hospitalizations and institutionalizations for its star. The script, reworked by new directors David Weisman and John Palmer as a kind of counterculture *Sunset Blvd.* (1950), now centered solely on Sedgwick's character, a drug-addled, washed-up ex-Superstar who lives in her mother's empty swimming pool in Santa Barbara.

Sedgwick's true sixties swan song, as well as her most haunting work, is her final star vehicle for Warhol, *Lupe*, filmed in December 1965. *Lupe* stemmed from Warhol's obsession with the mythology of star-driven classical cinema, itself a manifestation of the then-surging nostalgia for the star system of the thirties and forties as well as the accompanying realization that that system had ceased to exist. This recognition of its death throes was in turn supplemented by a slew of salacious new book and screen biographies that exposed Old Hollywood's icons as distressingly mortal. Warhol's major contribution to this deconstruction of star glamour was a series of films that parodied the secret offscreen lives of legendary Hollywood actresses. The immediate textual catalyst for this series was avant-garde filmmaker Kenneth Anger's book *Hollywood Babylon* (first published in America in 1965), a merciless broadside against movie star excess and self-destruction during the cinema's so-called golden era. Anger's poison-pen missive to the studio system inspired Warhol's *Harlot* (1964), a parody of two separate movie projects on the life of Jean Harlow; *More Milk, Yvette* (1966), an enactment of the 1957 scandal surrounding Lana Turner and the stabbing death of her mobster boyfriend by her own teenage daughter; *Hedy* (1966), a satire on Hedy Lamarr's January 1966 shoplifting arrest; and *Lupe*, a free adaptation of Anger's lurid (and oft discredited) account of the suicide of Mexican-born B-movie actress Lupe Vélez, who allegedly drowned in her toilet after attempting to overdose on barbiturates (Anger 232–38).

In *Harlot*, *Yvette*, and *Hedy*, the casting of a drag performer (Mario Montez) in the role of a great star in her decrepitude enabled Warhol to convey a necessary critical distance, in line with Ronald Tavel's observation that "Jean Harlow is a transvestite, as are Mae West and Marilyn Monroe, in the sense that their feminineness is so exaggerated that it becomes a commentary on womanhood rather than the real thing or representation of realness" ("The Banana Diary: The Story of Andy Warhol's *Harlot*,"*Film Culture*, Spring 1966, 44). In contrast, Sedgwick's presence in *Lupe* erases the distance between actress and role, a boundary also evoked by Warhol's experimentation with dual-image projection: *Lupe* consists of two film reels screened simultaneously, one next to the other. The image on the right in this thirty-six-minute character study is of a seemingly inebriated Sedgwick in long shot playing "Lupe," languorously decorating her luxurious residence with bouquets of flowers in preparation for her grand death scene. On the left is "Edie" herself, awakening, then applying makeup, making phone calls, and receiving a haircut from Factory "foreman" Billy Name. With Name she aimlessly discusses career opportunities, the murky sound track occasionally punctuated with pregnant phrases like "your agent situation" and "singing lessons." The poignancy of such moments from a contemporary viewpoint comes from the knowledge that *Lupe* marked not the penultimate rung on Sedgwick's climb to mainstream movie stardom, which had sorely tempted her in the waning months of 1965, but yet another milepost on her inexorable downward spiral. Appropriately, in the movie's three-minute coda both "Edie" (on the left) and "Lupe" (on the right) are pictured unconscious on a bathroom floor, head submerged in a toilet bowl. The "real" Edie now realizes (rather than simply reenacts) the ignominious fate of the thirties screen siren; for both women, a not fully realized stardom appears to end prematurely and in brutal fashion. Sedgwick would spend the next five years living out this finale until she herself overdosed on barbiturates in 1971 at the age of twenty-eight. *Lupe* both represents the sudden death of a star and documents the slow demise of a superstar, and thus retrospectively appears to damn its maker for indulging in the exploitation his other star exposés appear to critique. But such a formulation perhaps gives Warhol too much of the credit, and Sedgwick too little, for her own legend.

★★★★★ Pop as Fashion (and) Movement

At the time of its unfolding, the New York–based underground cinema of the 1960s was most commonly publicized and understood
not as art but as fashion. While cinéphiles were digesting the critical debates
on the underground's aesthetic accomplishments, published in the likes of
Jonas Mekas's "Movie Journal" column in the *Village Voice* and in the Mekas-
edited intellectual journal *Film Culture*, millions of Americans were encountering the underground as a "kicky" cultural phenomenon in the pages of
mass-circulated women's magazines and newsweeklies. The centrality of
stardom to the discursive formation of sixties underground cinema was
hugely important in translating the underground ethos for those beyond its
hardcore niche. Yet this centrality was long neglected in books on the
movement. Sheldon Renan, in one of the earliest published surveys on the
American experimental cinema of the sixties, downplays the significance of
stars; in his estimation, "it is the film-maker himself who is in the underground limelight" (197). Many later histories follow Renan's lead, analyzing and evaluating films of this period solely as the personal expressions of
their director-artisans. Yet the contemporaneous media coverage and discussion of the New York avant-garde reveals an intense preoccupation, even in
the specialized auteurist journals (see "Stars of 'New American Cinema,'"
Film Culture, Summer 1964, 25–40), with the stars of underground cinema.
The foregrounding of star performers in the texts and intertexts of the
sixties underground was one of the principal means by which this mode of
filmmaking distinguished itself among twentieth-century American avant-
garde trends.

The Edie Sedgwick phenomenon in particular was seen as a symptom
of the accelerating ephemerality of American culture in the 1960s, a period
in which art (as manifest in Pop Art and Happenings, two modes that
Warhol combined in his film practice) became as transitory and immediately obsolescent as fashion. Indeed, Warhol strove to dissolve art and fashion in the crucible of what David E. James labels "the publicity industry"
(58). Warhol's tireless cultivation of publicity early in his career, rooted in
his scandalously casual working methods and his unearthly pallor, itself
became by the mid-sixties one of the primary sources of that publicity.
Sedgwick's fortuitous appearance at the Factory cemented this objective.
Prior to her arrival, Warhol formulated the notion of film shoot as publicity stunt in the most literal way: by inviting dozens of guests from the New
York and national presses to witness the filming of such pictures as *Harlo*
("Saint Andrew," *Newsweek*, 7 December 1964, 103), *Screen Test II* (1965

(Tavel, "The Theatre of the Ridiculous," *Tri-Quarterly* 6, 1966, 105), and *Batman Dracula* (1964) (Malanga, "Interview with Jack Smith," *Film Culture*, Summer 1967, 13). The Sedgwick films, however, are subtler examples of underground cinema artistic production as a means of garnering publicity.

With the Sedgwick cycle, film shoot also became fashion shoot, a link enabled by her embodiment of shifts in the culture business. Sedgwick's reign as underground movie queen coincided with an unprecedented close identification of avant-garde artistic trends and countercultural fashion trends, an identification memorably announced by the April 1965 issue of *Harper's Bazaar*, guest-edited by renowned fashion photographer Richard Avedon. The April *Bazaar* integrated "now" couture and fine art on page after page; for example, a photo reproduction of George Segal's "Woman Washing Her Feet" called attention in its accompanying caption to the sandals affixed to Segal's sculpture: "vivid chrome yellow straw-like lace trimmed with matching patent leather. By Mademoiselle. About $21. At Neiman-Marcus" (187). This validation of "high fashion" and "style consumption" through comparison to the "genuine arts" and "art consumption" (Suárez 234) was repeated with regard to the cinema. Articles on underground film were commonplace in fashion publications by the mid-sixties, particularly in *Vogue*, in which such articles extended the magazine's longstanding commitment to profiles of modernist trends (Angeletti and Oliva 157). Accordingly, the Avedon issue of *Harper's Bazaar* featured a salute to American avant-garde cinema via a photo-montage, designed by filmmaker Stan Vanderbeek and featuring the images of Warhol, Mekas, Anger, Gregory Markopoulos, Marie Menken, Stan Brakhage, the Smiths (Harry and Jack), and the late Ron Rice ("Underground Film Makers," April 1965, 228–29).

In a logical extension of his longstanding obsession with and incorporation of classic Hollywood's manufactured glamour, Warhol actively sought to associate his art with fashion. In early 1965 a gallery show of his paintings served as backdrop for a *New York Herald Tribune* photo shoot advertising new dresses by trendy designers (Eugenia Sheppard, "Pop Art, Poetry and Fashion," *New York Herald Tribune*, 3 January 1965, 10–12). Warhol then began screening some of his silent films at similar fashion-related events, showing the minimalist *Eat* (1964) at a Happening thrown by hairdresser Kenneth Batelle (Enid Nemy, "A 'Happening' Happens to Replace a Hairdo Show," *New York Times*, 12 July 1965, 31) and *The Thirteen Most Beautiful Girls* (1964), a compilation of popular *Screen Tests*, at a party given by *Life*'s fashion editor Sally Kirkland (P.T., "13 Most Beautiful . . . ," *New York Herald Tribune*, 10 January 1965, 2:3). In gratitude, Kirkland rented a handful of film prints from the Factory for a spread in the 19 March issue of *Life*. The resulting feature, "Underground Clothes," depicted a bevy of chic young women modeling the latest "extreme" and "bizarre" designs from Seventh Avenue while sharing the frame with projected images from *Eat, Thirteen, Henry Geldzahler* (1964), and the unfinished *Batman Dracula* (116–19).

Among the beautiful girls displaying their underground clothes in *Life* was Warhol's first well-known film Superstar, a Park Avenue socialite known to the public as "Baby Jane" Holzer. A fashion magazine staple in 1964, instantly recognizable for her leonine features and immense head of hair, Holzer bridged the gap between old-money respectability and the new youth subcultures in ways that much appealed to Warhol, and that would be replicated by Sedgwick once Holzer drifted away from the Factory scene. Her seemingly inexplicable fame was the subject of Tom Wolfe's signature essay "The Girl of the Year," first published in the *Herald Tribune*, in which the author dismisses Baby Jane much in the same way highbrow trend-spotters would dismiss Edie eight months later: as a media fabrication, reflexively exploited by columnists and magazine editors, none of whom "have been able to do much more than, in effect, set down her name, Baby Jane Holzer, and surround it with a few asterisks and exploding stars, as if to say, well, here we have . . . What's Happening." But Holzer's utterly synthetic celebrity, deriving from her unconscious absorption of "new waves of style" (6 December 1964, 9), was the very raw material Warhol craved for his cinema, and her inescapable visage became a star attraction in some of the more widely screened Warhol pictures, including *Thirteen Most Beautiful Girls* and *Kiss* (1963). Indeed, the regular casting of female models—Holzer, Ivy Nicholson, Sedgwick, Nico, and Susan Bottomly—in Warhol's movies served, characteristically, both aesthetic and economic purposes. Fashion models, adept in the art of both physically graceful, glamorous posing and "being oneself," were well suited to the enactment of minimalist narrative situations. Their fame in other media also reflected well on the auteur. If their modeling notoriety preceded their appearances in Warhol's films (as with Holzer), he benefited from the publicity generated by their participation. If their modeling celebrity was the *result* of collaboration with Warhol (as with Sedgwick), his reputation as a star-maker—à la British fashion photographer David Bailey, whom Warhol envied (Wollen 146)—was confirmed.

Sedgwick's displacement of Holzer as the principal female Superstar further solidified the Factory's ties to the world of Pop fashion. Most of Sedgwick's media coverage in 1965 merely alludes to her work in underground films, as if their existence were an unsubstantiated rumor. (Almost none of her mass media profilers give any indication of having seen any of them, despite the films' semi-regular screening at the Factory and at the 41st Street Film-Makers' Cinematheque.) But her clothing, makeup, and accessories—especially the more bizarre accoutrements—are delineated in painstaking detail, starting from her much commented-upon April appearance at an opening at the Metropolitan Museum of Art. Though the black-tie affair was attended by Lady Bird Johnson and "260 titans of the art world and the Social Register," it was Sedgwick who caused a sensation in "a lilac jersey jump suit" with a "furry shoulder purse" (Marylin Bender, "First Lady Shops Here for Easter," *New York Times*, 8 April 1965, 48; see also "Edie & Andy," *Time*, 27 August 1965, 65).

The ubiquitous presence of Sedgwick at all types of gatherings was bemusedly chronicled on a seemingly daily basis by Manhattan society-page columnists and reporters, who alternately clucked and marveled at the coordinated silver outfit of pantsuit, earrings, and bra that Sedgwick wore to the Rainbow Room's "Mod Ball" (Angela Taylor, "Over the Rainbow Room: Modness," *New York Times*, 18 November 1965, 59) and at the ostrich-plumed cape she wore to a New York Film Festival screening, which to Joseph X. Dever made her resemble "a camp version of Mme. Dracula" ("Gotham-Go-Round," *New York World-Telegram and Sun*, 14 September 1965, 44). She came to be closely identified with some of the hipper designers of the era, especially the Austrian-born Rudi Gernreich. Her stunning appearance at an exhibition at Philadelphia's Institute of Contemporary Art in a "floor-length, shocking pink Rudi Gernreich sheath" (David Bourdon, "Help!," *Village Voice*, 14 October 1965, 13) with twelve-foot-long sleeves provoked the capacity crowd to nearly mob Warhol and his entourage as if they were rock stars. Sedgwick also favored costume jewelry by family friend Kenneth Jay Lane, particularly his very long and ornate earrings, which she modeled in the pages of *Life*, noting, "I swish them the way other girls swish their hair" (qtd. in "The Girl with the Black Tights," 26 November 1965, 48). Sedgwick's identification with outrageous clothing subsequently led to an association with Betsey Johnson of the Paraphernalia boutique on Madison Avenue. Paraphernalia's artificial, ready-to-wear esthetic, exemplified by its plastic, paper, and aluminum foil throwaway dresses, was strongly evocative of Pop's "disposability and impermanence" (Blackman 210) and its "glorification of the fleeting moment" (Lobenthal 8). It was thus a perfect fit not only for Warhol, who hosted the boutique's opening party at Johnson's request (Wollen 143), but also for Sedgwick, who became Johnson's first fitting model.

Aside from her *Life* profile, Sedgwick's most widely seen pictorials appeared in *Vogue*, the venerable women's magazine that, under the leadership of Diana Vreeland, had reoriented its focus from elegant haute couture for the older woman toward inexpensive, ready-to-wear, "Mod" apparel geared toward hedonistic youth (Marylin Bender, "These Are the Fashion Magazines and the Women Editors Who Run Them," *New York Times*, 25 July 1966, 18). *Vogue* in the mid-sixties applied a series of labels to the vivacious young female consumer whose tastes and desires were now occupying the center of the magazine's universe. One of Vreeland's early favored designations, the "Chicerino," defined as "cool, young, awed by nothing—the world's natural heiress, ready right now to claim her inheritance" (1 August 1965, 60), was supplanted by the more marketable "Youthquaker," a term coined in an August 1965 *Vogue* piece that featured a full-page photograph of Sedgwick in her apartment, perched gracefully on one leg atop her leather rhinoceros, clad in a sleeveless T-shirt and her signature black tights (1 August 1965, 91). Sedgwick's spread in the March 1966 *Vogue*, in which she models a bias chemise and a crêpe chemise-slip ("Edith Sedgwick Wears Small Starts for Small Clothes," 15 March 1966, 134–35), was intended as a tryout for a semi-regular presence in the magazine, but the invite was revoked due to reservations about her drug habit (Stein 243–44).

Sedgwick's impromptu arabesque for her "Youthquaker" profile embodies the qualities that Vreeland prized: movement, breathless activity, the "blaze of certainty" and "special dash" of youth (*Vogue*, 1 August 1964, 43). Animation was the aim of the new, freer style based around short skirts and stretch fabrics, because the Youthquaker's "body is strong and pliant and wonderfully pretty to see in motion—darting, springing, swinging curling and uncurling like a happy young cat" (1 August 1965, 60). The most celebrated of the sixties fashion photographers, men like Bailey and Avedon, were those most adept at capturing in a still image the quality of fleeting yet frenetic motion. Warhol mastered this skill as well, but within the cinematic medium. He likely grasped intuitively that Sedgwick, who shared with her contemporaries Mary Quant and Jean Shrimpton the ability to suggest movement in a snapshot, would be a perfect "model" for his famously unmoving moving pictures.

In their collaborations Warhol imposed numerous artificial constraints on Sedgwick's movements, forbidding her to leave the limits of the fixed frame and restricting her to the confined spaces of a trunk (*Vinyl*), a bed (*Beauty #2*), a sofa (*Afternoon*), and a chair (*Kitchen* and *Restaurant*). Sedgwick irrepressibility, not surprisingly, overrode those confines. In these films she explodes the stasis demanded by her surroundings with spontaneous body

Film shoot as fashion shoot: Sedgwick models her leopard-skin coat in *Poor Little Rich Girl* (Digital frame enlargement from *Andy Warhol: A Documentary Film*, PBS Paramount, 2006)

ily and facial expressions. Such gesticulations could be triggered even within the narrative films, often by "mistakes" that transgress their already unstable diegetic worlds. In *Kitchen*, Sedgwick smiles wickedly at the brazenly campy performance style of her friend Donald Lyons and grimaces broadly as she repeatedly knocks over her makeup mirror. (In other films she frequently upsets drinks and ashtrays.) In *Vinyl*, in a role requiring silence and stillness, Sedgwick introduces energetic movement into her per-formance via dance; her fluid, sinuous arm motions form an eloquent counterpoint to co-star Gerard Malanga's more exerting, strenuous moves. The Sedgwick films are also peppered with explicit references to modeling, as seen in most of the second reel of *Poor Little Rich Girl*, in which Sedgwick tries on various fur coats in anticipation of leaving her apartment. In *Kitchen*, the action is halted repeatedly as fashion photographer David McCabe walks onto the set from behind the camera and snaps both posed and action "stills" of the actors *during* their performance. Juan A. Suárez has classified the Factory's star vehicles as "street variants of *Vogue* and *Harper's*" (237) because they emphasize the tawdry and the unprettified. The fashion journals and the Warhol movies, however, also share common objectives related to the shattering of boundaries between the authentic and the manufactured, the timeless and the obsolescent, the unchanging and the always becoming. For Warhol, Edie Sedgwick proved invaluable in making this appropriation possible.

☆☆★★★ Edie Vérité

In the scripted Warhol-Sedgwick films, "text" often (d)evolves into a kind of publicity, and narrative becomes pretext or alibi for an ulterior signification. For David E. James, Warhol's fictional cinema was essential to his critical project, in that such films "allowed confrontation with the conventions of role playing and with the vocabulary of acting, and so provided the vehicle for an approach to Hollywood as a historical and economic institution" (70). Even in the Tavel pictures the goal of Warhol's cinema was, as Stephen Koch claims, "to evoke the presence and responses of the superstars" (64), rather than communicate a story through appropriate acting codes. This notion dates back to the earliest discourse on Warhol's sound films, which were rarely discussed as being "acted" in the traditional sense; rather, as expressed in a *New York Journal-American* feature, they were perceived as "merely focus[ing] on a single 'star' . . . doing what comes naturally" (Virginia Palmer, "Goddess of the Underground," 6 March 1966, 4). Warhol encouraged this notion through comments such as "I leave the camera running until it runs out of film because that way I can catch people being themselves" (qtd. in Mekas, "Notes" 141) and by disavowing any interest in conventional actors, labeling them as "all wrong for my movies" because "they have something in mind" (qtd. in P.T., "13 Most Beautiful . . . ," *New York Herald Tribune*, 10 January 1965, 2:3).

Because star quality in Warhol's fiction films was (over-) valued and projected at the expense of a coherent diegetic world, they can be classified as "improvised" in the sense that the main interest deriving from such films can be located independent of storyline. The Sedgwick "documentaries," on the other hand, are much more closely controlled and manipulated than they seem on the surface. This manipulation becomes manifest in part because of Sedgwick's greater participation in shaping the documentaries and in part because of the distinctive objective served by these texts: to document the very construction of Sedgwick's persona, a persona later subject to the constraints of narrative filmmaking in pictures like *Kitchen*. Whereas *Kitchen*'s absurdist storyline serves as a pretext for generating publicity for Warhol's artistic enterprise, based around the appeal of Edie Sedgwick, in the *Poor Little Rich Girl* cycle the act of observing and thus publicizing Sedgwick becomes the text itself. Each film in the series, therefore, is situated around a simple premise designed to elicit Sedgwick's reactions: Edie dines out with her Cambridge pals (*Restaurant*); Edie plays host to friends Ondine, Lyons, Arthur Loeb, and Dorothy Dean (*Afternoon*); Edie takes a handsome stud back to her apartment (*Beauty #2*).

Poor Little Rich Girl was the first of these sixty-six-minute portraits of Sedgwick being "herself." ("To play the poor little rich girl in the movie," Warhol later explained, "Edie didn't need a script—if she'd needed a script, she wouldn't have been right for the part" [Warhol and Hackett 110].) More specifically, she spends much of the film, and all of the first reel, performing the small rituals of her morning routine. In reel 2 she converses with Chuck Wein, who is positioned behind Warhol's camera, while she tries on clothes. The film was actually shot twice because the first attempt was severely out of focus; the final "cut" was assembled using the "ruined" first reel from the initial shoot and the in-focus second reel, resulting in a dichotomous view of the movie's subject. The metaphoric fragmenting or splitting of Sedgwick in her films has been analyzed by Wayne Koestenbaum, who finds it symptomatic of Warhol's need "to see desire centrifugally scattered into two separate bodies . . . echoing in heartless analogy" (93), a need that reflects Warhol's personal view of "human relationships as torture" (128). This schizoid divide is enacted on a more literal level in *Rich Girl* through the presence of a mirror, a featured prop in several other Sedgwick vehicles, including *Lupe*, a film that further doubles her image through dual-screen projection. The gesture's limit case is *Outer and Inner Space*, a dual-screen film in which Sedgwick's image is quadrupled through the framing of "each" Edie against her own, previously videotaped likeness.

The soft focus in *Poor Little Rich Girl*'s opening reel has the effect, as numerous critics have noted, of increasing Sedgwick's "mystique" (John Wilcock, "The Detached Cool of Andy Warhol," *Village Voice*, 6 May 1965, 23) and rendering her "alluring yet ungraspable" (Angell, "Andy" 132). The neglected second reel, however, allows more direct access to not only the star's materiality but also her personality. Because of its blur, reel 1 paints a portrait of Sedgwick as a bundle of indistinct tics and mannerisms, a ghostly apparition who makes telephone calls, ingests pills, smokes, stretches, pedals her legs in the air (a gesture she repeats in *Kitchen*), and bobs her head in time to an Everly Brothers record. In reel 2 we can see her clearly and are therefore in a better position to apprehend her unique physical quirks, like her comically pained mugging as she tries to end a phone conversation with a determined suitor. Furthermore, in her conversation with Wein she remarks upon many of the life events that helped form the public image she would promote throughout 1965 (see Marylin Bender, "Edie Pops Up as Newest Superstar," *New York Times*, 26 July 1965, 26; and Nora Ephron, "Woman in the News: Edie Sedgwick, Superstar," *New York Post*, 5 September 1965, 2:1): her personal life tragedies (she discusses her brother Bobby's death and her own serious car accident); her estrangement from both her class (she laments that her rich acquaintances are "all pigs") and her family; and her acting career.

From their very first exhibitions, the Sedgwick documentaries have been discursively linked to the cinematic movement most closely identified with ethnographic realism: cinéma vérité. This strategy was initiated by Jonas Mekas in his *Village Voice* column, in which he asserted that *Poor Little Rich Girl* surpassed anything yet attempted by "Leacock, Rouch, Maysles, Reichenbach" ("Movie Journal," 29 April 1965, 13); it then figured in the *Voice*'s promotion for a double bill of *Vinyl* and *Rich Girl* at the Astor Place Playhouse, in which the two films were marketed as "Pop style experiments in Cinema-Verite" (3 June 1965, 15). Mekas proclaimed Sedgwick "to be the most suitable person for such a film, with the proper personality," an acknowledgment of Sedgwick's importance and of Warhol's dependence on his star's personality for *Rich Girl*'s effects rather than those techniques (e.g., long take, direct sound, grainy black-and-white image) that signify an unmediated reality. This distinction was delicately downplayed in the publicity statements from the Warhol camp. Wein, serving as Factory spokesman, promoted the Sedgwick vehicles as exceptional in that they were spontaneous and truthful *because* they were contrived and synthetic. In Wein's estimation, one could "get down to the real nitty-gritty of cinematic truth only by creating a situation that is close to life as it is known to the actors" (qtd. in Douglas Sefton, "The Underground Movie: An Avant Garden of Eden," *New York Daily News*, 6 August 1965, 34). Yet this admission still fails to highlight the significance of Sedgwick's own agency. The example set by her films suggests that Callie Angell's thesis about the Warhol *Screen Tests*, that they "should be recognized as true collaborations, films in which the subjects have at least as much control as the artist in determining the outcome of the finished work" (*Andy* 14), should be extended to the features, as well.

Perhaps inevitably, Sedgwick's determination to take advantage of her position and more actively shape the direction of her career provoked considerable irritation on the part of her mostly male collaborators, hastening not only her own departure from the Factory but that of her primary adversary, Ronald Tavel, who chafed at writing scenarios to be so haphazardly and amateurishly performed by Warhol's recruits. Tavel's accounts of his acrimonious relationship with Sedgwick invariably deride her unrefined acting skills, which he attributes to her dependence on amphetamines and the attitude of entitlement enabled by her fawning coterie. But his comments also betray a stubborn unwillingness to share with his muse the objectives guiding his own creative output, as illustrated in his observation that "Edie started to annoy me when she asked" about the meaning under-lying his screenplays (qtd. in Stein 226). Like the other alpha males—Malanga, Wein, Paul Morrissey—jockeying for the position of Warhol's second-in-command, Tavel took pains to protect his turf, which ruled out alliances with other factions and especially with someone who, in the writer's view, "had absolutely no idea of what Andy was after or had ever done, of what the films effectively were or what they effectively would be . . . [someone] completely beyond grasping the simplest stage directions, knowing right from left in fact, let alone learning a role" ("*Shower*," http://www.ronald-tavel.com/pdf/012.pdf, accessed April 8, 2008). To Sedgwick's query as to what his scripts were about, Tavel curtly answered, "Nothing."

Sedgwick refused to accept this evasive response, and her retaliation became the subtext of their final movie as colleagues, *Space*. Though Tavel claimed the film was written chiefly to accommodate the increasingly in-capacitated Factory stock players, his later published comments suggest a more serious intent: a work of "abstraction" for which the author en-visioned eight performers arranged in a figure-eight, alternately speaking aphorisms selected at random from a typed page, thus commenting on "the broad mysticism in vogue at the time, Infinity, chance, the ordered and the arbitrary" ("*Space*," http://www.ronald-tavel.com/pdf/013.pdf, accessed April 8, 2008). Sedgwick's response upon being handed the *Space* script was to immediately tear it up (Stein 227). During shooting she and Donald Lyons concocted an improvised bit involving the Holy Commun-ion; their blatant subversion in turn inspired the other cast members to abandon the scenario and start a food fight and then a group sing-along. Revealingly, near the end of the second reel of shooting (long after a dis-gusted Tavel had walked out), Sedgwick picks up one of Tavel's mimeo-graphed sheets and mocks the screenwriter, sarcastically mimicking their earlier conversation ("'What does it *mean*?' 'Blah, blah, blah'"), and acidly suggests that the script must mean something profound but she isn't "allowed" to ask what. Tavel long blamed Sedgwick for the end of his asso-ciation with Warhol, saying as early as 1966 that "the day an actress starts dictating her scripts art goes out the window, and I gathered up my scripts and went out the door" ("The Theatre of the Ridiculous," *Tri-Quarterly* 6, 1966, 95). But certainly Tavel's reluctance to acknowledge Sedgwick's part in the success of, for example, *Kitchen* as a *film*, and his unwillingness to regard Sedgwick as a creative peer, played equally important parts in this dissolution.

Warhol's account of his own final falling out with his protégé reveals a similarly disheartening refusal to be upfront with Sedgwick about the terms of their cinematic collaboration. In his 1980 memoir, the artist recalls Sedgwick's objection that "everybody knows I just stand around in [these movies] doing nothing and you film it and what kind of talent is that?" Flustered, Warhol defended their work by denigrating it:

> I tried to make her understand that if she acted in enough of these underground movies, a Hollywood person might see her and put her in a big movie. . . . The funny thing about all this was that the whole idea behind making those movies in the first place was to be ridiculous. I mean, Edie and I both knew they were a joke—that was why we were doing them! . . . I kept reminding her that *any* publicity was good publicity.
>
> (Warhol and Hackett 123–24; emphasis in original)

Sedgwick's intransigence ultimately led Warhol to sever their personal and professional relationship. But for most of 1965 he used that intransigence to his artistic advantage. That Warhol chose to exhibit and publicize those films to which Sedgwick contributed the most of herself suggests that he realized (as Tavel could not) that his star's contestation over the authorship of her pictures itself constituted a textual element—both in scripted and unscripted productions—that further distinguished his cinema from that of his avant-garde counterparts.

The source of fascination for many of the Warhol cinema's devotees is the combustible psychodrama that results from the onscreen provocation of the Superstars. Tavel himself acknowledged in 1971 that the Warhol films' plot situations were determined on the basis of their capacity to bring forth extreme reactions from the actors: "There's a way of driving them to become very real because the script was geared in a way to make them just go insane, and then you pick people that are just on the verge of going nuts so that there is never any security" (qtd. in Wilcock, *Autobiography*). Surprisingly, given her own frequently precarious mental state, Sedgwick has often been identified by critics as the Superstar most unflappable and most immune to this tactic. For Stephen Koch, Sedgwick was "unique among the women superstars because she never played the female clown. . . . When she spoke she made sense; her response to a contretemps on screen . . . was never the customary hysteria but a visibly intelligent effort to cope" (67; see also Finkelstein and Dalton 101; and Edward Hood, "Edie Sedgwick," *Film Culture*, Summer 1967, 34). Indeed, what gives Sedgwick's films for Warhol their particular charge is her objection to the sado-masochistic relationship between author and subject they are designed to enact, via the imposition of deviously staged hostility and conflict. *Afternoon*'s third reel reveals both the mechanics behind this process and Sedgwick's resistance to it, as evidenced by her spontaneous reactions to Warhol's goading of the cast to

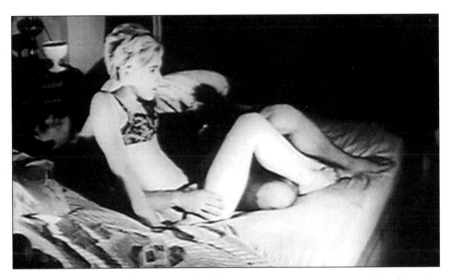

The center of unwanted scrutiny: Sedgwick's attention is torn between Gino Piserchio and Chuck Wein (offscreen) in *Beauty #2* (Digital frame enlargement from *Andy Warhol: A Documentary Film*, PBS Paramount, 2006)

physically and intellectually spar; she pleads for Ondine to quit assaulting Arthur ("I can't stand when people fight!") and moans when Dorothy suggests that they all "attack one another's shortcomings" ("That's what we do all day long!").

The most infamous of the Sedgwick psychodramas is *Beauty #2*, which was advertised by the Film-Makers' Cinematheque as one of "Andy Warhol's pseudoclinical explorations in pop art style" (*Village Voice*, 30 September 1965, 20). "Pseudoclinical" is an apt descriptor, as the film's premise suggests a sinister psychiatric experiment. *Beauty #2* opens on Sedgwick, in bra and panties, seated on a bed next to a reclining, shirtless companion she supposedly picked up at a club. As in *Poor Little Rich Girl* Chuck Wein sits offscreen and vies for Sedgwick's attention, his running commentary alternately encouraging and thwarting her seduction of her bedmate. After some preliminary small talk, Wein brings to the surface various long-harbored animosities regarding their offscreen friendship. He hammers away at Sedgwick's insecurities and personality flaws, accusing her of not listening to people, of being narcissistic and spoiled, of drinking and laughing too much. He berates her for only parroting what she's been directed to say by Gerard Malanga, who sits just outside the frame whispering stage directions. By the middle of the first reel Wein's taunts turn vicious, although his references to Sedgwick's possibly incestuous relationships with her father and recently deceased brother and to her possible pregnancy (and quest for an illegal abortion) are masked just enough to elude the understanding of the un-informed viewer.

In all of her Warhol productions after *Vinyl,* Sedgwick is the undisputed focus. Even in her "ensemble" films, the camera operator (often Warhol himself) keeps her centered within the frame and her fellow actors defer to her; even the acerbic attention-mongers she shares the screen with in *Afternoon* cease their verbal pyrotechnics for long enough to allow her to deliver a daffy yet utterly sincere rap about the need for humanity to "develop a suspension of mind" so that it may survive in outer space. When the spotlight threatens to shift, Sedgwick proves adept at shifting that attention back to herself by commandeering scripts and situations, a talent especially evident in *Space. Beauty #2,* however, places her in a position to which she is unaccustomed: the center of *un*wanted scrutiny. Consequently, her response to Wein's badgering is to deflect attention away from herself and redirect it toward her inquisitor. Sedgwick knowingly makes the film's disembodied "narrator," who never once appears within the image, into a corporeal subject—even as she herself superficially dominates the viewer's awareness as the film's main discursive subject and the occupant of the frame's central zone. Recognizing almost immediately that her male collaborators have a different, more menacing objective in mind than to indulge her monologues, she maintains her trademark effervescent façade while pointedly undercutting Wein's attempts to trap her in her own words, admonishing her old friend for misinterpreting everything she says and rebutting his attempts to patronize her. ("Why would I say 'what do you mean?' if I *knew* what you meant?") Though bombarded by lewd accusations, Sedgwick largely succeeds in keeping her cool throughout her ordeal, give or take a thrown ashtray, thus further focusing attention on her unseen tormentor, who strains to top each previous insult in order to elicit the desired aggravation.

Near the end of *Beauty #2,* Sedgwick mocks Wein with the question: "Do you think I'm performing for you?" Her query has broad implications, for "performance" was for Sedgwick a lifelong default mode of behavior, the result of a peculiar upbringing of luxury and privilege tempered by repressed family tragedies and abuse. Having adopted acting out as a psychological survival method, Sedgwick behaved like a star from childhood onward. The star image she performed in public was somewhat familiar, her prima donna's self-absorption and crippling anxieties replayed the offscreen existences of Marilyn Monroe and Judy Garland, the two mainstream movie stars most frequently cited in comparison to Sedgwick (see Edward Hood, "Edie Sedgwick," *Film Culture,* Summer 1967, 34; and Warho and Hackett 105–06). For their legions of followers, Monroe's and Garland's stardom is special because of the actresses' abilities to inject their screen performances with hints of their actual vulnerabilities and insecurities. Sedgwick, by virtue of the fact that she worked in experimental film production, was not constrained by the pressure to embody a character in the first place. The corpus of Warhol's film work illustrates just how difficult it is for a Superstar to sustain a shtick for an entire reel; for Sedgwick, in contrast, the more unnatural the filmic demands placed upon her, the more in command she appeared. When called upon to act as actresses in commercial properties do, she floundered. Reports of Sedgwick's dozens of blown takes and muffed lines on the *Ciao Manhattan* shoot indicate not only the ravages of heroin addiction but a temperament fundamentally unsuited to the discipline of "real" movie acting, and a performer paradoxically better equipped for a thirty-three-minute take than for a five-second line reading. Her screen appearances, therefore, seem much more direct and unmediated than those of the Hollywood stars Warhol worshipped. Yet they reveal not so much the "reality" of the performer but the fact that the performer's reality is that of constant performance. A close examination of her films suggests Edie Sedgwick's skill at signifying on this performance, confirming an agency that has been given short shrift ever since her indelible emergence.

ACKNOWLEDGMENTS

The author wishes to thank Greg Pierce at the Andy Warhol Museum and Tom Yoshikami for their invaluable assistance.

Eva and Zsa Zsa Gabor
Hungary Meets Hillbilly U.S.A.

DIANE PECKNOLD

When Eva Gabor died at seventy-four, the *New York Times* eulogized her as being "best known for her role as an out-of-place city socialite stuck on a farm on television's 'Green Acres' in the 1960s," but opined that she "probably achieved as much celebrity from being one of the three Gabor sisters as she did from her acting." This kind of assessment had dogged Eva throughout her career. As early as 1954, she described the difficulty she had overcoming her celebrity. "I've got to beat my glamour down. I've got to make the audience forget it, make them accept me as an actress," she averred in her autobiography (Gabor 213).

Eva Gabor. Courtesy Photofest.

Eva and Zsa Zsa Gabor stand in this volume as envoys of an emergent mode of stardom in which celebrity precedes film work, and then infiltrates and underscores (or undermines) screen stardom. Theirs is a pop-culture stardom no longer under the centralized control of Hollywood studios that came to the fore and troubled the lines between stardom and celebrity in the 1960s. Indeed, Zsa Zsa has been cited as "one of the first and easily among the most outstanding exemplars of . . . modern celebrity. [Hers] was a fame that required having to do no work to get it, save gaining media exposure" (Gabler, *Life* 163). Their unabashed cultivation of their own public personae was greeted with a form of indignant ridicule that revealed its threatening potential. "They all seem to have arrived [in America] carrying nothing but a slightly used mink coat, a bushel of orchids and a press agent," jibed one journalist (Tim Taylor, "I'm Bored with Gabors," *Cue*, 13 June 1953, 10–11). Another caustically suggested that "the Gabors measure success by the physical weight of newspaper notices the clipping bureaus turn over to them." But the real disdain was prompted by the fact that they had shrewdly created this publicity themselves. "The Gabors do not have a publicity agent. In the past, occasionally, they engaged the services of a professional, but long ago they came to the conclusion that all public relations counsels are mere amateurs in comparison to their own skills," *Esquire* reported in a mocking profile of the clan (John Mariot Graham, "Glamour Goulash," September 1953, 98).

Eva Gabor is, moreover, harbinger of a new mode of televisual stardom, combining film work and TV work; but with TV stardom always intertwined with film stardom and extra-textual celebrity. Though Gabors were fixtures of media culture throughout the 1950s, it was not until "Green Acres" (1965–1971) that Eva finally became a legitimate screen star, an accomplishment that, ironically, reflected her ability to embody the tension between celebrity and stardom in the post-studio era, and to mediate the larger anxieties about social and cultural authority such tension revealed.

At the same time that the Gabors participate in a repositioning of star discourse, their stardom is particularly relevant to the 1960s in another way, as their stardom is caught up in 1960s' discourses on race and class. Not only celebrity outcasts in the supposedly legitimate ranks of Hollywood stardom, they were also racially suspect ethnic whites in civil rights America. The Gabors could thus be imagined as the cultural detritus of, simultaneously, the breakdown of traditional class-cultural hierarchy and unexamined white privilege. In "Green Acres," Eva mobilized her status as an ersatz star to satirize increasingly unstable cultural mythologies—particularly cinematic ones—that had diffused and sustained class distinction and racial hegemony in the immediate postwar era.

★★★★★ Eva in the Barnyard: Casting Celebrity

"The first question popping into mind while watching Eva Gabor film a scene for a new TV series called 'Green Acres,'" television columnist Hal Humphrey wrote in 1965, "is, 'What's a chic Hungarian like her doing in a barnyard?'" ("Hungary Meets Hillbilly, U.S.A.," *Los Angeles Times*, 9 August 1965, 5: 20). His question both encapsulated the camp juxtaposition at the heart of the show's comedy and summarized the key features of class and ethnicity on which it relied. Following attorney Oliver Wendell Douglas (Eddie Albert) and his socialite wife Lisa (Eva Gabor) as they move from their Park Avenue apartment to a crumbling farmhouse in Hooterville to pursue Oliver's agrarian dream, the show continually mobilized the Gabor image of ethnic exoticism and wealth without class as the primary comic device through which it satirized social distinction. "That's where the humor comes in," Eva told a reporter. "It's the contrast between me and the farm. They see the chickens and they see me there in chiffon" (Morton Moss, "Eva Gabor Mixes Chiffon and Shenanigans in 'Green Acres,'" *TV Weekly*, 26 July 1970, 4). Her co-star agreed that her character was inseparable from her "real life" public persona. "Eva is playing herself," Eddie Albert opined. "The further she goes with her Hungarian accent and her regal mannerisms, the greater the comedy" (Isobel Ashe, "Good Living, Bad Farming on Green Acres," *Appleton [Wisc.] Post-Crescent*, 31 October 1965, n.p.).

At first blush, Eva might have seemed an odd choice to appeal to CBS's core audience. Since the advent of television broadcasting, the network had relied on a single principle: offering bankable but expensive stars to attract a mass audience, regardless of that audience's demographic characteristics (Roger Beardwood, "Bad Days at Black Rock," *Fortune*, May 1968, 175, 227). As critics derisively noted, this focus on obtaining the largest possible audience to cover the cost of star salaries meant that CBS, more than any other network, had to appeal to "'the folks in Iowa' . . . a trade term referring to the vast audience in the Middle West and all the rural states" (Bob MacKenzie, "My Consternation Worries Are Over," *Oakland Tribune*, 7 October 1965, 20; Slater 253–55; Edgerton 274–76). Until the end of the 1960s, when Nielsen began to break its ratings out by age, income, and other demographic factors, CBS consistently outstripped its network competition by capturing the great American middle, not only in terms of geography but socioeconomic status and life-cycle as well. Its programming roster famously emphasized low-brow rural sitcoms aimed at working- and lower-middle class audiences, at rural dwellers and recent migrants to the cities and suburbs, and at viewers old enough to have an established loyalty to stars like Lucille Ball and Jackie Gleason (Johnson 122–24).

In spite of the apparent disjuncture between the flamboyant glamour of the Gabor image and the characteristics of the CBS audience, the network clearly understood Eva as the celebrity upon whom "Green Acres" would rely. Producer Jay Sommers initially had reservations about whether she was appropriate for the part, which had been written for Martha Hyer, but by the time production started Eva was important enough to the package that she was able to negotiate not only for some of Hollywood's most expensive make-up artists and hairdressers, but also for a wardrobe budget large enough to costume her in gowns by French designer Jean Louis (Hal Humphrey, "Eva Has a 'Pooh' for Temperament," *Los Angeles Times*, 5 September 1966, D18). For the publicity department at Filmways, the show's production company, she was "the one stabilizing factor that the media accepted. . . . She was a Gabor." Ted Switzer, who handled the company's publicity for all of the Paul Henning rural sitcoms on CBS, remembered that Eva "was what elevated the show in the minds of the media" (Cox 147). Unlike the actors in "The Beverly Hillbillies," whom Henning hoped would "cease to exist as themselves" and who were therefore discouraged from creating public personae through entertainment columns and star-at-home photo layouts (Harkins 189), Eva's biography as a Hungarian immigrant and her home life as a millionaire sophisticate were central components of the show's publicity regime.

If Lisa Douglas had been a superior, New York snob who gets her come-uppance at the hands of wily hicks, or an exotic foreigner whose otherness marks and celebrates the boundary of normative American community, the mobilization of the Gabor persona to attract the older, rural, downscale audience to which CBS catered would have been a predictable populist strategy, especially in light of the emerging neoconservative vilification of "limousine liberals" and the intellectual "new class." But Lisa was intended as a sympathetic character, far more adaptable to the bucolic illogic of Hooterville than her husband, and generally allied with the hicks rather than the perennially flummoxed and fleeced Oliver. In fact, the cultural reasoning behind the casting was opaque enough to potential sponsors that they requested a battery of marketing tests "to establish a barometer of her acceptance by the average person," and she was given the role only when the results showed that "hostility was minimal" (Marian Christy, "Eva Gabor: Brains Beneath That Beauty," *Mansfield [Ohio] New Journal*, 7 October 1971, 4C). To the relief of CBS and Filmways, the role made Eva one of the most popular actresses on television, and contributed to a half-decade of top 30 rankings for "Green Acres." She had been an actress and a well-known celebrity before the series, but it was the show that made her a screen star proper (Cynthia Lowry, "Little Eva's Made the Grade: 'Green Acres' Gives Gabor Star Status," *Charleston [W.V.] Gazette*, 21 January 1968, 9A). That she could become an object of identification rather than antipathy for the CBS audience triggers Hal Humphrey's question: What *was* Eva doing in the barnyard?

Eva's counterintuitive popularity as Lisa Douglas revealed important shifts in American discourses of race, class, and gender during the 1960s, particularly those surrounding one of the largest internal migrations in the nation's history: the exodus of millions of rural whites to the west and urban north that began with the Dust Bowl and peaked in the late 1950s. Especially on "Green Acres," but also in *Country Music Holiday* (1958) and *Youngblood Hawke* (1964), the Gabors' performances connected their established personae as white others and class pretenders to the discourses of liminality associated with the migrants, whose move from south to north reconfigured the nation's cultural and political landscape, and whose relationship to narratives of American egalitarianism and pluralism was especially problematic (Gregory).

☆☆☆★★★ Glamour Girls and Gold Diggers: Gender and Class Mobility

The "Gabor legend," as it was often described, evoked "an aura of Bandit perfume, white mink, and sparkling jewels" (Lowry, "Little Eva's Made the Grade," 9A). In the publicity surrounding "Green Acres," Eva was clearly understood as a glamour girl, but she repeatedly stressed in interviews that she was, above all, a hard worker. "I come from the stage and I have discipline," she told Hal Humphrey ("Eva Has a 'Pooh' for Temperament," D18). "Darling, I live like a prize fighter," she told Cynthia Lowry. "I do nothing but work and keep in trim" ("Little Eva's Made the Grade," 21 January 1968, 9A). Profiles dwelt at length on the contrast between her image as a diva and her genuine professionalism: "Underneath that . . . fragile beauty there lies a sense of dedication vastly appreciated by anyone who has ever worked with [Eva]. She is organized. She is punctual. She is prepared. . . . She is, in short, the very essence of a pro," one such piece declared ("Little Eva—Hungarian Style," *Hayward [Calif.] Daily Review*, 21 May 1967, n.p.).

Eva's public insistence on hard work lay at the heart of her ability to represent a critique of class distinction that resonated with the experience of working-class whites in the 1960s. It was also a calculated corrective to her sister's reputation. Eva and Zsa Zsa were regularly conflated in the entertainment press and the popular imagination. Stories with titles such as "I'm Bored with the Gabors," "The Glamorous Fabulous Gabor Girls," and "Another Gabor" made the sisters interchangeable as icons of Hollywood celebrity. Audiences frequently struggled to distinguish between the sisters. "Are Eva Gabor and Zsa Zsa Gabor sisters, twins, or the same person?" asked a confused viewer in a TV question-and-answer column ("Queries," *Winnipeg Free Press*, 21–26 October 1967, 11). A typical instance of "Green Acres" reflexive humor parodically acknowledged that Eva's presence always summoned Zsa Zsa's persona as a tabloid celebrity and international playgirl. "When you married me, you knew I couldn't cook, I couldn't sew, and I couldn't keep house," Lisa complains to Oliver. "All I could do was talk Hungarian and do imitations of Zsa Zsa Gabor."

Because Eva and Zsa Zsa were treated as interchangeable, Eva indexed one of the most persistent comedic tropes of cross-class fantasy in the postwar era: the gold digger. The gold digger had emerged as a gendered mediator of class tension in the 1920s, when the stereotype of the conniving working girl in search of a rich husband had suppressed feminist critiques of the effects of urbanization and industrialization on women, concealing need born of structural disadvantage by substituting mere greed as the motive for the gold digger's machinations (Robertson, *Guilty* 75). Films such as *Gold Diggers of 1933* (1933) reasserted Progressive-era concerns about women trying to survive economic hardship during the Depression, but when prosperity returned after World War II, the gold digger once again became a parodic embodiment of suspect class aspirations and consumerism. In part, the stereotype reinforced the effort to return women to the domestic sphere by equating female independence with unbridled greed. But the gold digger also became a more general vehicle for relieving the "insecurities about class aspiration, status panic, patterns of consumption, and cultural taste" that characterized postwar film and television (Beach 132). In the figure of the gold digger, "visions of material and social success were literally mapped onto women's bodies as class relations were mapped onto gender relations" (Beach 129).

Thanks to her highly publicized personal life and the casting that resulted from it, Zsa Zsa was one of the most recognizable embodiments of the 1950s gold digger. Her marriage to hotel magnate Conrad Hilton had made her a fixture in the gossip and society press during the 1940s, well before she developed a screen persona; the very lucrative terms of her divorce settlement—and the even more lucrative settlement she requested but did not get—were the subject of much publicity ("Wife to Ask $10,000,000 from Hilton, Hotel Man," *Los Angeles Times*, 12 April 1945, 2). Eva's marriage to and divorce from millionaire real estate developer Charles Isaacs received less coverage, but made it easy for reporters to connect her to Zsa Zsa's tabloid image. Profiles with headlines like "The Glamorous Fabulous Gabor Girls: Pin Careers on Rich Husbands" abounded (Igor Cassini, *Los Angeles Examiner*, 16 July 1950, 1–2).

Hollywood studios eagerly inserted Zsa Zsa and her offscreen persona into the gold-digger comedies of the postwar era. In *Lovely to Look At* (1953), she plays a Parisian dress model (predictably named Zsa Zsa) who arrives at a nightclub with a boorishly ostentatious rich American and is introduced by her employer as "one of our more enterprising models." In *We're Not Married* (1953), she unsuccessfully attempts to fleece her devoted but naïve millionaire husband of his fortune. And in her most famous role as Jane Avril in *Moulin Rouge* (1953), she plays a bubbling showgirl whose innocent and oft-voiced class pretensions are juxtaposed with the characterization of Henri de Toulouse-Lautrec as a tragic figure destroyed by the rigid class hierarchies and hypocritical bourgeois morality of belle époque France. As in so many contemporaneous comedies, the buoyant gold digger whom Zsa Zsa enacts provides the comic relief that alleviated the rest of the film's melodramatic allegorization of the injuries of class.

Eva was also regularly cast as a gold digger and libertine, most notably as Liane d'Exelmans in *Gigi* (1958) and as Felicienne Courbeau in *A New Kind of Love* (1963). The latter film typified the way the Gabors' gold digger roles facilitated mythologies of class mobility. Felicienne Corbeau is a Parisian fashion broker hired to serve as a local guide by a contingent of buyers for a New York department store: Sam (Joanne Woodward), her boss, Joe Bergner (George Tobias), and his secretary, Leena (Thelma Ritter). All three of the central female characters explore variations of the gold digger—Sam masquerades as a prostitute, while Leena hopes to capture the attention of her wealthy boss—but only Felicienne is the genuine article. Unlike Sam, who is driven by loneliness, and Leena, who is genuinely in love, Felicienne simply enjoys romantic conquest and the gifts that go with it. She easily seduces Joe into proposing marriage, complete with an enormous diamond engagement ring. "It's so large it's beyond being in bad taste," she coos. Just as inevitably, her dubious sexual history is revealed and Joe breaks off the engagement, leaving him free to fall in love with Leena, who has been performing the caring functions of a good wife all along. Felicienne is not expressly Machiavellian. "When she gets her motor running, she can't turn it off," Leena remarks as Felicienn

Eva (right) plays the gold digger to Joanne Woodward's self-sufficient but romantically unfulfilled working girl and Thelma Ritter's lovesick secretary in *A New Kind of Love*. (Courtesy Photofest)

embarks on yet another tryst only moments after being spurned by Joe. But she nonetheless serves as a defining counterpoint to Leena's honest working woman, and her unmasking validates the cross-class union of the boss and the secretary as genuine affection rather than an economic and sexual bargain.

The comedic dismissal of the gold digger or the frustration of her schemes affirmed the essential class harmony represented by the married couple in suburban Cold War ideology. But while Hollywood used fantasies of romantic union to allay the real threat of class division, the Gabors' offscreen personae troubled such resolution and highlighted the connection between the gold digger masquerade and the class anxieties of the era. The postwar expansion of consumerism had led many observers to trumpet the arrival of a "classless society," but the shift in popular constructions of class relations was as much a cause of apprehension as celebration. In an age when professionals were no longer necessarily autonomous and self-employed, when geographic mobility undercut the social networks that might formerly have guaranteed recognition of class status, and when the rise in mass consumerism and middle-brow taste made commodity symbolism a much less effective means of class distinction, membership in the middle class no longer necessarily carried many of its former prerogatives (Beach 127–31).

Zsa Zsa revealed the class underpinnings of gold digger masquerade by self-consciously acknowledging and exposing to public scrutiny "her manipulation of that stereotype for her own ends" (Robertson, *Guilty Pleasures* 78). In a series of canny publicity maneuvers and interview statements, she slyly promulgated her own "low" reputation as a gold digger even as she indignantly denied it. One *Saturday Evening Post* profile purported to give Zsa Zsa's answer to "those undiscriminating persons who call her a gold digger," but instead featured her lament that, unlike her own, her former husband's business empire was evergreen: "My empire is my face and body, and nobody gets any younger," she matter-of-factly complained (Pete Martin, "I Call on Zsa Zsa Gabor," 13 September 1958, 105). This insistence on the gold digger masquerade as a form of feminized work reasserted the relationship between class and gender disadvantage at the heart of the figure's Progressive Era origins. In 1961, Zsa Zsa very publicly filed suit against a men's magazine for printing an article that she claimed "was calculated to defame and ridicule her" by unfairly depicting her "as a gold digger," but her loud protests served mainly to ensure that her name would appear alongside the epithet in news dailies across the country ("Zsa Zsa Gabor Files Suit for $6 Million," *Brainerd [Minn.] Daily Dispatch*, 22 April 1961, 2; "Zsa Zsa Gabor Claims False Stories Hurt," *Cumberland [Md.] Times*, 28 May 1961, 22). Indeed, she acknowledged to one reporter that "those stories are good for my career, dolling," before denying that she was a gold digger at all (Rick Du Brow, "Gold Digger? 'Not Me,' Says Gabor," *Salt Lake City Tribune*, 4 June 1961, 70). And while she insisted that she had married all her husbands for love alone, such declamations were as likely as not to be followed by vampish wisecracks, such as her quip that she and Conrad Hilton "had vun thing in common dollink. Ve both vanted his money" (May Mann, "Zsa Zsa Gabor's Surprising Confession: Success Has Ruined My Life as a Woman," *Modern Screen*, July 1970, n.p.).

But, like her sister, Zsa Zsa also insisted on her own status as a working woman and on the notion that class difference was a more deeply lived experience than the image of the gold digger's mobility through courtship or the Gabors' excessive performance of glamour, suggested. Her 1960 marriage to Joshua Cosden failed, she argued, because of irresolvable class difference. She had ultimately discovered that her husband had "completely different views and values" than she did. "Joshua came from an enormously rich family, and there you have the attitude of *expecting* goo‑

things to happen for you," she explained, and depicted herself, by contrast, as "a self-made woman" who "worked hard and achieved a new life" for herself (Mann, "Zsa Zsa Gabor's Surprising Confession," n.p.). And while she often enforced an ironic distance between herself and her masquerade as a gold digger in her dealings with the press, she also exposed the troublingly real consequences of that masquerade, in both her personal and professional life. She recognized that she was cast to "represent a definite personality—the Zsa Zsa I created," but when one reporter obliquely acknowledged that she was, in essence, a character actress, she passionately riposted, "I do not want to be a character actress. . . . I may be a character, but I do not want to be a character actress" (Frank 219; Martin, "I Call on Zsa Zsa Gabor," 105). In a particularly gendered form of double consciousness, she could wonder, "How shall I dress Zsa Zsa?" but at the same time find herself unable to distinguish her own sense of selfhood from externally constructed public and screen personae: "Jane Avril, Sari Gabor, Zsa Zsa. Who knows . . . what is really true and what is enchanting make-believe," she puzzled in her autobiography, itself someone else's ghost-written construction of her (Frank 284, 308).

Zsa Zsa's self-presentation as a working actress struggling against the ghettoizing burden of her own public persona spoke to a sense of class injury as lived experience that had largely fallen out of favor in the kinds of comedies and musicals in which the Gabors were cast as gold diggers (Beach 126). But in suggesting that class status was reducible to performed signs such as glamour, she also suppressed the notion that class really did make a difference: that it was a deeply lived social habitus rather than a mere masquerade. In this way, she glossed over socioeconomic anxieties in much the same way as contemporaneous gold digger films, where "the exterior signs of social class as cultural capital . . . [were] viewed as easily separable from economic wealth" (Beach 128).

By the time Eva emerged as a star on "Green Acres," her association with the gold digger image invested her character with an accumulation of conflicting meanings about the nature of class. Both she and Zsa Zsa could be read as venal pretenders whose wealth and success as celebrities reduced the meaning of class to mere performance, emptying it of its ability to signify meaningful social distinction. At the same time, their continued insistence on gendered performance as a form of work, whether onstage or off, limned an older narrative about status immobility that confirmed the enduring importance of cultural capital. As a result, Lisa Douglas could be read by audiences as both rejecting class differentiation and confirming its importance in lived experience.

★★★★★ "Bubbling Blonde Goulash": Racial Difference and White Ethnicity

The geographic mobility and mass commodity symbolism that threw class distinction into disarray during the 1950s and 1960s, combined with the challenge the civil rights movement posed to a previously invisible white privilege, also transformed the meaning of whiteness, and particularly ethnic whiteness, during those years. Just as their association with the gold digger had positioned the Gabors to simultaneously index and contain the era's class anxieties, the sisters' connections to gendered mediations of ethnicity and nation positioned them to deliver a meta-commentary on Hollywood's fables of assimilation and whiteness at a moment when the meaning of racial difference was undergoing a critical reevaluation.

As they became famous in the 1940s and 1950s, the Gabors were easily inserted into Hollywood's dominant discourses of white ethnicity. Cast in roles that positioned them as liminally but redeemably white, or that capitalized on their foreign accents to stitch them into fables of American global interventionism, both sisters were incorporated into a representational regime of whiteness that "symbolized the promise of American pluralism" even as it marked out the race-based limits of that pluralism (Negra, *Off-White* 3). When Eva signed with Paramount in 1939, the studio cultivated her specifically as an exotic import, describing her as a "Hungarian actress who was brought to this country by Paramount" in spite of the fact that she had actually arrived in Hollywood because of her husband's medical practice and only subsequently sought a career in film. The studio further emphasized her position in the system by juxtaposing the announcement with a note about Austrian-born Hedy Lamarr's most recent film and the arrival of French actor Victor Fancen, described as "another European acquisition" ("News of the Screen," *New York Times*, 13 February 1941, 25).

Even after the collapse of the studio system, press representations of the Gabors as exotic embodiments of Hungarian nationality and culture were utterly inescapable. "Along with goulash, veal paprika and Tokay," one profile suggested, the Gabors were "Hungary's most luxurious exports" (Lowry, "Little Eva's Made the Grade," 9A). Another declared, "After goulash, the Gabors are America's favorite Hungarian dish" (Joy Miller, "What's Behind Gabor Glamour?" *Ada [Okla.] Evening News*, 22 September 1961, 4). Whatever the reason, the Gabors continually performed their ethnicity for the publicity circuit. Zsa Zsa prepared goulash and sauerkraut on "The Steve Allen Show" in 1964, offering observations about Hungarian history, culture, and "gypsies," while Eva shared her recipe for "traditional Hungarian goulash" in newspaper television columns (Pullen 68; Johna Blinn, "Eva Gives Goulash Recipe," *Cedar Rapids Gazette*, 28 May 1967, 53).

The Gabors, however, also assiduously cultivated their ethnicity in their own self-promotion and public appearances. Indeed, Zsa Zsa's ghostwritten 1960 autobiography drew the very same parallel with Lamarr that Paramount's announcement had proposed. Reminiscing about the dazzling effect of seeing film and stage stars in the nightclubs of interwar Vienna when she was an aspiring teen actress, Gabor dwelt particularly on the night her escort pointed out "Hedy Mandl," whom she "was to know later in Hollywood as Hedy Lamarr." Lamarr is described in worshipful detail: she "wore a blue sequined dress which matched her eyes, her jet-black hair was set off by a superb diamond diadem, her face was incredible—I had never seen anything so beautiful" (Frank 49–50). Just as Paramount had done for Eva, Zsa Zsa sought to remind readers of studio-era Hollywood's tradition of female ethnic stardom, and to position herself as its inheritor.

The roles in which the sisters were cast throughout the 1950s and 1960s continued to reflect the structural position of ethnic white women in the Hollywood system. Eva regularly appeared in films where her accent and ethnicity defined her and distinguished her as one among a number of nationally or racially inflected "types" of women. In *Paris Model* (1953), she plays Gogo Montaine, the first of a series of women to wear the same dress in an effort to get what they want from men; Montaine dons the gown in her attempt to seduce the Rajah of Kim-Kepore, casting that clearly capitalized on the orientalist dimensions of Zsa Zsa's first marriage in Turkey. In *The Truth about Women* (1957), she plays a machinating French adulteress slotted between an enlightened British free-thinker, a tragic harem girl, and a grasping American belle. Even on television, where shorter time slots and the dominance of the racially homogenized suburban family sitcom would seem to have militated against this nominally pluralistic, if patently insulting, smorgasbord format, Eva's Hungarian heritage functioned as part of a gendered racial and ethnic continuum that emphasized the contingency and fluidity of racial categories. In a 1961 episode of the legal drama "The Defenders," she played one of six women suspected of murdering a millionaire. Alongside Chinese actress Tsai Chin and the Russian American Zohra Lampert, who was best known for her roles as working-class Italian Americans in *Pay or Die* (1960) and *Splendor in the Grass* (1961), Eva's ethnicity was presented both as part of an American pageant of difference and as inextinguishable otherness.

As such casting suggests, just as class difference had been mapped onto gender in the figure of the gold digger, so the Gabors provided a vehicle for articulating national and ethnic difference through gender conventions. Coverage of the Gabors' love lives continually emphasized that the democratic nature of American gender relations was just one more instance of difference from (and superiority to) Europe, a discourse the sisters themselves often reinforced. Eva, for instance, pointed out to one reporter that she had thoroughly assimilated, as evidenced by the fact that she expected her husband to fix his own breakfast. He may have thought he had married "a European woman" who would adhere to traditional gender roles, but, Eva claimed, "he didn't—I'm thoroughly American" (Miller, "What's Behind Gabor Glamour?" 4).

The lighthearted, celebratory rhetoric of ethnic pluralism the Gabors and sympathetic journalists promoted, however, could easily slide into more troubling modes that emphasized ethnic difference as irreducible, inassimilable, and potentially threatening. This shift was evident first in the way Zsa Zsa was cast as the alien counterpoint to Marilyn Monroe's ideal American girl in the publicity surrounding We're Not Married. Pale, blond, and fine-featured, the women appeared to be interchangeable incarnations of American femininity, and they were regularly pictured next to one another. But tabloid publicity revealed that Zsa Zsa's American looks were counterfeit. Her naturally dark hair was dyed blond and rumor suggested that her Eastern European nose had been reconstructed as a WASP-ish upturned button (John Mariot Graham, "Glamour Goulash," Esquire, September 1953, 98).

Eva's insistent references to the physical differences between American and Hungarian women challenged the efficacy even of such external transformation and edged the concept of ethnic difference closer to biological ideologies of race, a conception profoundly at odds with the diminishing rhetorical importance of ethnicity in the 1960s. "I never wear slacks," she explained to one reporter. "Slacks are for American girls with endless, fabulous long legs. European girls are round and feminine and should not wear slacks" (Bill Fiset, "Exotic Eva Gabor Scorns Sack Look," Oakland Tribune, 12 February 1958, 21D). In another interview she declared that she refused to wear slacks because "with my big Hungarian derriere, they've always looked ghastly on me" (Marilyn Beck, "Eva Likes Being Farm Wife," Winnipeg Free Press, 22 February 1969, 1). To another she remarked, "It doesn't make much difference what I eat. . . . I will always be round and Hungarian. I will never have long American legs and no hips" (Charles Witbeck, "Eva Gabor Thinks It's a Crime to Be Unattractive," Mansfield [Ohio] News Journal, 29 August 1968, 36). Whatever technology was applied to it, the Hungarian body remained, in such formulations, fundamentally different.

The same was true of the Gabors' accents, which Eva theatricalized to excess in her role as Lisa Douglas. Nearly every story on the sisters rendered their accents in literary dialect or commented on their malapropisms and mispronunciations. "Both [Gabors] still speak as if they had flunked a Berlitz course in Budapest," declared one, before noting that the sisters' accents were not only ineradicable but also contagious, quoting Eva's observation that she had "studied English at Columbia University" until "my professor turned gray and began speaking with a definite Hungarian accent" (Vernon Scott, "'Hello Dollink' Heard around Hollywood Now," *Great Bend [Kans.] Daily Tribune*, 21 February 1968, 8). Another recounted Eva's assertion that she had inadvertently taught her Mexican maid to speak English with a Hungarian accent. Even Hollywood's studios, America's crucibles of self-reinvention, had not been able to expunge Eva's accent. "Presumably the school for starlets went to work on her accent" during her stint as a contract player at Paramount, the profile speculated, "but with little result: it is still very charmingly Hungarian" (Joyce Haber, "Eva—Least Boring of the Gabors," *Los Angeles Times*, 25 August 1968, C12).

The Gabors' ethnic difference was thus not only cultural but physical and innate, and it excluded them from normative American-ness. A series of anthology and sitcom appearances by both sisters during the early 1960s indicated that the studio-era struggle to profitably manage white female ethnicity persisted into the television era, limiting the Gabors' roles and emphasizing their unfitness to embody the nation. In guest spots on the domestic sitcoms "Mr. Ed" and "The Joey Bishop Show" Zsa Zsa appeared once again as herself, and her exotic European excess was used as a foil to define middle-class American domesticity (Pullen). A failed pilot for a show called "Mickey and the Contessa" made a similar use of Eva. The show's premise revolved around a widower football coach who hires "a Hungarian refugee lady, ostensibly some older tomato" to keep house and help raise his children, but who ends up instead with the "lovely, shapely" Eva, whose European glamour hopelessly conflicts with the requirements of even surrogate domesticity (Earl Wilson, "Eva Gabor May Top Zsa Zsa If TV Series Is a Success," *Reno Evening Gazette*, 5 April 1961, 6). Zsa Zsa's appearance as herself on "December Bride" actually reflexively commented on such deployments of the Gabors' ethnicity. Seeking to convince her director that she can play Annie Oakley, Zsa Zsa acts out as parodic spectacle her inability to play "an American heroine"—her "Western 'drool'" is unintelligible through her thick Hungarian accent (Pullen71). Ironically, Zsa Zsa played out the very same conflict in real life shortly thereafter. "I'm dying to get a part in a western," one television columnist quoted her as saying. "After all,

Zsa Zsa was finally cast in a western on a 1967 episode of "Bonanza," but still in ethnic type as the gypsy fortuneteller Madame Marova. (Courtesy Photofest)

a lot of the American settlers had accents. Why shouldn't I do a 'Wagon Train' for instance?" The reporter's bemused tone, however, clearly ridiculed the very idea; the Gabors' ethnicity inescapably marked them as other, and as incapable of truly embodying the nation ("Zsa Zsa Gabor Wants to Do Western Show," *Troy [N.Y.] Record*, 1 September 1960, 41).

Though generally represented as humorous, the Gabors' lingering unassimilability also revived older constructions of contaminating ethnic whiteness associated with the nativist reaction to the massive immigration of eastern and southern Europeans in the late nineteenth and early twentieth centuries. Zsa Zsa, especially, became a gendered symbol of the limits of Americanization and the threat posed by immigrants. Reporting on a 1962 variety show appearance by Zsa Zsa, television columnist Rick Du Brow quoted the host's observation that "it would have been something if the three Gabor girls had married the three Kennedy boys," and noted that Zsa Zsa had "wisely avoided this line of humor," though it was unclear whether it was Zsa Zsa's Hungarianness or the Kennedys' Irish Catholicism, or both, that might besmirch the Americanness of the Office of the President (Rick Du Brow "Say, Zsa Zsa, Are You Hungarian?" *Oakland Tribune*, 25 July 1962, 18). The polluting threat of sexual congress between Americans and immigrants was similarly expressed in an article that depicted Conrad Hilton as "the perfect American representative," but for one flaw. "Who could be married to Zsa Zsa Gabor and still remain innocent and typically American?" the reporter's interlocutor asked (Lloyd Shearer, "Conrad Hilton: He's Americanizing the World," *Parade*, 21 July 1963, 13). Another article, about Peter Gogolak, a Hungarian football player whose career was said to demonstrate that "the 'American Dream' is just as glittering—and attainable—as ever," used Zsa Zsa as shorthand for the contrasting notion that some forms of ethnicity simply could not be incorporated into the national body politic: Gogolak fit right in, the article concluded, but most people found "goulash and Zsa Zsa Gabor indigestible" ("The Americanization of Pete Gogolak," *Parade*, 18 September 1966, 17–18). Such discourses of cultural indigestibility cut both ways in the civil rights era. On the one hand, they undermined the homogeneity and purported superiority of whiteness, but they also implicitly called into question the anti-biological interpretation of racial formation that had become the dominant liberal paradigm underlying integration (Omi and Winant 14–16).

Their physical and cultural failures meant that the Gabors could be perceived both as white and as not quite white enough, making them signifiers of the unstable and contingent nature of race, figures who potentially threateningly disconfirmed the inevitability . . . of whiteness as a form of social capital" (Negra, *Off-White* 5–6). That Zsa Zsa particularly featured in the popular imagination as someone whose whiteness was suspect was confirmed by Orson Welles's use of her cameo appearance in *Touch of Evil* (1958), a film devoted to probing the meaning of ethnic and racial difference, and particularly to interrogating the racialized tropes by which film noir had constructed the dark souls of its corrupt white characters (Lott; Dyer, "Colour of Virtue"). Welles cast both Zsa Zsa and Marlene Dietrich, one of the most recognizable archetypes of studio-era female ethnicity, in roles that emblematized the liminality of Hollywood's traditional constructions of white ethnic femininity. A strip club owner (Zsa Zsa) and a madam (Dietrich) in a Mexican border town, both actresses portray characters whose taint is racial and sexual. They are mired in a seamy and corrupt underworld where their implied sexual congress with nonwhites marks their fallen status and signifies the uncontainable threat of "color within whiteness" (Negra, *Off-White* 6).

As was so often the case, the role capitalized on Zsa Zsa's offscreen persona. A scandalous affair with Dominican diplomat Porfirio Rubirosa had eclipsed her emergent image as a legitimate actress in the early 1950s, so that the slightly seedy nature of her celebrity in the early 1960s seemed to give confirmation of the polluting dangers of sexual and social connection with racial Others, and positioned ethnic whiteness as especially vulnerable. The imagined threat posed by such transgressions of the color line was reiterated by a second scandal at the turn of the decade. As Congress was considering renewing aid to the Dominican Republic—one of a number of Latin American and Caribbean dictatorships the United States supported in the name of containing communism—newspapers began to report that the president's son, Ramfis Trujillo, had showered Zsa Zsa with tens of thousands of dollars in gifts, including a car and a mink coat. Congressman Wayne Hays denounced Gabor as "the most expensive courtesan since Madame de Pompadour" and introduced an amendment to remove the Dominican Republic from the foreign aid authorization bill ("National Affairs: A Romp with Pompadour," *Time*, 26 May 1958, 18). Coverage of the story connected the old world decadence once associated with the "new immigrants" to a more modern and pointedly racialized political and moral corruption: Ramfis was described as a "Latin playboy" and "a mustachioed Latin" ("Gifts Nobody's Business but His, Says Trujillo," *Los Angeles Times*, 11 May 1958, 1; "Zsa Zsa's Coat Mink, Not Chinchilla, Trujillo Says," *Los Angeles Times*, 13 May 1958, 2). Zsa Zsa thus became an updated, Cold War version of the immigrant as racial, political, and cultural contaminant and cemented the Gabors' association with a gendered discourse of inassimilable ethnicity and unsuccessful whiteness.

★★★★★ Eva in the Barnyard: Race, Class, and the Southern White Migration

Both onscreen and off, the Gabors made a spectacle of social failure and flouted hierarchies, whether in the form of the Hollywood star system, the taste distinctions of traditional class order, or the racial hegemony of the postwar era. As a result, they were perfectly positioned to reflect the experiences of the millions of rural-to-urban white migrants whose arrival in the urban, blue-collar industrial centers of the north and west prompted a reexamination of American formulations of race and class. Frequently cast as impoverished, illiterate, and lazy, the migrants unsettled popular belief in the inexorable advance of postwar consumerism. Observers wondered over the migrants' apparent inability to integrate into the modern industrial order: Ohioans, one researcher found, stereotyped southern migrants as "indolent . . . and too often found enjoying the benefits of relief," while Californians worried that impoverished Okies and their children would overwhelm the state's economic resources.

Popular constructions of the migrants also troubled ideologies of fixed racial difference. The combination of their "undeniable physical whiteness [and their] failure to conform to the unstated social norms associated with that category" created a disjuncture that disturbed notions of racial difference (La Chapelle 23–24; Negra, *Off-White* 6). They were viewed, in the succinct formulation of one journalist, as "a disgrace to their race" (Berry 176). By the 1960s, the southern white migrant and his hillbilly cousin were becoming the preeminent symbols of prosperity's failure to lift all boats in its rising tide, even among whites who expected class respectability as a prerogative of their race. The migrants thus partook of what Richard Dyer has characterized as "a damaged identity" (Dyer, *White* 165). Prior to migration, and before civil rights demands for racial justice, rural white southerners "could subscribe to . . . widely held notions of white superiority that gave [them] real advantages over people of color at home" (La Chapelle 24). But as migrants, their white privilege was largely stripped in discourses that depicted them as an "ethnoregional group with a shared set of seemingly racial character flaws," including a purportedly natural combination of violence, viciousness, and clannishness that took expression as virulent racism (La Chapelle 24).

Critical responses to "Green Acres" confirmed the show's popularity among rural-to-urban white migrants even as they inadvertently revealed the cultural anxiety the migrants elicited. Puzzling over how such an "overdone" and "heavy-handed" show could rate among the ten most popular programs in the nation, one critic blamed the baleful influence of the migrants' bad taste: "Census statistics continue to show a plummeting rural population so it's to be assumed that when people move to the city they take their bucolic tastes with them," he noted (Ernie Kreiling, "Green Acres," *Pasadena Independent Star News*, 21 November 1965, 15). Another observer echoed Dust Bowl–era fears that California would be socially, economically, and culturally inundated by Okies when he feigned shock that CBS would deliberately target "the folks in Iowa," since he "assumed that Iowa was an empty state, all its inhabitants having moved to Orange County" (MacKenzie, "My Consternation Worries Are Over," 20). Even sympathetic critics noted the cultural and political impact of the migration in their coverage of the show's popularity. Hal Humphrey ventriloquized the sentiment of many northerners when he suggested that a southern drawl was even more foreign than Eva's Hungarian accent. "People say they don't always understand my accent," he gleefully quoted Eva as saying. "Migawd! I haven't understood a word said yet on that Petticoat show [*Petticoat Junction*]. Is that English?" He went on to caution, beneath the bold header "Hillbilly Influence Spreading," against "underestimating the power of our hillbilly dialect, which has been growing more widespread in this country every year. A form of it is even spoken in the [Lyndon Johnson] White House now" ("Hungary Meets Hillbilly, U.S.A.," 5: 20).

As Lisa Douglas, Eva simultaneously indexed and lampooned for this audience the narratives of racial and class assimilation, and failure, in which she and her sister had been cast during the preceding decades. By connecting those narratives explicitly with rural-urban conflict, she offered a kind of metacommentary on the promise of assimilation from which the migrants were often excluded. Like the peplum films produced for working-class Italian audiences of approximately the same era, which "mobilize[d] whiteness as a balm to damaged male class identity," Eva's satire of white ethnic assimilation could express the migrants' resentment that the promise of white privilege had been withdrawn "while also dissociating [them] from a discredited politics of whiteness" (Dyer, *White* 165). Though this discourse sustained claims on white privilege, it also denaturalized whiteness, revealing it as a constructed and contingent identity and exposing the cultural work underlying racial hegemony.

Initially, the Gabors were inserted into the cultural mediation of the migration in predictable roles as class enemies. In 1958, Zsa Zsa appeared opposite country music stars Ferlin Husky and June Carter in *Country Music Holiday* (1958), a low-budget throwaway that became a surprisingly durable hit among the "peripheral southern drive-in and small-town trade" a which it was aimed; in Boone, North Carolina, the film was still enjoying an annual week-long run as late as 1970 (Williamson 50). Once again taking the part of a character named Zsa Zsa to highlight the reflexive connection between the role and her star persona, she played a movie star socialite who takes an unexpected romantic and financial interest in an aspiring country singer named Verne Brand (country music star Ferlin Husky). The film reversed the gender dynamics of the postwar gold digger by positioning Zsa Zsa as the wealthy sugar daddy and Husky as the aspiring showgirl, and many of the gags revolved around Husky's extension of his well-known comic alter-ego, Simon Crum, a character who satirized aspirations of middle-class upward mobility. But Brand is an essentially honest and naïve country boy in danger of being corrupted by the decadence in which he suddenly finds himself; Zsa Zsa's manipulation of him for her own economic benefit and her condescending interest in Brand's "American peasant music" served as a populist reminder of the dangers of class ambition and the bankruptcy of consumerist cultural hierarchy.

Eva served a nearly identical function in a melodramatic rather than comic register as the socialite wife of a publisher in *Youngblood Hawke* (1964). Adapted from Herman Wouk's best-selling novel, the movie told the story of a young writer from the hills of Kentucky who moves to New York, joins café society, and achieves acclaim and wealth before, inevitably, succumbing to the moral corruption of his new surroundings. As the catty Mrs. Fannie Prince, Eva symbolizes the illegitimacy of elite judgment of the hillbillies. Upon Hawke's arrival in New York, she invites him to her annual Christmas party, which his mentor (Suzanne Pleshette) warns is "a kind of command performance" demonstrating his ability to adapt to the mores and culture of the rich. Perhaps not surprisingly, Eva's appearance combines ostentatious glamour with a blinding whiteness, as the light dances off her diamonds, her blond hair, and her white satin dress. Hawke is clearly there, in the words of one party guest, in the role of amusing "backwoods, savage-type genius," and when he foolishly pretends to full membership in the fraternity of the wealthy, he fails spectacularly. Fannie is always present at his moments of humiliation, and is conspicuously shown watching him as he endures them. In both *Country Music Holiday* and *Youngblood Hawke,* the Gabors symbolized the impossibility of class mobility, even as they represented the fraudulence of class distinctions and cultural hierarchies.

In many ways, however, the Gabors' offscreen personae invoked the class failings of Youngblood Hawke and Verne Brand far more than they partook of the class-based cultural authority wielded, however illegitimately, by the characters of Zsa Zsa and Fannie Prince. The sisters had successfully

A resplendently white Eva as New York socialite Fannie Prince in *Youngblood Hawke.* (Courtesy Photofest)

parlayed sensationalist interest in their "private" lives into a marquee status they otherwise would have been unlikely to attain, but they could never fully overcome their déclassé position as tabloid celebrities and gold diggers to become legitimate stars. Their presence thus contradictorily indexed both the breakdown of American cultural hierarchy as it was expressed in the pecking order of Hollywood stardom and the persistence of immobility within that framework of prestige. In her role as Lisa Douglas Eva drew on both of these conflicting significations to reconcile incompatible desires for egalitarian classlessness, on one hand, and respectability within established hierarchies of cultural distinction, on the other. In this way "Green Acres," like other fantastic sitcoms of the era, became "a cultural space in which anxieties about everyday life could be addressed" and Eva the embodied canvas upon which ideological contradictions could be projected and resolved (Spigel 117).

In the first two episodes of "Green Acres," Lisa is a believable sophisticate, genuinely exasperated by the backwardness of Hooterville and clearly condescending, if haughtily polite, to its denizens. In "Lisa's First Day on the Farm," for instance, she occupies the center of the viewer's attention, watching from the background as an exchange between Oliver and the future farmhand Eb reveals their ineptitude. Her knowing amusement functions as an invitation to the audience to see both men, as she clearly does, as ridiculous in comparison to her polish and intelligence. For this moment, she essentially reprises her role as Fannie Prince, a wealthy sophisticate visibly scrutinizing the failures of her social inferiors. Within a few episodes, however, Lisa has become fully domesticated, taking on the vacant wackiness that made her a parody rather than a representative of the upper-class cultural authority she might otherwise have embodied. By the fifth episode, Lisa is hare-brained enough to forget that she doesn't know how to drive; she spouts Hungarian malapropisms; and she loses her adult grace to wide-eyed astonishment and a bouncing, childish totter.

Taming the most threatening aspects of the Gabor glamour through camp allowed Eva to distance herself from the sisters' associations with ruthless gold-digging, exoticism, and tabloid excess. The show's popularity, she told Hal Humphrey, "gives me a chance to spoil my image. Everyone always thinks I am the temperamental actress. " Indeed, Lisa's drift toward camp apparently occurred at Eva's own insistence. She told Humphrey, "I established this character when I wore a chiffon negligee . . . to chase a chicken across the barnyards" instead of the ordinary robe the script called for in the season's third episode. And she explicitly sought to identify herself with Lisa's good-natured harmlessness. "I know this character . . . because she is like me," she declared ("Eva Has a 'Pooh' for Temperament," D18).

The camping of Eva's glamour made a mockery of class distinction, but it was in its commentary on the cultural mythologies and star system of Hollywood, and the Gabors' place in them, that the show most pointedly lampooned class-based cultural hierarchies. Many episodes satirized the low-brow status of television or called into question the authenticity of star personae and even stardom itself. In "A Star Named Arnold Is Born," Lisa arranges for Arnold the pig to go to Hollywood for a screen test with a "big-time Hollywood producer." As in many such episodes, in spite of Oliver's skepticism, Lisa and the rubes unexpectedly manage to take over the machinery of mass media for their own purposes. The producer discovers, of course, that Arnold is a pig but, much to Oliver's surprise, this disturbs him not at all. Rather than dismissing Arnold, the producer sets in motion a publicity campaign that makes him a star overnight so he can replace a horse who is demanding a better contract. As Lisa says, "Just because you're not human, that doesn't mean you can't be a movie star." Lisa is similarly the impetus behind Oliver's unwitting television stardom in "How to Succeed in Television without Really Trying," in which he becomes Hooterville's highest-rated actor when broadcasts of him getting ready for bed and imitating barnyard animals are accidentally beamed all over the valley. Episodes like these exposed the industrial system that produced stardom and suggested that anyone who could capture the machinery of celebrity could be a star: a pig, a bumbling farmer, and, in real life, even a Hungarian gold digger whose fame derived from a television panel show.

Eva also became a vehicle for interrogating Hollywood's narrative conventions of class, particularly in the flashback episodes in which Lisa relates what turn out to be mostly fabricated bits of her personal and family past. Invariably, her listeners confuse her story with a movie they've seen, a device that draws attention to the concealed publicity work that had allowed studios to conflate stars and characters, real and fictional personae. These episodes frequently referenced the Gabors' history as actresses. In "A Royal Love Story," for instance, Lisa's improbable claim to have auditioned for the Moulin Rouge and considered posing for Henri de Toulouse-Lautrec recalls Zsa Zsa's most famous film role, virtually requiring the audience to recognize the way the Gabors specifically had participated in the construction of cinematic mythologies.

"Das Lumpin" directly inserted Lisa into the narrative convention that had most defined the Gabors: the postwar gold digger. Here, Lisa saves Oliver from the Nazis during World War II and then accidentally runs into him again in a seedy café after the war. In a spoof of the impoverished showgirl whose gold-digging is her only economic alternative, she is playing the cello, very badly, in the house trio, but making her real living as a "hostess," and she carefully details for Oliver her commission on each service she encourages him to purchase. Kisses are 35 cents. At the end of the episode, Lisa recounts how Oliver ultimately rescued her from a lecherous bandleader. At this point Oliver interjects—his voice interrupts the flashback's sound track, yelling "Hold it!" as the image begins to jump and slur like a reel caught in a projector—to explain that Lisa has made this part of the story up based on the late-late movie. "The Broadway Gaieties of 193? with Slim Summerville and Sally Eilers!" he exclaims. Though the film is fictional, Summerville and Eilers were real B-movie actors, and the reference to them, like Eva's participation in satirizing the gold digger she had played in publicity and earlier films, implicitly acknowledged that the Hollywood fables with which the sisters had been associated were cultural fictions that reconciled and defused contradictory ideologies.

Unlike the whiteness in the peplum films of which Dyer writes, however, the whiteness Eva offered as a salve for the migrants' damaged class identity was also imperfect. Just as the class satire on "Green Acres" relied on the Gabors' immobility within Hollywood's class system to call into question national mythologies of egalitarianism, so its parody of racial fiction depended for its substance on the Gabors' Hollywood history of limin whiteness, unassimilability, and inability to embody the nation onscreen. On the surface, Eva's Hungarian camp on "Green Acres" would seem to be of a piece with ethnic oddballs such as Ricky Ricardo on "I Love Lucy" or Buddy Sorrell on "The Dick Van Dyke Show," but her connection with Zsa Zsa's troublesome racial status offscreen imbued the role with a reflexive dimension that those portrayals lacked (Jacobson 30). And while Lisa was isolated as an ethnic character in Hooterville, the show featured a recurring plot device in which wily Hungarians, all of them friends of Lisa's from the old country, seem to turn up everywhere. In "A Star Named Arnold Is Born," Lisa is able to arrange Arnold's screen test because the Hollywood producer is an old school friend from Hungary. In the "Hungarian Curse," a guest arrives at the Douglases' house, speaks a few words to Lisa in Hungarian, and then submits meekly as she squeals, throws her arms around him, and kisses him. "Who's this?" asks Oliver. "I don't know," replies Lisa. "Well, what are you kissing him for?" he demands to know. "Because he's Hungarian!" she exclaims, as if forced to explain that water is wet.

In "The Vulgar Ring Story," another flashback episode, Lisa relates the story of her great-great-grandmother, Lastfogel Gronyitz (played by Eva), a Hungarian gypsy who marries an American (played by Eddie Albert). The slippage between "Volga" and "vulgar" is thoroughly intentional, as the episode both repeats and satirizes Eastern European and Roma stereotypes. As had been the case in publicity surrounding the Gabors' ethnicity, Lisa's Gypsy heritage is both racialized and unalterable: "Once you're a Gronyitz you're always a Gronyitz; there is no escaping that," Lastfogel tells the American. But while the running gag of the episode is the Gypsies' incorrigible thievery, the script also draws attention to the cultural narratives that underpin racialization: "It's not our idea to steal," Lastfogel's father explains to her suitor, "but everybody says that Gypsies steal, so if it makes them happy, we steal. When you got an image you have to live up to it."

And, as was regularly the case in the show's flashbacks, the Hooterillians misunderstand the story as the plot summary of a studio-era Hollywood film. "I think I saw this movie. Are you sure it wasn't a movie? Because I remember seeing Alice Faye in it. Only she wasn't a Gypsy," says the county extension agent. The comment emphasized the centrality of assimilation mythologies to American identity even as it pointed to the irreducibility of some kinds of ethnic difference. During the 1930s and 1940s, Faye had frequently been cast as a sympathetic showgirl who successfully negotiated upward class mobility, and her much-publicized biographical origins in the German and Irish communities of New York's Hell's Kitchen positioned her as an avatar of white assimilation. The contrast between

Faye, as the embodiment of mobility and assimilation, and the stubbornly resistant lowness and racialization of Eva and Zsa Zsa could not be more evident: Faye would never be a Gypsy.

As was the case with its satire of class assimilation, "Green Acres" also aimed specifically at Hollywood's traditional narrative conventions of ethnic difference. In "A Royal Love Story," Eva plays Lisa's grandmother, a silent-era actress who is cast in role after role as a threatening vamp, Hollywood's dominant trope of ethnic femininity during the 1920s. Among these parts is a turn as Cleopatra, one of most enduring cinematic icons of exotic otherness and racial indeterminacy and a defining role for the original vamp, Theda Bara (Royster 60–92). Here, Eva satirized the same typing of ethnic femininity to which she and her sister had been subjected and which had limited their careers. She thus activated and interrogated for her audience older mythologies of contaminating immigrants that were, by that time, regularly applied to working-class white migrants from the South.

Since the early 1950s, film actors had used occasional sketch-comedy appearances on television as opportunities to impersonate their own star identities and thereby acknowledge the artificiality of their public "private" personae (Becker 35). Unlike the personae those actors gently mocked, however, the discursive construction of Eva's offscreen identity had precluded rather than guaranteed star status. As a result, the satire of Hollywood's myths presented in "Green Acres" was far more pointed than that of earlier star appearances. Viewed from the perspective of failure rather than success, such mythologies became cultural lies that reified and obscured existing inequalities rather than harmless narrative fictions that reflected an American spirit of self-reconstruction.

In 1971 CBS cancelled its entire roster of "corn," including "Green Acres," "Hee Haw," and "The Beverly Hillbillies," in favor of realist programming it thought would appeal to a young, urban, middle-class demographic advertisers increasingly viewed as their most important market. Though Eva continued to make guest appearances on television serials and talk shows, and enjoyed a successful run voicing patrician female characters in Disney animated films, she largely faded from view after "Green Acres" ended.

Eva had found her greatest success performing a burlesque of the exotic, gold-digging, ostensibly inauthentic celebrity she and Zsa Zsa shared, lampooning Hollywood's fictions of stardom, its fables of class assimilation, and its discourses of white ethnicity. She represented both the promise and limits of class mobility by performing class simultaneously as a reflection of deep cultural habitus and as an inconsequential surface mobilization of the signs of wealth. By summoning the Gabors' liminal whiteness, she sanctioned the migrants' claims to white privilege even as she undermined naturalized conceptions of whiteness, mediating the transition to what Geoff Mann has described as the reactionary "pose of historically 'innocent' . . . American whiteness" that has become central to the politics of race in the post–civil rights era (89–90). She had, in the ideological sense, become a real star, whose image managed the central political contradictions of her era.

In the Wings

PAMELA ROBERTSON WOJCIK

By discussing stars according to decade, this series enables us to see trends in Hollywood, and to capture aspects of the zeitgeist through analyses of star images. In this volume, we can see changing aesthetics, changing mores, and changing industry practices working together to alter and expand the concept of the star.

The periodization of stars is a tricky business, however. Most stars do not fit neatly into single decades but work across two or more decades. In many cases, we can analyze how a star's meaning changes over time. Joan Crawford, for example, shifts from being an iconic flapper in the 1920s to a "shopgirl's dream" of class rise in the 1930s to an image of neurotic dissatisfaction in the 1940s and becomes eventually, in the 1950s and 1960s, a camp grotesque (Robertson, *Guilty* 85–114). In a different vein, Frank Sinatra's image transforms from that of something of a sexual innocent in the 1940s, with a fan base of bobbysoxers, to more of a tough but vulnerable alienated guy—in alternation with a playboy image—in the 1950s, growing his iconic status as an image of masculine cool, finally settling into a tough guy Rat Pack persona in the late 1960s. Other stars enter into different genres as they age, and thus alter or deepen their star image. For example, Jimmy Stewart moves from predominantly light romantic comedy in the 1930s and 1940s into Hitchcockian thrillers and dark westerns in the 1950s and, conversely, both Meryl Streep and Robert De Niro are associated with deep meaningful dramas in the 1970s but have increasingly turned to light comedy in the new century.

Like the business practices and ideologies discussed in the introduction, stars can also be thought in terms of Raymond Williams's notion of residual, dominant, and emerging cultures. The star, and his or her attendant meanings, may gain and lose cultural ascendancy, even as he or she remains active on the scene. Our by-the-decades breakdown attempts to locate the star at his or her moment of cultural dominance. While Rock Hudson and Doris Day, for example, are certainly still active in the 1960s, screen stars, maintaining box office success, their cultural dominance and attendant meaning are more deeply tied to the 1950s than the 1960s; and, therefore, they are not included here. Often, the moment at which a star becomes residual to the culture is when that star ascends into camp, achieving subcultural dominance. For example, Judy Garland attains significance for gay men as a camp icon only after she is fired from MGM in the 1950s (Dyer, *Heavenly* 142–43). Her 1960s roles—which are largely nonsinging—are not, in and of themselves, what would define her stardom. In reverse, some stars who emerge in the 1960s will not achieve their dominance (by which I mean their star image will not fully cohere or achieve its full cultural impact) until the 1970s and beyond. These emergent stars are "in the wings."

Some stars are viewed as emergent because they make relatively few films in the 1960s, as compared to their overall output. One such star is Barbra Streisand. Streisand emerges full-blown as a star in *Funny Girl* (1968) and as a star who asserts her talent in her first number singing "I'm the Greatest Star." And all the components of the Streisand persona are in place—her characterization as ethnic, or culturally Jewish, and not conventionally attractive; her dominance onscreen and attendant difficulties finding a mate who can match her; her anger and unruliness (Robertson "Star"). But Streisand only appears in two musicals in the 1960s—*Funny Girl* and *Hello Dolly!* (1969). Streisand in the 1960s is similar to Julie Andrews—insofar as she gains star billing in films based on Broadway success and emerges as a star in the seemingly outmoded genre of the costume musical, working with directors like William Wyler and Gene Kelly associated with Old Hollywood. But unlike Andrews, Streisand's star moves easily into the 1970s, as she works with New Hollywood directors like Peter Bogdanovich, and in contemporary genres with contemporary social mores—playing a hooker in *The Owl and the Pussycat* (1970) and an unhappy neurotic housewife in *Up the Sandbox* (1972). To fully comprehend the coherence of her star image, one needs to consider the way in which the components of her star image recur across her career, even as she revises and comments upon the musical in remaking *A Star Is Born* (1976) or making the musical numbers in *Yentl* (1983) wholly interior; or as she crosses into romantic comedy with films such as *What's Up, Doc?* (1972) or *The Main Event* (1979); and as she moves into nonmusical dramas like *The Way We Were* (1973) or *Nuts* (1987). Further, Streisand needs to be understood in relation to the impact of Second Wave feminism in popular culture, and as an auteur, both of which make her image readable as feminist. For this reading, her control over her career and choices in the 1970s are key. Streisand becomes a producer, forming First Artists Production Company with Paul Newman and Sidney Poitier in 1969, then her own production company, Barwood, in 1972. And, finally, she becomes a director with *Yentl*.

Faye Dunaway makes a few more films than Streisand in the 1960s, but, like Streisand, makes her splash at the end of the decade and proves her mettle in the 1970s and 1980s. Initially appearing in small roles in *Hurry Sundown* (1967) and *The Happening* (1967), Dunaway's most memorable roles of the sixties are *Bonnie and Clyde* (1967) and *The Thomas Crown Affair* (1968). These two films reflect the changing tastes and aesthetics of the 1960s, signalled by their forthright sexuality, seemingly callous attitude toward crime, and daring visual style. Dunaway's credentials are furthered in two smaller films of the late sixties—the realist French Italian co-production *Amanti* (1968) and the Method-born *The Arrangement* (1969). But Dunaway, like Streisand, flourishes in the seventies when there is a new emphasis on the female star as serious actress, a belated Method-influenced turn to "character" for women. Her biggest roles range across genres: the film noir *Chinatown* (1974), the satire *Network* (1976), the disaster movie *The Towering Inferno* (1974), the thriller *The Eyes of Laura Mars* (1978), and the Joan Crawford biopic *Mommie Dearest* (1981).

Dunaway's co-star in *Bonnie and Clyde*, Warren Beatty, similarly flourishes most fully in the 1970s. Beatty makes a striking entry into Hollywood filmmaking early in the 1960s with the racy *Splendor in the Grass* (1961). The film was a commercial success and Beatty was nominated for a Golden Globe award. But his career stalled in the mid-1960s, as he made a few largely unnoticed appearances until *Bonnie and Clyde*. *Bonnie and Clyde* was followed by roles in New Hollywood productions like Robert Altman's *McCabe and Mrs. Miller* (1971). Crucially, with *Bonnie and Clyde*, Beatty assumed the role of the actor/auteur, serving as producer for the film. After that, he served as writer, producer, or director on a number of films that defined his image and career, such as *Shampoo* (1975), for which he was writer and producer, and *Heaven Can Wait* (1978) and *Reds* (1981), for both of which he was writer, director, and producer.

Where some stars are perceived as emergent in the 1960s because they make relatively few films in that decade, others are characterized as "in the wings" because they have not yet achieved the star image that will come to be dominant. Jane Fonda, like Streisand and Dunaway, will come to be identified most strongly with the strong female roles of the 1970s. He 1960s roles are emblematic of the period but not as fully emblematic of what we come to view as the Fonda persona. Fonda is a star, like Madonna who can be characterized through dramatic changes in her persona and appearance. In Fonda's case, these changes are often related to the men in her life and her marriages. In her first film in 1960, *Tall Story*, Fonda is very much perceived as Henry Fonda's daughter, continuing on a family tradition, having been groomed by director Joshua Logan who urged her to appear alongside her father in her first play, "The Country Wife." Married to Roger Vadim in 1965, Fonda initially appears in light comedies such as *Cat Ballou* (1965) and *Any Wednesday* (1966) in which she plays the sex kitten, culminating in the outrageous Vadim-directed science fiction erotic fantasy *Barbarella* (1968). Only at the tail end of the 1960s do we see Fonda as a "serious" actress, in her first Oscar-nominated role, in *They Shoot Horses, Don't They?* (1969). Neither her affiliation with "serious" filmmaking nor her image as activist will become dominant until the 1970s, when she is married to activist Tom Hayden. Beginning with *Klute* (1971) and *Tout va bien* (1972) and continuing in projects such as *Julia* (1977), *Coming Home* (1978), and *The China Syndrome* (1979), Fonda will become increasingly regarded as a serious and talented actress who puts her star power to work for leftists causes and in leftist quasi-feminist films. Then, as she becomes increasingly identified with fitness routines in the 1980s and becomes Ted Turner's wife in the 1990s, she will turn into more of a residual presence in Hollywood.

Like Fonda, Jack Nicholson works steadily throughout the 1960s, but his star image will not be highly regarded until the seventies when his independent background and quirky style merge with the mainstream in the New Hollywood. Where Fonda enters as Hollywood royalty, Nicholson approaches through the back door, via exploitation films and low budget B-movies. In the 1960s, Nicholson gains his apprenticeship as part of Roger Corman's cadre of actors, writers, and directors. He stars in such Corman films as *The Broken Land* (1962), *The Raven* (1963), and *The Terror* (1963), then partners with Corman's protégé Monte Hellman for such pictures as *Flight to Fury* (1964), *Back Door to Hell* (1964), *Ride in the Whirlwind* (1965), and *The Shooting* (1967). Nicholson serves as writer for *Flight to Fury, Ride in the Whirlwind*, and Corman's *The Trip* (1967), then the psychedelic Monkees movie *Head* (1968). His breakout role in the 1960s is a minor role in Dennis Hopper's countercultural road movie *Easy Rider* (1969). In 1970, he still plays a minor role alongside Streisand in *On a Clear Day You Can See Forever*. In the 1970s he becomes a full-fledged star, famous for offbeat, slightly mad characters in a string of hits including *Five Easy Pieces* (1970), *Carnal Knowledge* (1971), *The King of Marvin Gardens* (1972), *Chinatown*, and *One Flew Over the Cuckoo's Nest* (1975).

Another star who works steadily throughout the 1960s but becomes dominant in the next decade is Clint Eastwood. Eastwood is a real journeyman actor. Beginning in film and TV in the 1950s, he gets his first big break with a starring role on the TV show "Rawhide" (1959–65). From there, he reverses the trend of importing foreign stars into Hollywood and becomes an export, appearing as "The Man with No Name" in Sergio Leone's trilogy of Italian spaghetti westerns—*A Fistful of Dollars* (1964), *For a Few Dollars More* (1965), and *The Good, the Bad and the Ugly* (1966). *Coogan's Bluff* (1968), directed by Don Siegel, begins to cement and Americanize Eastwood's image as a taciturn tough guy, to make him a kind of western outlaw hero in urban police environments. This thread will be furthered in the 1970s, notably with Siegel's iconic *Dirty Harry* (1971). Most important for Eastwood's star image, though, will be his transformation into a director who, for most of his career, directs himself as star and shapes his image, in films like *Play Misty for Me* (1971), *High Plains Drifter* (1973), *The Outlaw Josey Wales* (1976), and forward. Overall, he makes over thirty films as director, most, until this century, with him in a starring role.

Remarkably, all the actors discussed here have either continued working steadily—in the case of Dunaway, Nicholson, and Eastwood—or, having left Hollywood for some time, reappeared onscreen in this century—as with Beatty (*Town and Country* [2001]), Streisand (*Meet the Fockers* [2004], *Little Fockers* [2010]), and Fonda (*Monster-in-Law* [2005] and *Georgia Rule* [2007]). The arc of their careers—like those of other stars discussed in this book, and especially Newman, Hoffman, Poitier, and Farrow—extend well past their moment of supposed dominance. No longer necessarily at the top, these stars are still relevant.

WORKS CITED

★★★★★★★★★★★★

Fan magazines and other primary or archival materials are cited in the text of individual essays.

Amburn, Ellis. *The Most Beautiful Woman in the World: The Obsessions, Passions, and Courage of Elizabeth Taylor*. New York: Cliff Street Books, 2000.

Andrews, Julie. *Home: A Memoir of My Early Years*. New York: Hyperion, 2008.

Angeletti, Norberto, and Alberto Oliva. *In Vogue: The Illustrated History of the World's Most Famous Fashion Magazine*. New York: Rizzoli International Publications, 2006.

Angell, Callie. "Andy Warhol, Filmmaker." *The Andy Warhol Museum*. New York: Distributed Arts Publishers, 1994. 121–45.

———. *Andy Warhol Screen Tests: The Films of Andy Warhol Catalogue Raisonné*, Volume 1. New York: Harry N. Abrams, 2006.

Anger, Kenneth. *Hollywood Babylon*. New York: Bell Publishing Company, 1975.

Armbruster, Frank E. *The Forgotten Americans: A Survey of Values, Beliefs, and Concerns of the Majority*. New Rochelle, N.Y.: Hudson Institute, 1972.

Baecque, Antoine de. *La Nouvelle Vague*. Paris: Flammarion, 1998, 2009.

Baldwin, James. *The Devil Finds Work: An Essay*. New York: Laurel, 1976.

———. "Sidney Poitier." *Look* 23 July 1968. 50–54, 56, 58.

Balio, Tino. "Hollywood's Takeover of the US Art Film Market in the 1960s." Unpublished ms.

Bardot, Brigitte. *Initiales B. B.* Paris: Grusset, 1996.

Baron, Cynthia. "The Method Moment: Situating the Rise of Method Acting." *Popular Culture Review* 9.2 (August 1998): 89–106.

Beach, Christopher. *Class, Language, and American Film Comedy*. New York: Cambridge UP, 2002.

Becker, Christine. *It's the Pictures That Got Small: Hollywood Film Stars on 1950s Television*. Middletown, Conn.: Wesleyan UP, 2008.

Bender, Marylin. *The Beautiful People*. New York: Coward-McCann, 1967.

Berry, Chad. *Southern Migrants, Northern Exiles*. Urbana: U of Illinois P, 2000.

Bingham, Dennis. *Whose Lives Are They Anyway? The Biopic as Contemporary Film Genre*. New Brunswick, N.J.: Rutgers UP, 2010.

Blackman, Cally. "Clothing the Cosmic Counterculture: Fashion and Psychedelia." *Summer of Love: Psychedelic Art, Social Crisis and Counterculture in the 1960s*. Ed. Christoph Grunenberg and Jonathan Harris. Liverpool: Liverpool UP, 2005. 201–22.

Bogle, Donald. *Toms, Coons, Mulattoes, Mammies, and Bucks: An Interpretive History of Blacks in American Films*. New York: Continuum, 1994.

Boorstin, Daniel. *The Image: A Guide to Pseudo-Events in America*. New York: Harper Colophon Books, 1961.

Bordwell, David, Janet Staiger, and Kristin Thompson. *The Classical Hollywood Cinema: Film Style and Mode of Production to 1960*. New York: Columbia UP, 1985.

Bordwell, David, and Kristin Thompson. *Film History: An Introduction*. 2nd ed. New York: McGraw-Hill, 2003.

Brake, Elizabeth. "'To Live Outside the Law, You Must Be Honest': Freedom in Dylan's Lyrics." *Bob Dylan and Philosophy*. Ed. Peter Vernezze and Carl J. Porter. Chicago: Open Court Publishing, 2006. 78–89.

Braudy, Leo. *The Frenzy of Renown*. New York: Oxford UP, 1986.

Brodsky, Jack, and Nathan Weiss. *The Cleopatra Papers: A Private Correspondence*. New York: Simon and Schuster, 1963.

Carnes, Valerie. "Icons of Popular Fashion." *Icons of America*. Ed. Ray Browne and Marshall Fishwick. Bowling Green, Ohio: Popular Press, 1978. 228–39.

Cohan, Steven. *Masked Men: Masculinity and the Movies in the Fifties*. Bloomington: Indiana UP, 1997.

Combs, Steven C. "The Tao of Rhetoric: Revelations from *The Tao of Steve*." *Intercultural Communication Studies* 11.1 (2002): 117–35.

Cook, David A. *Lost Illusions: American Cinema in the Shadow of Watergate and Vietnam, 1970–1979*. Berkeley: U of California P, 2000.

Cox, Stephen. *The Hooterville Handbook: A Viewer's Guide to "Green Acres."* New York: St. Martin's, 1993.

Cuomo, Chris. "Spinsters in Sensible Shoes: *Mary Poppins* and *Bedknobs and Broomsticks*." *From Mouse to Mermaid: The Politics of Film, Gender, and Culture*. Ed. Elizabeth Bell, Lynda Haas, and Laura Sells. Bloomington: Indiana UP, 1995. 212–23.

Danan, Martine. "The Studio, the Star and International Audiences: Paramount and Chevalier." *Journeys of Desire: European Actors in Hollywood*. Ed. Alastair Phillips and Ginette Vincendeau. London: BFI, 2006. 53–60.

De Cordova, Richard. *Picture Personalities: The Emergence of the Star System in America*. Champaign: U of Illinois P, 1990.

Deleuze, Gilles. *Cinema 2: The Time-Image*. Minneapolis: U of Minnesota P, 1985.

Denkert, Darcie. *A Fine Romance: Broadway & Hollywood*. New York: Watson Guptill, 2005.

Derry, Charles. "Mia Farrow." *International Dictionary of Films and Filmmakers* (2001). www.encyclopedia.com/doc/1G2–3406801700.html.

Dunne, John Gregory. *The Studio*. 1970. Reprint, New York: Vintage, 1998.

Dyer, Richard. "The Colour of Virtue: Lillian Gish, Whiteness, and Femininity." *Women and Film: A Sight and Sound Reader*. Ed. Pam Cook and Philip Dodd. Philadelphia: Temple UP, 1993. 1–9.

———. *Heavenly Bodies: Film Stars and Society*. London: Macmillan, 1986.

———. *Stars*. London: BFI, 1979.

———. *White*. New York: Routledge, 1997.

Eaves, Elizabeth. "The McQueen Resurrection." *Forbes* (29 October 2007). www.forbes.com/2007/10/26/steve-mcqueen-comeback-biz-media-deadcelebs07_cx_ee_1029cool.html.

Edgerton, Gary. *The Columbia History of American Television*. New York: Columbia UP, 2009.

Elsaesser, Thomas. "The Pathos of Failure: American Films in the 1970s: Notes on the Unmotivated Hero." *The Last Great American Picture Show*. Ed. Thomas Elsaesser, Alexander Horwath, and Noel King. Amsterdam: Amsterdam UP, 2004. 279–92.

Epstein, Edward, and Joe Morella. *Mia: The Life of Mia Farrow*. New York: Dell Publishing, 1991.

Epstein, Rebecca L. "Sharon Stone in a Gap Turtleneck." *Hollywood Goes Shopping*. Ed. David Desser and Garth S. Jowett. Minneapolis: U of Minnesota P, 2000. 179–204.

Erickson, Glenn. "DVD Savant Review: *Hawaii*." 12 April 2005. http://www.dvdtalk.com/dvdsavant/s1554hawa.html. Accessed 15 August 2009.

Farrow, Mia. *What Falls Away*. London: Doubleday, 1997.

Finkelstein, Nat, and David Dalton. *Edie: Factory Girl*. New York: VH1 Books, 2006.

Fischer, Lucy. "Birth Traumas: Parturition and Horror in *Rosemary's Baby*." *Cinema Journal* 31. 3 (Spring 1992): 3–18.

Frank, Gerold. *Zsa Zsa Gabor: My Story*. New York: World Publishing, 1960.

Frank, Thomas. *The Conquest of Cool: Business Culture, Counterculture, and the Rise of Hip Consumerism*. Chicago: U of Chicago P, 1998.

Funke, Lewis, and John E. Booth. "Sidney Poitier." *Actors Talk about Acting: Fourteen Interviews with Stars of the Theatre*. New York: Random House, 1961. 371–94.

Gabler, Neal. *Life: The Movie*. New York: Knopf, 1998.

———. *Walt Disney: The Triumph of the American Imagination*. New York: Knopf, 2006.

Gabor, Eva. *Orchids and Salami*. New York: Doubleday, 1954.

George, Nelson. *Blackface: Reflections on African-Americans and the Movies*. New York: Harper-Collins, 1994.

Gitlin, Todd. *The Twilight of Common Dreams*. New York: Metropolitan Books, 1995.

Gleason, Philip. "American Identity and Americanization." *Concepts of Ethnicity*. Cambridge, Mass.: Harvard UP, 1980. 127–52.

Goudsouzian, Aram. *Sidney Poitier: Man, Actor, Icon*. Chapel Hill: U of North Carolina P, 2004.

Grant, Barry Keith. "Introduction: Movies and the 1960s." *American Cinema of the 1960s: Themes and Variations*. Ed. Barry Keith Grant. New Brunswick, N.J.: Rutgers UP, 2008. 1–21.

Gregory, James. *The Southern Diaspora: How the Great Migrations of Black and White Southerners Transformed America*. Chapel Hill: U of North Carolina P, 2005.

Gundle, Stephen. "Sophia Loren, Italian Icon." *Stars, the Film Reader*. Ed. Lucy Fischer and Marcia Landy. New York: Routledge, 2004. 77–96.

Hansen, Miriam. "Introduction." *Theory of Film: The Redemption of Physical Reality*, by Siegfried Kracauer. Princeton, N.J.: Princeton UP, 1997. i–xxviii.

Harkins, Anthony. *Hillbilly: A Cultural History of an American Icon*. New York: Oxford UP, 2003.

Harris, Mark. *Pictures at a Revolution: Five Movies and the Birth of the New Hollywood*. New York: Penguin Press, 2008.

Haskell, Molly. *From Reverence to Rape*. 1974. Reprint, Chicago: U of Chicago P, 1987.

Heffernan, Kevin. *Ghouls, Gimmicks, Gold: Horror Films and the American Movie Business, 1953–1968*. Durham, N.C.: Duke UP, 2004.

Henriksen, Margot A. *Dr. Strangelove's America: Society and Culture in the Atomic Age*. Berkeley: U of California P, 1997.

Hernton, Calvin C. *White Papers for White Americans*. 1966. Westport, Conn.: Greenwood Press, 1982.

Heymann, C. David. *Liz: An Intimate Biography of Elizabeth Taylor*. Secaucus, N.J.: Citadel Star Books, 1996.

Hirsch, Foster. "The Actor as Auteur." *Kansas Quarterly* 4.2 (1972): 31–38.

———. *A Method to Their Madness: The History of the Actor's Studio*. New York: Da Capo Press, 1984.

Horwath, Alexander. "The Impure Cinema: New Hollywood 1967–1976." *The Last Great American Picture Show*. Ed. Thomas Elsaesser, Alexander Horwath, and Noel King. Amsterdam. Amsterdam UP, 2004. 9–18.

Isserman, Maurice, and Michael Kazin. *America Divided: The Civil War of the 1960s*. 3rd ed. New York: Oxford UP, 2008.

Jacobson, Matthew Frye. *Roots Too: White Ethnic Revival in Post–Civil Rights America*. Cambridge, Mass.: Harvard UP, 2006.

James, David E. *Allegories of Cinema: American Film in the Sixties*. Princeton, N.J.: Princeton UP, 1989.

Johnson, Victoria E. *Heartland TV: Prime Time Television and the Struggle for U.S. Identity*. New York: New York UP, 2008.

Johnston, Claire. "Women's Cinema as Counter-Cinema." *Film Theory*. Ed. Philip Simpson, Andrew Utterson, and Karen J. Shepherdson. New York: Taylor and Francis, 2004. 183–92.

Kael, Pauline. *Kiss, Kiss, Bang, Bang*. New York: Bantam, 1969.

Kemp, Peter. "How Do You Solve a 'Problem' Like Maria Von Poppins?" *Senses of Cinema* 22 (September-October 2002). http://www.sensesofcinema.com/contents/02/22/andrews.html. Accessed 3 May 2007.

Kelley, Kitty. *Elizabeth Taylor: The Last Star*. New York: Simon and Schuster, 1981.

Kenner, Hugh. *Flaubert, Joyce and Beckett: The Stoic Comedians*. Boston: Beacon Press, 1963.

Kerbel, Michael. *Paul Newman*. New York: Pyramid Communications, 1974.

Kinder, Marsha. *Close-Up: A Critical Perspective on Film*. New York: Harcourt Brace Jovanovich, 1972.

Klaprat, Cathy. "The Star as Market Strategy: Bette Davis in Another Light." *The American Film Industry*. 2nd ed. Ed. TinoBalio. Madison: U of Wisconsin P, 1985. 351–76.

Knight, Arthur. *Disintegrating the Musical: Black Performance and American Musical Film*. Durham, N.C.: Duke UP, 2002.

———. "'It Ain't Necessarily So That It Ain't Necessarily So': African American Recordings of *Porgy and Bess* as Film and Cultural Criticism." *Soundtrack Available: Essays on Film and Popular Music*. Ed. Pamela Robertson Wojcik and Arthur Knight. Durham, N.C.: Duke UP, 2001. 319–46.

Koch, Stephen. *Stargazer: The Life, World and Films of Andy Warhol*. Rev.ed. New York: Marion Boyars, 1991.

Koestenbaum, Wayne. *Andy Warhol*. New York: Viking Penguin, 2001.

Krein, Kevin, and Abigail Levin. "Just Like a Woman: Dylan, Authenticity, and the Second Sex." *Bob Dylan and Philosophy*. Ed. Peter Vernezze and Carl J. Porter. Chicago: Open Court, 2006. 53–65.

La Chapelle, Peter. *Proud to Be an Okie: Cultural Politics, Country Music, and Migration to Southern California*. Berkeley: U of California P, 2007.

Lax, Eric. *Paul Newman: A Biography*. Atlanta: Turner Publishing, 1996.

Lederer, Susan. *Flesh and Blood: Organ Transplantation and Blood Transfusion in Twentieth Century America*. New York: Oxford UP, 2008.

Lenburg, Jeff. *Dustin Hoffman: Hollywood's Antihero*. New York: St. Martin's, 1983.

Levine, Andrea. "Sidney Poitier's Civil Rights: Rewriting the Mystique of White Womanhood in *Guess Who's Coming to Dinner* and *In the Heat of the Night*." *American Literature* 73.2 (June 2001): 365–86.

Lewis, Roger. *The Life and Death of Peter Sellers*. New York: Applause, 1997.

Lobenthal, Joel. *Radical Rags: Fashions of the Sixties*. New York: Abbeville Press, 1990.

Lott, Eric. "The Whiteness of Film Noir." *American Literary History* 9.3 (Autumn 1997): 542–66.

Luck, Richard. *Steve McQueen: The Pocket Essential*. Haselden: Oldcastle, 2000.

Luckett, Moya. "A Moral Crisis in Prime Time: *Peyton Place* and the Rise of the Single Girl." *Television, History, and Culture.* Ed. Mary Beth Haralovich and Lauren Rabinovitz. Durham, N.C.: Duke UP, 1999. 75–97.

Lytle, Mark Hamilton. *America's Uncivil Wars: The Sixties Era from Elvis to the Fall of Richard Nixon.* New York: Oxford UP, 2006.

Maddox, Brenda. *Who's Afraid of Elizabeth Taylor?* New York: M. Evans, 1977.

Maltby, Richard. *Hollywood Cinema.* 2nd ed. Malden, Mass.: Blackwell, 2003.

Mann, Geoff. "Why Does Country Music Sound White? Race and the Voice of Nostalgia." *Ethnic and Racial Studies* 31.1 (January 2008): 73–100.

Mast, Gerald. *Can't Help Singin': The American Musical on Stage and Screen.* Woodstock, N.Y.: Overlook Press, 1987.

McDougal, Dennis. *The Last Mogul: Lew Wasserman, MCA, and the Hidden History of Hollywood.* New York: Da Capo Press, 2001.

Medevoi, Leerom. "Marx and McQueen: Racing against Communism in Fordist America." *International Journal of Motorcycle Studies* 6.1 (Spring 2010). ijms.nova.edu.

Medved, Harry, and Michael Medved. *The Hollywood Hall of Shame: The Most Expensive Flops in Movie History.* New York: Peregee Books, 1984.

Mekas, Jonas. "Notes after Reseeing the Movies of Andy Warhol." *Andy Warhol.* Ed. John Coplans. New York: Graphic Society, 1970. 139–56.

Metcalf, Greg. "Discounting the '60s: Hollywood Revisits the Counterculture." *Beyond the Stars: Studies in American Popular Film.* Vol. 5, *Themes and Ideologies in American Popular Film.* Ed. Paul Loukides and Linda K. Fuller. Bowling Green, Ohio: Popular Press, 1996.

Monaco, Paul. *The Sixties, 1960–1969.* Berkeley: U of California P, 2001.

Morella, Joe, and Edward Z. Epstein. *Paul and Joanne: A Biography of Paul Newman and Joanne Woodward.* New York: Delacorte Press, 1988.

Morley, Sheridan. *Elizabeth Taylor: A Celebration.* New York: Pavilion, 1988.

———. *The Private Lives of Noel and Gertie.* London: Oberon, 1999.

Negra, Diane. *The Irish in Us: Irishness, Performativity, and Popular Culture.* Durham, N.C.: Duke UP, 2006.

———. *Off-White Hollywood: American Culture and Ethnic Female Stardom.* New York: Routledge, 2001.

Novak, Michael. "Pluralism in Human Perspective." *Concepts of Ethnicity.* Cambridge, Mass.: Harvard UP, 1980. 43–68.

O'Brien, Daniel. *Paul Newman.* London: Faber and Faber, 2004.

Omi, Michael, and Howard Winant. *Racial Formation in the United States: From the 1960s to the 1990s.* 2nd ed. New York: Routledge, 1994.

Oumano, Elena. *Paul Newman.* New York: St. Martin's, 1989.

Painter, Melissa, and David Weisman. *Edie: Girl on Fire.* San Francisco: Chronicle Books, 2006.

Phillips, Alastair. "Changing Bodies, Changing Voices: French Success and Failure in 1930s Hollywood." *Journeys of Desire: European Actors in Hollywood.* Ed. Alastair Phillips and Ginette Vincendeau. London: BFI, 2006. 85–94.

Poitier, Sidney. *Life Beyond Measure: Letters to My Great-Granddaughter: An American Icon Shares His Experience, Wisdom, and Hope.* New York: Harper One, 2008.

———. *The Measure of a Man: A Spiritual Autobiography.* New York: Harper SanFrancisco, 2000.

———. *This Life.* New York: Ballantine Books, 1980.

Porter, Darwin. *Steve McQueen, King of Cool: Tales of a Lurid Life.* Staten Island, N.Y.: Blood-Moon, 2009.

Pullen, Kirsten. "Guest-Starring Excess: Zsa Zsa Gabor and the Domestic Sitcom." *Women & Performance* 15.2 (2005): 63–78.

Quirk, Laurence J. *The Films of Paul Newman.* New York: Citadel Press, 1971.

Renan, Sheldon. *An Introduction to the American Underground Film.* New York: E. P. Dutton, 1967.

Rigelsford, Adrian, and Geoff Tibballs. *Peter Sellers: A Celebration.* London: Virgin Books, 1997.

Robertson [Wojcik], Pamela. *Guilty Pleasures: Feminist Camp from Mae West to Madonna.* Durham, N.C.: Duke UP, 1996.

———. "A Star Is Born Again, or How Streisand Recycles Garland." *Falling for You: Essays on Cinema and Performance.* Ed. Lesley Stern and George Kouvaros. Sydney, NSW, Australia: Power Institute, 1999. 177–208.

Rocheleau, Jordy. "'Far Between Sundown's Finish an' Midnight's Broken Toll': Enlightenment and Postmodernism in Dylan's Social Criticism." *Bob Dylan and Philosophy.* Ed. Peter Vernezze and Carl J. Porter. Chicago: Open Court Publishing, 2006. 66–77.

Royster, Francesca T. *Becoming Cleopatra: The Shifting Image of an Icon.* New York: Palgrave, 2003.

Sandford, Christopher. *McQueen: The Biography.* Lanham, Md.: Taylor Trade Publishing, 2003.

Schwartz, Vanessa. *It's So French! Hollywood, Paris, and the Making of Cosmopolitan Film Culture.* Chicago: U of Chicago P, 2007.

Segal, Ronald. *The Americans: A Conflict of Creed and Reality.* New York: Viking, 1968.

Sellers, Michael. *P.S. I Love You: An Intimate Portrait of Peter Sellers.* New York: Dutton, 1982.

Sexton, Jared. "The Ruse of Engagement: Black Masculinity and the Cinema of Policing." *American Quarterly* 61.1 (March 2009): 39–64.

Sheppard, Dick. *Elizabeth: The Life and Career of Elizabeth Taylor.* New York: Warner Books, 1974.

Sikov, Ed. *Mr. Strangelove: A Biography of Peter Sellers.* New York: Hyperion, 2002.

"Silver *Star!*" *Star!* Special Edition laser disc. Fox Video, 1995. On *Star!* DVD. Beverly Hills, Calif.: Twentieth Century-Fox Home Entertainment, 2004.

Simon, John. *Private Screenings.* New York: Berkeley, 1967.

Simon, Marie. *La Mode: 1945–1975.* Geneva: Aubanel, Editions Minerva, 2009.

Slane, Andrea. "Pressure Points: Political Psychology, Screen Adaptation, and the Management of Racism in the Case-History Genre." *Camera Obscura* 15.3 (2001): 70–113.

Slater, Robert. *This . . . Is CBS: A Chronicle of 60 Years.* Englewood Cliffs, N.J.: Prentice Hall, 1988.

Smith, Jeff. *The Sounds of Commerce.* New York: Columbia UP, 1998.

Sontag, Susan. "Notes on 'Camp.'" *Against Interpretation.* New York: Farrar, Straus and Giroux, 1966. 275–92.

Spigel, Lynn. *Welcome to the Dreamhouse: Popular Media and Postwar Suburbs.* Durham, N.C.: Duke UP, 2001.

Spoto, Donald. *A Passion for Life: The Biography of Elizabeth Taylor.* New York: HarperCollins, 1995.

Starr, Michael. *Peter Sellers: A Film History.* Jefferson, N.C.: McFarland, 1991.

Steele, Valerie. *Paris Fashion: A Cultural History.* 2nd ed. Oxford: Berg, 1998.

Stein, Jean. *Edie: An American Biography.* Ed. Jean Stein and George Plimpton. New York: Dell, 1982.

irling, Richard. *Julie Andrews: An Intimate Biography.* New York: St. Martin's, 2007.

udlar, Gaylyn. "'Chi-Chi Cinderella': Audrey Hepburn as Couture Countermodel." *Hollywood Goes Shopping.* Ed. David Desser and Garth S. Jowett. Minneapolis: U of Minnesota P, 2000. 159–78.

uárez, Juan A. *Bike Boys, Drag Queens, and Superstars: Avant-Garde, Mass Culture, and Gay Identities in the 1960s Underground Cinema.* Bloomington: Indiana UP, 1996.

Supercalifragilisticexpialidocious: The Making of *Mary Poppins.*" *Mary Poppins* 40th Anniversary Edition DVD. Burbank, Calif.: Buena Vista Home Entertainment, 2004.

wartz, Omar. *The View from On the Road: The Rhetorical Vision of Jack Kerouac.* Carbondale: Southern Illinois UP, 1999.

araborrelli, J. Randy. *Elizabeth.* New York: Warner Books, 2006.

aylor, Elizabeth. *Elizabeth Takes Off: On Weight Gain, Weight Loss, Self-Image, and Self-Esteem.* New York: G. P. Putnam's Sons, 1987.

———. *Elizabeth Taylor: An Informal Memoir.* New York: Harper and Row, 1964.

aylor, Greg. *Artists in the Audience: Cults, Camp, and American Film Criticism.* Princeton, N.J.: Princeton UP, 1999.

errill, Marshall. *Steve McQueen: The Life and Legend of a Hollywood Icon.* Chicago: Triumph, 2010.

———. *Steve McQueen: Portrait of an American Rebel.* Rev. ed. London: Plexus, 2008.

offel, Neile McQueen. *My Husband, My Friend: A Memoir.* Bloomington, Ind.: Author House, 2006.

.S. Congress. House of Representatives.Committee on Education and Labor. *Employment-Practices in the Performing Arts.* Washington, D.C.: U.S. Government Printing Office, 1963.

an Hees, Martin. "The Free Will in Bob Dylan." *Bob Dylan and Philosophy.* Ed. Peter Vernezze and Carl J. Porter. Chicago: Open Court, 2006. 115–23.

incendeau, Ginette. "Hot Couture: Brigitte Bardot's Fashion Revolution." *Fashioning Film Stars: Dress, Culture, Identity.* London: BFI, 2005. 134–46.

———. *Stars and Stardom in French Cinema.* London: Continuum, 2000.

Walker, Alexander. *Elizabeth: The Life of Elizabeth Taylor.* New York: Grove Press, 1997.

———. *Peter Sellers: The Authorized Biography.* New York: Macmillan, 1981.

Wanger, Walter, with Joe Hyams. *My Life with Cleopatra.* New York: Bantam, 1963.

Warhol, Andy, and Pat Hackett. *POPism: The Warhol '60s.* San Diego: Harcourt Brace, 1980.

Wasson, Sam. *A Splurch in the Kisser: The Movies of Blake Edwards.* Middletown, Conn.: Wesleyan UP, 2009.

White, Patricia. "Supporting Character: The Queer Career of Agnes Moorehead." *Out in Culture: Gay, Lesbian and Queer Essays on Popular Culture.* Ed. Corey Creekmur and Alexander Doty. Durham, N.C.: Duke UP, 1995. 91–114.

Whitmer, Peter O. "Foreword." *Steve McQueen: The Life and Legend of a Hollywood Icon,* by Marshall Terrill. Chicago: Triumph, 2010.

Wilcock, John. *The Autobiography and Sex Life of Andy Warhol.* New York: Other Scenes, 1971.

Williams, Raymond. *Marxism and Literature.* New York: Oxford UP, 1978.

Williamson, J. W. *Hillbillyland: What the Movies Did to the Mountains and What the Mountains Did to the Movies.* Chapel Hill: U of North Carolina P, 1995.

Windeler, Robert. *Julie Andrews: A Life on Stage and Screen.* Secaucus, N.J.: Birch Lane Press, 1997.

Wojcik, Pamela Robertson. "Typecasting." *Movie Acting: The Film Reader*. Ed. Pamela Robertson Wojcik. New York: Routledge, 2004. 169–90.

Wolf, Stacy. *A Problem Like Maria: Gender and Sexuality in the American Musical*. Ann Arbor: U of Michigan P, 2002.

Wollen, Peter. "Plastics: The Magical and the Prosaic." *The Warhol Look: Glamour, Style, Fashion*. Ed. Mark Francis and Margery King. Boston: Bulfinch Press, 1997. 142–51.

CONTRIBUTORS
★☆★☆★☆★☆★★★

LESLIE H. ABRAMSON holds a doctorate from the University of Chicago and is an independent film scholar. She is the author of chapters in the volumes *American Cinema of the 1960s* (2008) and *In the Limelight and Under the Microscope: Forms and Functions of Female Celebrity* (2011). Her work has appeared in *Literature/Film Quarterly*, among other publications.

CYNTHIA BARON is an associate professor in the Department of Theatre and Film and affiliated faculty in the American Culture Studies Program at Bowling Green State University. She is the author of *Denzel Washington* (forthcoming), co-author of *Food in Film Matters: Food as Sign, Symbol, and Subject in Cinema* (forthcoming), and co-author of *Reframing Screen Performance* (2008); co-editor of *More Than a Method: Trends and Traditions in Contemporary Film Performance* (2004); and editor of *The Projector*, an electronic journal on film, media, and culture.

CHRISTINE BECKER is an associate professor in the Department of Film, Television, and Theatre at the University of Notre Dame. She is the author of *It's the Pictures That Got Small: Hollywood Film Stars on 1950s Television* (2009) and has published work on stardom and television history in such journals as *Framework* and the *Journal of Popular Culture*.

DENNIS BINGHAM teaches English and Film Studies in the IU School of Liberal Arts at Indiana University Purdue University Indianapolis. He is the author of *Whose Lives Are They Anyway? The Biopic as Contemporary Film Genre* (2010) and numerous writings on stardom, acting, genre, and gender in cinema.

KELLEY CONWAY is an associate professor in the Department of Communication Arts at the University of Wisconsin–Madison. She is the author of *Chanteuse in the City: The Realist Singer in French Film* (2004). Her scholarly interests include French cinema of all eras, notably the work of Agnès Varda, documentary, and the relationship between cinema and the other arts.

ALEXANDER DOTY is a professor in the Gender Studies and Communication and Culture Departments at Indiana University. He has written *Making Things Perfectly Queer* (1993) and *Flaming Classics* (2000), co-edited *Out In Culture: Gay, Lesbian and Queer Essays in Popular Culture* (1995), and served as the special issue(s) editor for two volumes of *Camera Obscura*, "Fabulous! Diva Issues I and II."

INA RAE HARK, Distinguished Professor Emerita at the University of South Carolina, is the author of *Star Trek* (2008) and *Deadwood* (forthcoming). She has edited or co-edited four books of film and media criticism, including *American Cinema of the 1930s* (2007). Among her forty journal articles and book chapters is the essay on Errol Flynn and Olivia de Havilland in *Glamour in a Golden Age: Movie Stars of the 1930s* (2011).

ARTHUR KNIGHT is an associate professor of American Studies and English at the College of William & Mary. He is the author of *Disintegrating the Musical: Black Performance and American Musical Film* (2002) and co-editor, with Pamela Robertson Wojcik, of *Soundtrack Available: Essays on Film and Popular Music* (2001). His current work is on the cultural history of African American fame, stardom, and celebrity.

DIANE PECKNOLD is an assistant professor in the Department of Women's and Gender Studies at the University of Louisville. She is author of *The Selling Sound: The Rise of the Country Music Industry* (2007) and co-editor, with Kristine McCusker, of *A Boy Named Sue: Gender and Country Music* (2004). She has contributed a number of essays to collections on popular music and culture, including *Old Roots, New Routes: The Cultural Politics of Alt. Country Music* (2008) and *The Year's Work in Lebowski Studies* (2009).

CHRISTOPHER SIEVING is an assistant professor in the Department of Theatre and Film Studies at the University of Georgia. He is the author of *Soul Searching: Black-Themed Cinema from the March on Washington to the Rise of Blaxploitation* (2011).

DANIEL SMITH-ROWSEY teaches film studies at Folsom Lake College in California. He completed his doctorate at the University of Nottingham in Film and Television Studies in December 2010 with a thesis entitled "Representing Rough Rebels: How Star-Actors Defined the Hollywood Renaissance." He completed his master's degree in Critical Studies at the University of Southern California's School of Cinematic Arts in 2004. His academic interests include cinematic performance, new media, postcolonial studies, and emergent genres.

PAMELA ROBERTSON WOJCIK is professor in the Department of Film, TV, and Theatre and director of Gender Studies at the University of Notre Dame. She is the author of *The Apartment Plot: Urban Living in American Film and Popular Culture, 1945 to 1975* (2010) and *Guilty Pleasures: Feminist Camp from Mae West to Madonna* (1994), editor of *Movie Acting: The Film Reader* (2004), and co-editor, with Arthur Knight, of *Soundtrack Available: Essays on Film and Popular Music* (2001).

I N D E X

★☆★☆★☆★☆★☆★☆★